PRAISE FOR

The Complete Infidel's Guide to ISIS

"The first rule of warfare—indeed, of *survival* in a dangerous world— is to know your enemy. As always, Robert Spencer is scholarly, thorough, fearless, and insistent in making sure we know the Islamic State. *The Complete Infidel's Guide to ISIS* dispenses with the politically correct handwringing and connects the dots between jihadist ideology and savage action. Don't say you haven't been warned."
> **—Andrew C. McCarthy**, contributing editor of *National Review* and *New York Times* bestselling author of *The Grand Jihad*, *Willful Blindness*, and *Islam and Free Speech*

"Robert Spencer's *The Complete Infidel's Guide to ISIS* contains everything the people of the free world need to know about the Islamic State. Islam is the foremost threat to freedom, and to every free person, in the world today. This book shows how ISIS plans to sow murder and mayhem in our countries, how it is setting out to realize those plans, why it is so appealing to Islamic youths in the West, and above all, how it can and must be stopped, namely by confronting its Islamic ideology. As Robert Spencer writes, we should challenge mosques and Islamic schools in the West and act upon the knowledge that our ideas, our way of life, and our civilization are better than the Islamic ideology of ISIS. Everyone should read this fantastic book by one of the most courageous Islam experts of our time."
> **—Geert Wilders**, member of parliament in the Netherlands and leader of the Dutch Party for Freedom (PVV)

"Robert Spencer has been telling, and warning, us of the activities of the jihadists since 2003. Every single day for twelve years he has kept a vigilant eye on all the barbarisms of the Islamic terrorists and is surely the best informed and almost the only truly qualified expert capable of analyzing the emergence, development, and ideology of the monstrous death cult known as ISIS. Spencer also offers ways to combat this group, a group that President Obama refuses to recognize as posing any threat to American security and interests. On so many sad occasions when he was not taken seriously enough, Spencer was forced to remind us, 'I told you so.' It is time to listen to Robert Spencer."

—**Ibn Warraq**, author of *Why I Am Not a Muslim* and
Defending the West

"Robert Spencer has given us a series of immensely informative and accurate books, enlarging our knowledge on vital current issues. This latest one adds a potent analysis of ISIS, the most pressing danger of our time, which Spencer knows to its core. This essential book provides us with the intellectual tools that are indispensable for successfully overcoming this threat to our civilization, and should be widely read. It is an urgent necessity."

—**Bat Ye'or**, author of *Eurabia: The Euro-Arab Axis* and
Islam and Dhimmitude: Where Civilizations Collide

"Here is everything you need to know about the gravest threat to the U.S. and the free world today. Spencer goes way beyond the superficial cable headlines and the misleading conventional news reports into the deepest levels of ISIS that no other analyst has ever gone before. It is an eye opening masterpiece that will leave you absolutely shocked. Robert Spencer is truly amazing in how he breaks through the fog of denial and peels away layer upon layer of misinformation surrounding ISIS; how he shows the unparalleled savagery of ISIS and why Western leaders are living in lala land when they ludicrously assert that ISIS has nothing to do with Islam; and discards and destroys the political correctness in Washington that has masked the existential danger to our society by the continued growth of ISIS and the continued charade that it is merely a 'death cult.' If you want to know the truth and full story, you have to read Spencer's book. If you want to blind yourself to reality and the true danger to your family and friends, then ignore this book at your peril. I have been investigating Islamic terrorism for nearly twenty-five years and I can honestly state that this book is one of the most important books on terrorism I have ever read. Buy copies for your family members, for your friends, and last but not least for your elected political leaders."

—**Steven Emerson**, author of *American Jihad* and *Jihad Incorporated*

"ISIS is here. The threat it poses is real. It means to bring blood and chaos to the US, while our leaders deny and dissemble about what the group is, why its appeal is so strong, and what can and should be done about it. Robert Spencer is a singular voice unafraid to tell these unwelcome truths. If sanity still prevailed in our government and media, this book would be required reading for all elected officials and journalists. Here at last are the truths they're afraid to tell and abjectly ignorant of how to confront."

—**Pamela Geller**, president of the American Freedom Defense Initiative

The COMPLETE INFIDEL'S GUIDE to ISIS

The
COMPLETE
INFIDEL'S GUIDE

to

ISIS

ROBERT SPENCER

REGNERY
PUBLISHING
A Division of Salem Media Group

Regnery® is a registered trademark of Salem Communications Holding Corporation

Library of Congress Cataloging-in-Publication Data

Spencer, Robert, 1962- author.
 The complete infidel's guide to ISIS / Robert Spencer.
    pages cm
 Summary: "ISIS is on a campaign to destroy the Western world of "infidels." Who is ISIS? What do its leaders believe? And why exactly do they hate us? New York Times bestselling author Robert Spencer, author of The Complete Infidel's Guide to the Koran, takes on the Islamic State in The Complete Infidel's Guide to ISIS"-- Provided by publisher.
 ISBN 978-1-62157-453-8 (paperback)
 1. IS (Organization) 2. Terrorism--Religious aspects--Islam. 3. Religious fundamentalism. 4. Jihad. 5. Terrorism--Iraq. 6. Terrorism--Middle East. I. Title.
 HV6433.I722S64 2015
 363.32509567--dc23
                          2015026643

Published in the United States by
Regnery Publishing
A Division of Salem Media Group
300 New Jersey Ave NW
Washington, DC 20001
www.Regnery.com

Manufactured in the United States of America

10 9 8 7 6 5 4 3 2 1

Books are available in quantity for promotional or premium use. For information on discounts and terms, please visit our website: www.Regnery.com.

Distributed to the trade by
Perseus Distribution
250 West 57th Street
New York, NY 10107

For all the people around the world
whom the Islamic State is threatening to kill or enslave:
may you prevail and prosper

CONTENTS

AN ISIS TIMELINE

The Historical Antecedents and Meteoric Rise of the Islamic State

632

Death of Muhammad.

632–661

The Rightly Guided Caliphs.

661

The fourth caliph, Muhammad's son-in-law Ali, is killed. Controversy over Ali will lead to the division of Muslims into Sunni and Shia (Shīʿatu ʿAlī, the Party of Ali).

661–750

Umayyad Caliphate.

750–1258 and 1261–1517

Abbasid Caliphate (restored in the latter period under the Mamluk sultans).

909–1171

Rival Fatimid Caliphate in North Africa.

1147–1269

Rival Almohad Caliphate in North Africa and Spain (where the Umayyads also had a revived caliphate from 929 to 1031).

1517–1924

Ottoman Caliphate.

1744

Muhammad ibn Saud, whose family will one day rule Saudi Arabia, undertakes a mutual pact of allegiance with ʿAbd al-Wahhab, a reformist Sunni preacher leading an Islamic revival movement.

1924

Mustafa Kemal Atatürk, founder of the Republic of Turkey, abolishes the Ottoman Caliphate.

1928

Egyptian schoolteacher Hassan al-Banna founds the Muslim Brotherhood, which aims to restore the caliphate and return "Andalusia [Spain], Sicily, the Balkans, the Italian coast, as well as the islands of the Mediterranean . . . all of them Muslim Mediterranean colonies . . . to the Islamic fold."

1938

Oil, which will enrich the Saud family and finance their $100 billion worldwide campaign of Wahhabi propaganda instrumental in the resurgence of Islam in the late twentieth century, is discovered at Daharan, Saudi Arabia.

1966

Ahmed Fadhil Nazar al-Khalaylah, who will become internationally famous as Abu Musab al-Zarqawi, the founder of the precursor organization to ISIS, is born in Jordan.

1979

The Islamic Revolution in Iran and the seizure of the U.S. embassy there bring resurgent Islam to the attention of the West.

1989

In the first effective attempt to apply Islamic blasphemy law in the West, Iran's Ayatollah Khomeini issues a fatwa calling for the death of novelist Salman Rushdie; Rushdie goes into hiding. Zarqawi travels to Afghanistan to join the mujahideen fighting against the Soviets.

1992

Zarqawi, having returned to Jordan and founded the Jund-al-Sham (Soldiers of the Levant) jihadi group, is arrested when firearms and explosives are found in his house.

1999

Zarqawi is released from prison in a general amnesty. Upon the Jordanian authorities' discovery of the "Millennium Plot" to bomb a luxury hotel and tourist attractions, he flees to Pakistan and then to Afghanistan, where he runs a training camp funded by Osama bin Laden and founds Jama'at al-Tawhid wa al-Jihad (the Party of Monotheism and Jihad), the forerunner organization to ISIS.

2001

Al-Qaeda strikes New York and the Pentagon, and the U.S. invades Afghanistan.

2002

Party of Monotheism and Jihad members are arrested for plotting to kill Jews in Germany, and Zarqawi goes to Iraq, where he expects a U.S. invasion.

2003

The U.S. invades Iraq, and Zarqawi takes a leading role in the bloody insurgency. His Party of Monotheism and Jihad serves as a hub for foreign jihadis flocking to Iraq.[1] Their terror attacks on U.S. forces and Iraqis who cooperate with the Americans (or who have religious differences with Zarqawi's brand of Sunni Islam) will kill thousands of people.[2]

2004

The First and Second Battles of Fallujah, after Blackwater contractors' burnt bodies are hung from a Euphrates River bridge. The Nick Berg beheading video is released, bringing international attention to Zarqawi's leadership in the insurgency in Iraq and to his gruesome tactics. Zarqawi formally aligns himself with Osama bin Laden and changes his group's name to Tanzim Qai'dat al-Jihad fi Bilad al-Rafidayn, al-Qaeda in the Land of Two Rivers, which will become infamous as al-Qaeda in Iraq, or AQI.

2005

The U.S. puts a $25 million bounty on Zarqawi.

2006

Zarqawi is killed in a U.S. airstrike, and al-Qaeda in the Land of Two Rivers, better known as al-Qaeda in Iraq (AQI), renames itself the Islamic State of Iraq (ISI). In what comes to be known as "the Anbar Awakening," Sunni tribal leaders in Anbar Province turn against the brutal AQI/ISI jihadis and ally themselves with the U.S. and the Shia-led government of Iraq.

2007

"The Surge" of U.S. troops in Iraq.

2010

The self-immolation of a Tunisian vegetable cart proprietor who has been abused by the police sparks the Arab Spring.

2011

Arab Spring protests spread to Syria, Syrian President Bashar Hafez al-Assad attempts to suppress them with violence, and civil war breaks out. Jihadis associated with the Islamic State of Iraq travel from Iraq into Syria to take part in the fight.[3] In December, the last U.S. troops leave Iraq. President Barack Obama, celebrating the withdrawal as a "moment of success," claims that "we're leaving behind a sovereign, stable, and self-reliant Iraq."

2012

Obama draws a "red line" but takes no effective action on the war in Syria, other than to arm anti-Assad "rebel" groups that are often aligned with the Islamic State of Iraq.

2013

Reports emerge of Islamic Sharia law being imposed in areas around Raqqa, Syria, held by rebels fighting against Assad's government.[4] The Islamic State of Iraq renames itself the Islamic State of Iraq and the Levant/al-Sham (ISIL or ISIS), signaling its claim to Syrian territory. In July, hundreds of jihadis escape from Abu Ghraib and another prison just outside Baghdad, and ISIS claims credit, boasting the long-planned prison break was effected using suicide bombers and a dozen car bombs.[5]

2014

JANUARY

Taking advantage of clashes between the Shia-controlled government of Iraq and Sunni tribes in Anbar Province, ISIS seizes control of Fallujah. Asked by an interviewer for the *New Yorker* about the jihadi flag flying over the city, where Americans had sacrificed so much in 2004, President Obama compares ISIS to "a jayvee team."

FEBRUARY

ISIS and al-Qaeda officially split.

JUNE

ISIS begins a lightning offensive across northern Iraq with the bombing of a police station south of Samarra.[6] The jihadis seize Iraqi population centers and gain control of territory on the border between Iraq and Syria. Mosul, the capital of Nineveh Province and one of the largest cities in Iraq, falls to ISIS, demonstrating the weakness of the Iraqi armed forces (who are routed despite outnumbering the jihadis fifteen to one),[7] leaving significant American military materiel and approximately half a billion dollars in ISIS hands, and creating as many as half a million refugees. The jihadi group bulldozes the border between Iraq and Syria and, on June 29, ISIS declares a new caliphate, renaming itself the Islamic State.

JULY

The new Caliph Ibrahim (Abu Bakr al-Baghdadi) gives his inaugural speech, rallying the worldwide Muslim ummah to fight "the camp of the Jews, the crusaders, their allies, and with them the rest of the nations and religions of kufr [unbelievers], all being led by America and Russia, and being mobilized by the Jews." The Islamic State attacks Kobani in the autonomous Rojava region of Syrian Kurdistan; in the next three months, three hundred thousand Kurds from this area will flee into Turkey.[8]

AUGUST

ISIS routs Kurdish Peshmerga forces in northern Iraq and perpetrates a genocidal campaign against the Yazidi religious minority, driving tens of thousands from their homes into the Sinjar Moutains—where hundreds of children die from thirst and exposure to the elements—carrying out forced conversions and massacres, and making thousands of women sex slaves. The U.S. begins bombing raids against ISIS; Peshmerga and Iraqi forces recapture the Mosul dam, but not the city of Mosul. On August 14, al-Qaeda in the Arabian Peninsula (AQAP) in Yemen aligns itself with the Islamic State. On August 18, a video is posted to YouTube showing the beheading of American journalist James Foley—and threatening to kill Steven Sotloff (a threat that is carried out two weeks later).

SEPTEMBER

President Obama tells the American people, "We will degrade, and ultimately destroy, ISIL through a comprehensive and sustained counter-terrorism strategy." Islamic State spokesman Abu Muhammad Adnani calls Muslims living in the West to mount jihad attacks in their home countries.

OCTOBER

The FBI detains three Denver teenagers on their way to the Islamic State, presumably to become jihadi brides.[9] "Lone wolf" jihadi Zale Thompson, apparently inspired by the urgings of ISIS, attacks four police officers with a hatchet in Queens, New York.

2015

JANUARY

Said and Cherif Kouachi, affiliates of al-Qaeda in the Arabian Peninsula, murder twelve people in Paris at the offices of the satirical magazine *Charlie Hebdo*, which has published cartoons of Muhammad. Two days later, in an attack coordinated with the Kouachis (who by this time are cornered with a hostage at a printing shop outside Paris), their associate Amedy Coulibaly, an Islamic State supporter, takes hostages at the Hyper Cacher kosher supermarket in Paris and murders four Jewish men there. On January 27, the ISIS siege of Kobani is broken by Kurdish forces and U.S. airstrikes.

MARCH

Boko Haram pledges allegiance to the Islamic State.

MAY

Jihadis attack a Muhammad cartoon contest in Garland, Texas; the Islamic State takes credit and vows to kill contest sponsor Pamela Geller and anyone who harbors her. ISIS seizes Ramadi, the capital of Iraq's Anbar Province, and the ancient city of Palmyra in Syria and launches a surprise offensive in Syria's Aleppo Province. A United Nations report reveals that more than twenty-five thousand jihadis, from over half the countries in the world, have flocked to join either al-Qaeda or the Islamic State—and the numbers are rising "sharply."[10] An article in the Islamic State's online magazine *Dabiq* suggests that ISIS may be able to acquire a nuclear weapon from Pakistan in the next year.[11] And the Pentagon acknowledges that, for lack of ground intelligence on targets, approximately 75 percent of bombing runs against ISIS return without dropping a bomb.

JUNE

President Obama admits that "we don't yet have a complete strategy" for defeating the Islamic State.

AUTHOR'S NOTE

In December 2014, ISIS issued a list of rules for Christians living in the Islamic State's de facto capital of Raqqa, Syria. Those who dare disobey risk calling down on themselves the full force of the Islamic State's brutal enforcement mechanisms—as inhabitants of that tortured city are well aware, accustomed as they have become to public beheadings and crucifixions; the torture of women who are found insufficiently covered or breastfeeding in public; and the stoning of homosexuals (if, that is, they survive being thrown from rooftops). In the ISIS rules, Christians are forbidden to worship in public and to build or repair churches. They are not allowed to pray where Muslims can hear them, to display the cross, or to ring bells. They are not allowed to prevent anyone from converting to Islam. They must not aid the Islamic State's enemies.

One more thing is absolutely forbidden in the capital of the Islamic State: mocking Muslims or Islam.

And on May 3, 2015, jihadis loyal to ISIS attempted to impose the death penalty on offenders against that rule—including some Christians, a Jewish woman, and an atheist—who had dared to mock Islam and its Prophet. But the criminals who were guilty of flouting the absolute respect that the Islamic State demands for their religion on pain of death were not in Raqqa. We were in Garland, Texas—as were our would-be executioners.

Just four days after I submitted the manuscript of this book to the publisher, I was with Pamela Geller at the American Freedom Defense Initiative/Jihad Watch Muhammad Art Exhibit and Cartoon Contest when two jihadis, one of whom had formally pledged allegiance to ISIS, traveled from Phoenix to enforce the respect they demand for Islam, and opened fire outside the venue for our event. Fortunately, thanks to the clear-headed and courageous actions of the security team, the only people killed were the jihad attackers.

Their terror masters in the Islamic State, however, followed up the attack with a chilling promise:

> The attack by the Islamic State in America is only the beginning of our efforts to establish a wiliyah [actually wilayah, administrative district] in the heart of our enemy. Our aim was the khanzeer [pig] Pamela Geller and to show her that we don't care what land she hides in or what sky shields her; we will send all our Lions to achieve her slaughter. This will heal the hearts of our brothers and disperse the ones behind her. To those who protect her: this will be your only warning of housing this woman and her circus show. Everyone who houses her events, gives her a platform to spill her filth are legitimate targets. We have been watching closely who was present at this event and the shooter of our brothers. We knew that the target was protected. Our

intention was to show how easy we give our lives for the Sake of Allah.

Ultimately, the justification for the cartoon contest in Garland, as well as for the quixotic idea of writing a breezy book about a group devoted to mass murder, rape, slavery, and other far-from-light-hearted topics, is this: in the face of evil, especially evil that demands respect and obeisance at the point of a gun, mockery is not only justified, but required.

Thomas More said, "The devil…the proud spirit…cannot endure to be mocked." But the lovers of life, and of humanity, and of freedom must mock humorless evil—and its enablers in our willfully blind intelligentsia and political leadership—for not to do so would be to leave unpunctured its pride, its hubris, its arrogance, its hatred of all that is good, decent, vibrant, and alive. It would be to grant evil the victory, to concede that death will overcome life.

It will not. Life will overcome death. And it will triumph with a laugh.

INTRODUCTION

The Islamic State, a.k.a. ISIS, is the wealthiest, most successful, and most dangerous terror group in the world—and the most mysterious. Al-Qaeda shocked the world and staggered the United States when it destroyed the Twin Towers and struck the Pentagon on September 11, 2001. Hamas and Palestinian Islamic Jihad maintain steady pressure upon Israel with attacks on Israeli civilians and rockets lobbed from Gaza. Hizballah menaces Israel from Lebanon. In the Philippines, Islamic jihad groups have succeeded in compelling the government to grant Muslims an autonomous region in Mindanao. In Nigeria, Islamic jihadists horrified the world and moved Michelle Obama to take to Twitter with the hashtag #BringBackOurGirls by kidnapping infidel girls and pressing them into sex slavery. Other jihad groups around the world wage jihad campaigns against various non-Muslim and non-Sharia governments, all for the goal of establishing an Islamic state.

But one jihad terror group has outdone them all by actually establishing that Islamic state—and embarking upon a reign of terror unmatched in recent memory—rivaling the atrocities of Hitler, Stalin, Mao, and Pol Pot.

This, of course, is the group that calls itself the Islamic State, that most of the rest of the world calls ISIS, and that Barack Obama and his administration call ISIL. ISIS constitutes a threat to the U.S. greater than that of al-Qaeda, Hamas, Hizballah, Boko Haram, and all other jihad groups *combined*. Undeniably, its success has already been far greater than that of any of them. The Islamic State has become the first jihad terror group to rule over a significant expanse of territory for any extended period. It has won the loyalty of other jihadis far outside its domains—in Libya and Nigeria, and even as far away as the Philippines. It has called for attacks in the West, and Muslims in the U.S., Canada, Britain, and France have heeded its call.

On June 29, 2014, the group that had up to that point called itself the Islamic State of Iraq and the Levant (or *al-Sham* in Arabic; hence the synonymous acronyms ISIL and ISIS) announced that it was forming a new caliphate—a single unified government of all the Muslims, according to Sunni Muslim thought—and would henceforth drop the second half of its name and call itself simply the Islamic State.[1]

This claim to constitute a new caliphate became the basis of the Islamic State's appeal to Muslims worldwide, the inspiration for them to travel in unprecedented numbers to Iraq, Syria, and Libya to join ISIS. Once the Islamic State declared itself the new caliphate, it swiftly began to consolidate control over the large expanses of Iraq and Syria that it had taken by military force—an area larger than the United Kingdom, with a population of eight million people.[2] Blithely disregarding the world's universal condemnation of its pretensions, it has moved to assemble the accouterments of a state: currency, passports, social services, and the like. Its control of oil wells in Iraq quickly gave it a sizeable and steady source of wealth.

And ISIS has achieved remarkable military success. Despite a promise from the president of the world's only remaining superpower to "degrade and ultimately destroy the terrorist group known as ISIL,"[3] the new caliphate continues to add to its territory.

By May 2015 it had taken both Fallujah and Ramadi—reversing gains America had won over the Islamic State's precursor organization al-Qaeda in Iraq (AQI) at a huge cost in our blood and treasure and the lives and confidence of our local allies. In the north toward Turkey, it was also in control of the formerly million-inhabitant city of Mosul, half of whose residents were driven out as refugees. The Islamic State had captured American tanks, artillery, and thousands of U.S.-made armored vehicles from the hapless Iraqi Army. As ISIS forces stood within seventy miles of Baghdad, the Pentagon and the Iraqi government exchanged mutual accusations of incompetence and lack of commitment to the fight. In Syria, the Islamic State occupied half the nation's territory, carried out mass public executions in the ancient Roman amphitheatre in Palmyra, and threatened Damascus. Coalition pilots were able to drop their bombs on only one out of four bombing runs because of a lack of ground intelligence on targets, and American airstrikes seemed to be no match for armored bulldozers and suicide bombers—some of them citizens of Western countries who had abandoned comfortable lives for the glamor of the new caliphate.

The Islamic State's conquests have been accompanied by savage brutality that commands the attention of the world. ISIS has beheaded Americans on video, burned a captured Jordanian pilot alive in a metal cage, and made sex slaves of thousands of women and young girls. It executes men for smoking and tortures women for the tiniest infractions against covering themselves in public.

Yet despite all this and more, most Americans know very little about ISIS. And that's not just Americans who know what they know about world affairs from watching network news shows. Even the nation's highest authorities and our intelligence apparatus have shown that they know very little about the Islamic State.

Back in January 2014, less than six months before ISIS declared itself a new caliphate, Barack Obama dismissed the group with a now-infamous analogy. After the group took over the Iraqi city of Fallujah, Obama declared that he did not take them seriously: "The analogy we use around here sometimes, and I think is accurate, is if a jayvee team puts on Lakers uniforms that doesn't make them Kobe Bryant." He added: "I think there is a distinction between the capacity and reach of a bin Laden and a network that is actively planning major terrorist plots against the homeland versus jihadists who are engaged in various local power struggles and disputes, often sectarian."[4]

Just a few months later, this JV team that was supposed to be "engaged in various local power struggles" controlled a nation-sized expanse of Iraq and Syria and had organized a police force, amassed an army of over one hundred thousand fighters, and become the world's richest (and best-armed) jihad terror group.

Obama wasn't the only person surprised by the sudden growth and stunning success of this group; its rapid advance shocked the world. No one, however, should have been shocked at all: the group's success has been a long time in the making. Nonetheless, even after the Islamic State established its hold on so much territory, Western authorities continued to disparage it. "Whether you call them ISIS or ISIL, I refuse to call them the Islamic State, because they are neither Islamic or a state," said Hillary Clinton.[5] President Obama, Secretary of State John Kerry, Vice President Joe Biden, British Prime Minister David Cameron, and virtually every other politician in the Western world agreed with Clinton that the Islamic State had nothing to do with Islam. All the major Muslim groups in the West likewise condemned the Islamic State and questioned its claims not just to be the caliphate, but to be Islamic at all.

Despite this chorus of condemnation, however, the Islamic State is drawing Muslims from around the world to join it in unprecedented numbers. By February 2015, over twenty thousand Muslims from all over the world had traveled to Iraq and Syria to wage jihad for the Islamic State—an outpouring of support that no other jihad group, or in fact terror group of any kind, had ever inspired.[6]

In this book I explain the roots of its success—in the political situation created by the removal of Saddam Hussein from power in Iraq, the war against Bashar Assad in Syria, and the resulting chaos—but also in the deep currents of Islamic thought. I demonstrate how the Islamic State's rapid success would never have been possible without its claim to reconstitute the caliphate, a claim that has proven to be extraordinarily potent among Muslims worldwide.

I'll take you inside the mindset of the leaders of ISIS, of those who have killed in its name, and of the Muslims from Western countries who have been inspired to give up everything they have known and leave their families in order to move to the Islamic State and take up its jihad.

Wherever possible, I'll let the Islamic State speak for itself. I'll use the words of the people who have joined it and who run it (as well as of those who have been victimized by it)—so that you can see directly what they think of themselves and of their actions. You will also see what they think of you. I'll bring you the Islamic State's own explanations of what it has done, and why, and—most chilling of all—its plans for the future.

I show what constitutes its appeal among young Muslims, and why the condemnations of ISIS from Muslim groups have been completely ineffective in stopping young Muslims from traveling thousands of miles from all over the globe to join the group. The Islamic State is likely to be around for years to come, but it can be defeated, and indeed must be; in this book, I'll detail how it can be stopped, and what is likely to follow in its wake once it is defeated. You'll also discover the shocking extent of the nature and magnitude of the ISIS threat within the United States.

Above all, I show why the Islamic State is nothing less than the most pressing danger of our time. And why our struggle against it is a struggle against a force so purely evil, so focused, and so determined that our struggle against ISIS is, without exaggeration, a struggle for the survival of civilization itself.

We can win. And we *must* win. For the sake of a society that preserves humane values. For the sake of the continued existence of free societies that maintain respect for the dignity of every human person. For our children's sake.

Chapter One

BORN OF BLOOD
AND SLAUGHTER

T he organization now known as the Islamic State was born in the
    struggles of Muslim hard-liners in the Middle East in the 1990s to
    topple the relatively secular Arab nationalist governments that
dominated the region and restore the rule of Islamic law. But the blood and
ruin wreaked by the Islamic State have their ultimate origin in the battles
and raids that Islamic tradition ascribes to Muhammad, the prophet of
Islam, and in the jihad conquests of the Abbasid, Umayyad, and Ottoman
caliphates.

ISIS began as an Iraqi jihad group known as the *Jama'at al-Tawhid wa
al-Jihad*, the Party of Monotheism and Jihad. It was founded in 1999 by a
Muslim named Ahmed Fadhil Nazar al-Khalaylah, who became internationally famous as Abu Musab al-Zarqawi. His career in jihad is illuminating

not only of the background of the Islamic State, but of the goals of jihad terrorists in general.

From Small-Time Criminal to Terror Master

Zarqawi's *nom de jihad* means "Musab's father from Zarqa," and the man who would become for a time one of the two most renowned and feared jihad terrorists in the world was indeed born in the Jordanian town of Zarqa, on October 30, 1966. Zarqawi's father died when he was seventeen, leaving his mother with ten children to raise and the future terrorist with an angry, bitter heart. Zarqawi was jailed for possession of drugs and sexual assault, whereupon he found religion, gave up drinking and drugs, memorized the Qur'an, and embarked upon the path that would lead him to become one of the most notorious men in the world.[1]

Zarqawi's first taste of jihad came fighting against the Soviets in Afghanistan in the 1980s, but he saw little action there, and in 1992 he returned to Jordan to wage jihad at home.[2] He founded a jihad group named *Jund al-Sham* (Soldiers of the Levant), which foreshadowed ISIS in its dedication to overthrowing a relatively secular government (that of Jordan) and uniting a larger territory (the Levant) in a single Islamic state. Arrested after a cache of weapons was discovered in his home, Zarqawi was given a fifteen-year sentence in March 1994 at the end of a trial during which he showed his contempt for authorities who did not govern according to Islamic law by handing the judge a paper on which the terror mastermind had written out an indictment naming Jordan's king and the judge himself as defendants.[3]

While in prison, Zarqawi became the leader of a group of Muslims upon whom he imposed strict discipline and to whom he was fanatically devoted. A fellow jihadi who knew Zarqawi in those days recalled that he was "well-known for loving his brothers in God more than his relatives."[4]

In May 1999, Zarqawi was released from prison after serving only a third of his sentence, under a general amnesty granted by Jordan's King Abdullah. The wisdom of that amnesty was immediately cast into doubt when Zarqawi got involved in a jihad scheme known as the "Millennium Plot"; plotters intended to bomb a luxury hotel and other sites in Jordan frequented by tourists.[5] The plot was foiled; Zarqawi fled to Pakistan and eventually ventured into Afghanistan, where he founded the Party of Monotheism and Jihad.[6] In Afghanistan he met Osama bin Laden, who decided to set him up with funding for a jihad training camp for Zarqawi in Herat, where he trained jihadis from Jordan, Syria, the Palestinian territories, and elsewhere for actions in Europe.[7]

After 9/11, Zarqawi and his men crossed from Afghanistan into Iran, where they were able to operate until April 2002. At that point, eight of his jihadis were discovered in Germany, plotting jihad mass murder attacks against Jewish targets.[8] Expelled from Iran as a result of this discovery, Zarqawi made his way to Iraq, where he anticipated that an American attack was imminent. He trained his Party of Monotheism and Jihad to be an anti-American jihad force and positioned himself as the leader and guide of the jihadis from all over the world who had begun to stream into Iraq to fight the Americans.

Thus Zarqawi's ascent to international fame began. He became infamous as a pioneer of the media jihad for which ISIS has now become feared and hated and was personally responsible for one of the first decapitation videos to be posted on the internet and capture the attention of the West—that of American hostage Nicholas Berg in May 2004.

THE COMMON TOUCH

Pious and emotional, Zarqawi was committed to the well-being of his men. Their awareness that he was one of them who had come from a similar background won him a loyalty that rivaled that given to Osama bin Laden—whose status as a wealthy, aristocratic Saudi placed a distance between him and his rank-and-file jihadis that was never a problem for Zarqawi.

A few months later, Zarqawi's group also filmed and distributed the beheadings of two other Americans, contractors Eugene Armstrong and Jack Hensley.[9]

Zarqawi was morally responsible for many murders, but in the cases of Berg and Armstrong it appears that he actually wielded the murder weapon as well. According to the caption of the Nicholas Berg video and the Party of Monotheism and Jihad online announcement of Armstrong's murder, Zarqawi himself is the masked figure who is seen sawing those victims' heads off with a knife.[10]

The Alliance with al-Qaeda

On October 17, 2004, with his notoriety at its peak, Zarqawi pledged his loyalty and that of his organization to Osama bin Laden and renamed his group *Tanzim Qai'dat al-Jihad fi Bilad al-Rafidayn*, al-Qaeda in the Land of Two Rivers. Soon it became popularly known as al-Qaeda in Iraq (AQI).

The Zarqawi group's declaration of allegiance to al-Qaeda stressed the importance of Muslim unity, something that would also be a priority of the Islamic State. The declaration began with an epigraph from the Qur'an: "Hold fast to the rope of God and you shall not be divided" (3:103), and then added, "Praise be to God, the Cherisher

NOT THAT THIS HAS ANYTHING TO DO WITH ISLAM

"Is it not time for you [Muslims] to take the path of jihad and carry the sword of the Prophet of prophets? ... The Prophet, the most merciful, ordered [his army] to strike the necks of some prisoners in [the Battle of] Badr and to kill them.... And he set a good example for us."

—Zarqawi invoking Muhammad's example in defense of the murder of Nicholas Berg[11]

and Sustainer of worlds, and let there be no aggression except upon the oppressors"—that is, no aggression between Muslims.

The statement boasted that the alliance was "undoubtedly an indication that victory is approaching, God willing, and that it represents a return to the glorious past. We shall, with great fury, instill fear in the enemies of Islam, who consider that through their war in Iraq they have nearly uprooted Islam from its recent stronghold. For this, we will turn [the war] into a hell for them."

By this time, Zarqawi's unapologetic embrace of terror as a tactic of war had made him a virtual folk hero among jihadis worldwide; he rivaled his new chief as the world's most renowned and reviled jihad terrorist. The U.S. considered Zarqawi so important that it placed a $25 million bounty on his head—the same amount as that offered for bin Laden.

Ultimately, Zarqawi—but not his movement—was killed in a U.S. airstrike on June 7, 2006. No jihad group depends upon a charismatic leader—even one as fanatically devoted to his cause and able to galvanize others to join it as Zarqawi. Such organizations are rather, as we shall see, ideologically driven. Thus Zarqawi's group survived him.

On October 13, 2006, al-Qaeda in the Land of Two Rivers reconstituted itself as the Islamic State of Iraq (ISI).[14] It continued to harass American troops in Iraq, biding its time until the inevitable day when the Americans would leave. That day came on December 14, 2011, when Barack Obama, speaking at Fort Bragg,

MUTUAL ADMIRATION SOCIETY

• • •

In October 2004 Zarqawi's group vowed allegiance to Osama bin Laden: "By God, O sheikh of the mujahideen, if you bid us plunge into the ocean, we would follow you. If you ordered it so, we would obey. If you forbade us something, we would abide by your wishes. For what a fine commander you are to the armies of Islam, against the inveterate infidels and apostates!"[12]

Late in December of the same year, Al Jazeera broadcast an audiotape, purportedly of Osama bin Laden, declaring, "The dear mujahed brother Abu Musab al-Zarqawi is the prince of al Qaeda in Iraq, so we ask all our organization brethren to listen to him and obey him in his good deeds."[13]

North Carolina, to some of the last soldiers to come home from Iraq, boasted about ending the war and called the withdrawal of all American troops a "moment of success."[15]

But the jihadis of the Islamic State of Iraq didn't agree that the war was over. They weren't walking away or folding up shop—in fact, they were expanding. They seized the opportunity that uprisings against Syrian dictator Bashar al-Assad provided to move into that neighboring country and on April 9, 2013, renamed their organization again as the Islamic State of Iraq and the Levant (ISIL, or ISIS).[16] They then took advantage of the successes of the Sunni rebels in Syria (for whom Obama had asked Congress to authorize military support in the summer of 2013) and the weakness of the Shi'ite regime in Baghdad to assert control over territory in both Syria and Iraq. Both Assad and the Iraqi government in Baghdad were too weak to stop them.

WAIT, MAYBE YOU DON'T WIN WARS BY RETREATING?

. . .

"We're leaving behind a sovereign, stable, and self-reliant Iraq with a representative government that was elected by its people. We're building a new partnership between our nations and we are ending a war not with a final battle but with a final march toward home. This is an extraordinary achievement."

—President Barack Obama, December 14, 2011[17]

Rift between Islamic State and al-Qaeda Becomes Official, Western Leaders and Media Overjoyed

Early in 2014, al-Qaeda attempted to reassert control over ISIS. Osama bin Laden had been killed in May of 2011, but the organization continued to operate under the leadership of his successor, Ayman al-Zawahiri, a scholarly Egyptian eye surgeon who had served as bin Laden's personal physician. Zawahiri demanded that ISIS stand down and leave the jihad in Syria to another al-Qaeda–allied group, Jabhat al-Nusra.[18] When ISIS did not comply, al-Qaeda made the announcement on February 2, 2014: "ISIS is not a branch of the Qaidat al-Jihad group, we have no organizational relationship with it, and [our] group is not responsible for its actions."[19]

Now this formal break came long after the alliance had ceased to exist anywhere but on paper. ISIS hadn't even used the name "al-Qaeda" in over seven years. Nonetheless, Western leaders and the mainstream media made all they could out of the split between ISIS and al-Qaeda.

In the midst of its lengthy campaign to convince Americans that the Islamic State was not Islamic at all, the Obama administration (and its willing enablers in the mainstream media) welcomed the rift between the two terror organizations as proof for its theory that ISIS was distorting and hijacking the religion of peace. "They're more extreme than al-Qaeda," said Secretary of State John Kerry in June 2014. This became a recurring

FLUIDITY

On April 16, 2015, Abdirahman Sheik Mohamud, a Muslim who lived in Columbus, Ohio, was indicted for plotting to carry out a jihad terror attack in the United States—he had talked about attacking a military base and murdering American soldiers "execution style."[20]

Mohamud had returned to the United States from Syria, where he had received training from Jabhat al-Nusra, the al-Qaeda group that Ayman al-Zawahiri had insisted that ISIS defer to in Syria—leading directly to the split between the two groups.

Before he left for Syria, Mohamud posted on his Facebook page the black flag of jihad in the design that has become associated with the Islamic State, as well as another photograph also containing the Islamic State symbol. Authorities said that he went to Syria intending to join the Islamic State, but ended up in Jabhat al-Nusra instead.[21] Exactly how and why this happened is unclear, but it does indicate that the gulf between the two groups is not so wide as to prevent jihadis from moving from one to the other. They share the same religious perspectives, ideology, and goals, and that's good enough.

theme in the media coverage of the jihadi groups.[22] MSNBC's David Gregory said in August 2014 that ISIS was "cast off by al-Qaida because this group is considered too extreme."[23] The UK's *Guardian* told readers that "The Islamic State in Iraq and the Levant (Isis) is so hardline that it was disavowed by al-Qaida's leader, Ayman al-Zawahiri."[24] The UK's *Daily Mail* noted that "lying among a pile of papers at the hideout in Pakistan where Osama Bin Laden was shot dead was a carefully worded 21-page letter" written by one of Osama's men in 2011. This letter found at bin Laden's Abbottabad compound warned that ISIS "had such complete disregard for civilian life that it could damage the reputation of Al Qaeda," listing as some of the acts that were beyond the pale "the use of chlorine gas as a chemical weapon, bombing mosques and a massacre in a Catholic church in Baghdad."[25]

The al-Qaeda letter did complain about some of the bloody tactics ISIS was using. But its putative author, al-Qaeda spokesman Adam Gadahn, better known as "Azzam the American," seemed chiefly concerned with

GEE, I WONDER WHY CATHOLICS AREN'T RUSHING TO CONVERT TO ISLAM?

"The Catholics are a fertile ground for call of God and to persuade them about the just case of the Mujahidin, particularly after the rage expanding against the mother church (Vatican) as a result of its scandals.... But the attacks on the Christians in Iraq, like the Baghdad attack and what took place earlier in Mosul and others, does not help us to convey the message. Even if the ones we are talking to have some grudge against the mother church, they will not grasp in general the targeting of their public, women, children and men in their church during Mass."

—from pages 6–7 of the twenty-one-page 2011 al-Qaeda letter detailing differences with ISIS the PR fallout. The massacre of Catholics at the church in Baghdad, for example, had come at a particularly inopportune moment—just as the author of the letter was doing the preparatory research for an appeal to fast-secularizing Irish Catholics to embrace Islam. He had also been "thinking of preparing an Arabic message to the Christians of the Arab region, calling them to Islam, and to caution them from cooperating with invader enemies of Islam who oppose the Islamic State."[26] So the timing was terrible.

The Obama administration and the media were taking a dispute primarily about timing and tactics and making it into something that it clearly wasn't: a principled condemnation of the world's most notorious terror group of the 2010s by the most notorious terror group of the 2000s on the grounds that it had transgressed the bounds of Islamic law.[27]

OSTRICH ALERT

"It is a corruption of the Islamic faith. It is a distortion of it. It does not represent the Muslim community or Islam."

—CIA Director John Brennan, explaining how ISIS is not Islamic[28]

Steamrolling to the Caliphate

The split with al-Qaeda did not slow ISIS down. On June 10, 2014, ISIS jihadis posted online photos of the bulldozing of the Syria-Iraq border, under the title "Smashing the Sykes-Picot border."[29] They were referring to the Sykes-Picot Agreement of 1916, which had delineated the British and French spheres of influence in the post–World War I Middle East, with France getting Syria and northern Iraq and Britain, southern Iraq—and thus had ultimately demarcated the border between the nations of Syria and Iraq. The Islamic State did not recognize the Syria-Iraq border: they considered it to be an artificial construction of the West and saw it as a symbol of how the non-Muslim West had oppressed the Muslims of the world by, among other things, dividing them into artificial nation states and destroying the divinely ordained unity they had enjoyed under a single political leader, the caliph.

The destruction of the border was a manifestation of the belief that Muslims should be united in a single state under a single ruler. And once the Syria-Iraq border was no more, the next step was essentially inevitable. On June 29, 2014, ISIS declared the formation of a new caliphate and dropped the second half of its name, rebranding itself yet again—this time, as simply the Islamic State.[30] That new name was a claim to the loyalty of the entire *Ummah*, the community of all Muslims worldwide. *The* Islamic State was laying claim to be *the* Islamic government in the world and demanding all Muslims' allegiance. The revival of the caliphate was a return to the form of government of the glory days of Islam—from Muhammad's death through Islam's Golden Age up until the breakup of the Ottoman Empire after the end of World War I—when Muslims were ruled by a caliph, the successor to Muhammad as spiritual and political leader of Islam.

Abu Bakr al-Baghdadi

And who was that leader? Abu Bakr al-Baghdadi, the Islamic State's leader since 2010 and its new Caliph Ibrahim, proclaimed as such in June 2014 with the declaration of the caliphate. He is a supremely shadowy figure, and virtually nothing that has been reported about him is known for certain; the material here has been widely reported, but none of it is unquestionable.

The most noteworthy fact reported about Baghdadi is that he has a Ph.D. in Islamic law from the Islamic University in Baghdad and comes from a family of Muslim clerics.[31]

Even before his rise to the leadership of the group that Zarqawi had founded, the future caliph was not entirely unknown to America. It seems that Baghdadi was actually arrested and imprisoned by U.S. forces at Camp Bucca under his given name Ibrahim Awad Ibrahim al-Badri (Abu Bakr al-Baghdadi is a *nom de guerre*)—not as a known terrorist, however, but as a "civilian internee," that is, someone who had been linked to jihad terrorists but not found to be engaging in terror activity himself.[32] Nevertheless, it has been reported that before his arrest in 2004 the future caliph had played a role in founding "a militant group, Jeish Ahl al-Sunnah al-Jamaah, which had taken root in the restive Sunni communities around his home city."[33]

Camp Bucca was the model U.S. prison camp to which inmates from the notorious Abu Ghraib prison were transferred after the scandal there.[34] Unfortunately, while the crimes at Abu Ghraib provided a huge propaganda coup for the jihadis, the relatively relaxed conditions at Camp Bucca seem to have provided networking opportunities that would be at least as valuable in advancing the cause of jihad. Apparently al-Baghdadi was a natural leader who seemed to his American guards like a model prisoner. "He was respected very much by the US army," a man who claims to have been one of his prison associates and colleagues in ISIS has said. "If he wanted to visit people in another camp he could, but we couldn't. And all the while, a new strategy, which he was leading, was

NOT THAT THIS HAS ANYTHING TO DO WITH ISLAM

"O ummah of Islam, indeed the world today has been divided into two camps and two trenches, with no third camp present: The camp of Islam and faith, and the camp of kufr (disbelief) and hypocrisy—the camp of the Muslims and the mujahidin everywhere, and the camp of the jews, the crusaders, their allies, and with them the rest of the nations and religions of kufr, all being led by America and Russia, and being mobilized by the jews."

—Abu Bakr al-Baghdadi, the Islamic State's Caliph Ibrahim, in his inaugural message upon being named caliph, "A Message to the Mujahedin and the Muslim Ummah in the Month of Ramadan," July 1, 2014 (capitalization as in the original)

rising under their noses, and that was to build the Islamic State. If there was no American prison in Iraq, there would be no IS now. Bucca was a factory. It made us all."[35]

According to some reports, which may or may not be more reliable than anything else reported about him, al-Bagdadi may have made an interesting remark in Bucca. As he left, he is said (although this could be legend born of his later notoriety) to have given a hint of what he had in mind for the future, telling his guards:

"I'll see you guys in New York."[36]

Cheering the Hearts of Jihadis Everywhere

The new caliphate galvanized opinion worldwide. Jihadis took fresh energy from the declaration of the Islamic State. It seemed like a giant step forward toward the fulfillment of their dreams and plans. The reestablishment of the caliphate had long been an aspiration dear to the hearts of many jihadi terrorists—including al-Qaeda.

As bin Laden lieutenant Ayman al-Zawahiri had written to Zarqawi in a July 9, 2005, letter, "It has always been my belief that the victory of Islam will never take place until a Muslim state is established in the manner of the Prophet in the heart of the Islamic world, specifically in the Levant, Egypt, and the neighboring states of the Peninsula and Iraq; however, the center would be in the Levant and Egypt."[37]

In that letter Zawahiri had heaped praise on Zarqawi for helping bring that state—the revived caliphate—closer to reality: "If our intended goal in this age is the establishment of a caliphate in the manner of the Prophet and if we expect to establish its state predominantly—according to how it appears to us—in the heart of the Islamic world, then your efforts and sacrifices—God permitting—are a large step directly towards that goal."

Zawahiri then offered Zarqawi his "humble opinion that the Jihad in Iraq requires several incremental goals," the first of which was to "expel the Americans from Iraq." The second stage, wrote Zarqawi, would be exactly what the Islamic State ended up doing nine years later:

> The second stage: Establish an Islamic authority or amirate, then develop it and support it until it achieves the level of a caliphate—over as much territory as you can to spread its power in Iraq, i.e., in Sunni areas, is in order to fill the void stemming from the departure of the Americans, immediately upon their exit and before un-Islamic forces attempt to fill this void, whether those whom the Americans will leave behind them, or those among the un-Islamic forces who will try to jump at taking power.

Following the establishment of this state, the third stage would be to "extend the jihad wave to the secular countries neighboring Iraq," followed by the fourth stage, which "may coincide with what came before: the clash with Israel, because Israel was established only to challenge any new Islamic entity."

Zawahiri wrote in an extremely deferential manner to Zarqawi, repeatedly assuring the Iraq commander that his analysis was not "infallible." Nonetheless, he did not hesitate to give him direction, emphasizing that "the mujahedeen must not have their mission end with the expulsion of the Americans from Iraq, and then lay down their weapons, and silence the fighting zeal." If they did that, "we will return to having the secularists and traitors holding sway over us. Instead, their ongoing mission is to establish an Islamic state, and defend it, and for every generation to hand over the banner to the one after it until the Hour of Resurrection."

Zawahiri summed up the "two short-term goals" as "removing the Americans and establishing an Islamic amirate in Iraq, or a caliphate if possible." Attaining them, he wrote, would ensure possession of "the strongest weapon which the mujahedeen enjoy—after the help and granting of success by God," which was "popular support from the Muslim masses in Iraq, and the surrounding Muslim countries."

He Who Hesitates Is Lost

But al-Qaeda hesitated to declare a caliphate for fear that the Americans would nip it in the bud.

As a letter apparently from Osama bin Laden, found in the trove of documents at the Abbottabad compound and declassified in May 2015, explained,

> We should stress on the importance of timing in establishing the Islamic State. We should be aware that planning for the establishment of the state begins with exhausting the main influential power that enforced the siege on the Hamas government, and that overthrew the Islamic Emirate in Afghanistan and Iraq despite the fact this power was depleted. We should keep in mind that this main power still has the capacity to lay siege on any Islamic State, and that such a siege might force the people to overthrow their duly elected governments. We have to continue with exhausting and depleting them till they become so weak that they can't overthrow any State that we establish. That will be the time to commence with forming the Islamic state.

Bin Laden saw the restoration of the caliphate as the ultimate goal of al-Qaeda's activities: "the result that we deployed for" was "to reinstate the wise Caliphate and eliminate the disgrace and humiliation that our nation is suffering from." But he argued against "insisting on the formation of an Islamic State at the time being"—and instead wanted his followers "to work on breaking the power of our main enemy by attacking the American embassies in the African countries, such as Sierra Leone, Togo, and mainly to attack the American oil companies" first.[38]

In the event, bin Laden's appraisal of the risks of declaring a caliphate appears to have been overcautious. (Perhaps, after America's strong initial response to the September 11 attacks, he was in once-burned-twice-shy mode.) So far, the Islamic State has survived and thrived. America may "still ha[ve] the capacity to lay siege on any Islamic State," but we don't seem to have the political will—or, perhaps, the necessary understanding of the threat—to do so effectively.

Al-Qaeda Still Hearts ISIS

When the Islamic State did boldly go where Osama bin Laden was afraid to, declaring the caliphate on June 29, 2014, at least some members of bin Laden's organization were apparently so heartened that they were ready to paper over the rift between al-Qaeda and ISIS. In August 2014, just six months after al-Qaeda's declaration that it had no organizational relationship with ISIS, "al-Qaeda in the Arabian Peninsula" (AQAP), al-Qaeda's branch in Yemen, declared its "solidarity" with the Islamic State: "We announce solidarity with our Muslim brothers in Iraq against the crusade. Their blood and injuries are ours and we will surely support them. We assert to the Islamic Nation [that is, to all Muslims worldwide] that we stand by the side of our Muslim brothers in Iraq against the American and Iranian conspiracy and their agents of the apostate Gulf rulers."[39]

But then the AQAP leadership apparently had second thoughts. Just a couple of months later, in November 2014, Harith bin Ghazi al-Nadhari, a Muslim cleric affiliated with the al-Qaeda branch in Yemen, denounced the Islamic State for claiming Yemen as part of its new caliphate. "We did not want to talk about the current dispute and the sedition in Syria," said al-Nadhari, "however, our brothers in the Islamic State...surprised us with several steps, including their announcement of the caliphate [and] they announced the expansion of the caliphate in a number of countries which they have no governance, and considered them to be provinces that belonged to them."[40]

Al-Nadhari asserted that "the announcement of the caliphate for all Muslims by our brothers in the Islamic State did not meet the required conditions." Like Adam Gadahn (or whoever the author really was) in the twenty-one-page letter found in the Abbottabad compound, he seemed to be concerned about the particularly bloodthirsty tactics ISIS was becoming known for. He complained that the Islamic State was "going too far in inter-pretations in terms of spilling inviolable blood under the excuse of expand-ing and spreading the power of the Islamic State."[41]

And the next month, Nasr bin Ali al-Ansi, a senior AQAP commander, criticized the Islamic State's practice of filming its beheadings: "Filming and promoting it among people in the name of Islam and Jihad is a big mis-take and not acceptable whatever the justifications are. This is very barbaric. Sheik Osama bin Laden used to say anyone with sound instincts cannot stand watching scenes of killings."[42]

However, at the same time that he denounced the Islamic State's behead-ings, al-Ansi also declared that al-Qaeda in the Arabian Peninsula still supported the Islamic State's "jihad against crusaders."[43]

The new caliphate was bloody and brutal—like its antecedents going back to the beginning of Islamic history.

The Assassins

Though the Obama administration, the media, and Muslim spokesmen in the West often suggest that ISIS is not authentically Muslim, the history of Islam abounds with similar groups that have spread terror with their ruthless brutality and their rigorist fidelity to the cruelest tenets of Islamic law. The Islamic State may have begun in the aftermath of the U.S. defeat of Saddam Hussein in Iraq, but its antecedents in Islamic tradition go back much farther than that. One Muslim group that was almost as notorious (and as hated and feared) as ISIS is today was a Shi'ite Muslim sect, the Nizari Ismailis of the Middle Ages—popularly known as the Assassins.

The Assassins flourished in the twelfth and thirteenth centuries in territory now in Iran and Syria. By their activities—particularly the planned murders of many of their opponents—they gave the English language its word for one who commits a planned and deliberate murder, especially a public killing for political or ideological reasons.

The word *Assassin* is derived from *Hashashin*, "hashish smokers," a name given to the group by its opponents on the basis of stories about their leader, a mysterious figure known as the Old Man of the Mountain, and his novel method for recruiting new members. The fullest account comes from Marco Polo's *Travels*:

> Mulehet is a country in which the Old Man of the Mountain dwelt in former days; and the name means *"Place of the Aram."* I will tell you his whole history as related by Messer Marco Polo, who heard it from several natives of that region.
>
> The Old Man was called in their language ALOADIN. He had caused a certain valley between two mountains to be enclosed, and had turned it into a garden, the largest and most beautiful that ever was seen, filled with every variety of fruit. In it were erected pavilions and palaces the most elegant that can be imagined, all covered with gilding and exquisite painting. And there were runnels too, flowing freely with wine and milk and honey and water; and numbers of ladies and of the most beautiful damsels in the world, who could play on all manner of instruments,

and sung most sweetly, and danced in a manner that it was charming to behold. For the Old Man desired to make his people believe that this was actually Paradise. So he had fashioned it after the description that Mahommet gave of his Paradise, to wit, that it should be a beautiful garden running with conduits of wine and milk and honey and water, and full of lovely women for the delectation of all its inmates. And sure enough the Saracens of those parts believed that it *was* Paradise!

Now no man was allowed to enter the Garden save those whom he intended to be his ASHISHIN. There was a Fortress at the entrance to the Garden, strong enough to resist all the world, and there was no other way to get in. He kept at his Court a number of the youths of the country, from 12 to 20 years of age, such as had a taste for soldiering, and to these he used to tell tales about Paradise, just as Mahommet had been wont to do, and they believed in him just as the Saracens believe in Mahommet. Then he would introduce them into his garden, some four, or six, or ten at a time, having first made them drink a certain potion which cast them into a deep sleep, and then causing them to be lifted and carried in. So when they awoke, they found themselves in the Garden.[44]

According to the legend that surrounded the Assassins, the "potion" that made these young men susceptible to the suggestion that they had visited Paradise was hashish.[45] The Old Man would get his potential recruits high on the drug—an experience for which they had no cultural referent in those pre–*Sgt. Pepper* days—and then introduce them to his gardens, which, as Marco Polo related, had been scrupulously designed to correspond to the Qur'an's descriptions of Paradise—fruits, women, and all:

Indeed, you [disbelievers] will be tasters of the painful punish-
ment,
And you will not be recompensed except for what you used to
do—
But not the chosen servants of Allah.
Those will have a provision determined—
Fruits; and they will be honored
In gardens of pleasure
On thrones facing one another.
There will be circulated among them a cup from a flowing
spring,
White and delicious to the drinkers;
No bad effect is there in it, nor from it will they be intoxicated.
And with them will be women limiting [their] glances, with
large eyes,
As if they were eggs, well-protected. (37:38–49)

The Old Man of the Mountain, according to Marco Polo's account, used
his young recruits' experience of Paradise to manipulate them into doing
his murderous bidding:

When therefore they awoke, and found themselves in a place
so charming, they deemed that it was Paradise in very truth.
And the ladies and damsels dallied with them to their hearts'
content, so that they had what young men would have; and
with their own good will they never would have quitted the
place.

This elaborate ruse was all in aid of the Old Man's recruitment program:

Now this Prince whom we call the Old One kept his Court in grand and noble style, and made those simple hill-folks about him believe firmly that he was a great Prophet. And when he wanted one of his *Ashishin* to send on any mission, he would cause that potion whereof I spoke to be given to one of the youths in the garden, and then had him carried into his Palace. So when the young man awoke, he found himself in the Castle, and no longer in that Paradise; whereat he was not over well pleased. He was then conducted to the Old Man's presence, and bowed before him with great veneration as believing himself to be in the presence of a true Prophet. The Prince would then ask whence he came, and he would reply that he came from Paradise! and that it was exactly such as Mahommet had described it in the Law. This of course gave the others who stood by, and who had not been admitted, the greatest desire to enter therein.

Thus the young men were induced to commit murder:

So when the Old Man would have any Prince slain, he would say to such a youth: "Go thou and slay So and So; and when thou returnest my Angels shall bear thee into Paradise. And shouldst thou die, natheless even so will I send my Angels to carry thee back into Paradise." So he caused them to believe; and thus there was no order of his that they would not affront any peril to execute, for the great desire they had to get back into that Paradise of his. And in this manner the Old One got his people to murder any one whom he desired to get rid of. Thus, too, the great dread that he inspired all Princes withal, made them become his tributaries in order that he might abide at peace and amity with them.[46]

STILL CHASING THE SAME CARROT

Wissam Haddad, the former head of the al-Risalah Islamic Centre in Bankstown, Australia, and a supporter of the Islamic State, was asked in December 2014 what he thought about four Muslim brothers from Australia who had gone to Syria to join the Islamic State. Haddad explained: "There is something that Allah is offering more than any person or country can offer and that's paradise. One of the scholars said how can you fight a people who look down the barrel of a gun and see paradise. It's what we are all after, eternal bliss, eternal paradise, which is a lot better than the world we live in."[47]

Abu Mariam, a Muslim from Toulouse, France, who also left his home to travel to Syria and join the Islamic State, echoed Haddad's sentiments: "I am but a contribution to the conquest of Islam, and I also look forward to reach[ing] paradise via jihad for the cause of Allah. We [Muslims] are all promised paradise because we listened to the words of Allah. Islam is a really great religion. It includes all aspects of life. It gives meaning to human life." His voice cracked as he continued: "I have devoted my entire life to jihad...I am only looking up to paradise; is there anything better than this?"[48]

The Old Man of the Mountain would have been pleased.

The Old Man's promise to these young men that they would enter Paradise if they were killed in the process of killing for him would already have been familiar to them—because that same promise is in the Qur'an: "Indeed, Allah has purchased from the believers their lives and their properties; for that they will have Paradise. They fight in the cause of Allah, so they kill and are killed" (9:111).

The Islamic State doesn't engage in such elaborate ruses as the Old Man of the Mountain, but it does lure young Muslims with the same promise of Paradise, offered in the same way to those who "kill and are killed" for Allah.

The Khawarij

The Kharijites (or Khawarij) are another of the most often-mentioned ancient Muslim sects, since in their violence and rigorousness they resemble today's jihad movements. Muslim spokesmen in the West frequently brand groups such as the Islamic State and al-Qaeda "neo-Kharijites," implying that the jihadis are Islamic heretics with no standing in the religion.

But reality is not quite that simple.

The Khawarij, or "those who go out," left the Muslim community during the civil strife known as the First Fitna (disturbance, unrest) in the late 650s, when Ali ibn Abi Talib, and Muawiya, the governor of Syria, were vying for the caliphate. Finding the behavior of both to be unacceptable on Islamic grounds, the Kharijites left—and then plotted to kill them both.

The Khawarij held that Muslims must not obey a sinful ruler and that they have a duty to overthrow him. They considered those who did not do so to be unbelievers.

On the one hand, this idea is directly contradicted by numerous statements attributed to Muhammad:

> You should listen to and obey your *Imam* (Muslim ruler) even if he was an Ethiopian (black) slave whose head looks like a raisin.[49]

> There will be leaders who will not be led by my guidance and who will not adopt my ways. There will be among them men who will have the hearts of devils in the bodies of human beings.... You will listen to Amir and carry out his orders; even if your back is flogged and your wealth is snatched, you should listen and obey.[50]

On the other, however, some hadiths depict Muhammad mandating an obedience that was not quite so unconditional:

It is obligatory upon a Muslim that he should listen (to the ruler appointed over him) and obey him whether he likes it or not, except that he is ordered to do a sinful thing. If he is ordered to do a sinful act, a Muslim should neither listen to him nor should he obey his orders.[51]

The hadith literature was first published around two hundred years after Muhammad is supposed to have died, and around 180 years after the Kharijites first "went out." In those days, rival factions among the Muslims fabricated sayings of Muhammad to support their own positions.

The conflict between the nascent Muslim establishment—both Muawiya's camp, which became the Sunnis, and Ali's party, which became the Shi'ites—and the Kharijites gave rise to these conflicting hadiths. The ones depicting Muhammad enjoining absolute obedience even to an unjust ruler were placed in his mouth by supporters of the caliphate, while those in which Muhammad forbids obedience to a ruler who orders Muslims to sin are likely to have come from the Khawarij and their supporters.

Also favorable to the Khawarij are Qur'an verses such as this one, enjoining Muslims to fight against Muslims who oppress their brethren: "And if two factions among the believers should fight, then make settlement between the two. But if one of them oppresses the other, then fight against the one that oppresses until it returns to the ordinance of Allah. And if it returns, then make settlement between them in justice and act justly. Indeed, Allah loves those who act justly" (49:9).

Numerous Islamic authorities have branded the Islamic State and other jihad groups neo-Khawarij for their rejection of the legitimacy of relatively secular Muslim rulers such as Hosni Mubarak and Saddam Hussein, who did not govern in accord with Islamic law, and sinful rulers such as the House of Saud, the most conspicuous of all conspicuous consumers. Muslim spokesmen frequently label modern-day jihad groups "*takfiris*" because, like the Khawarij, they are eager to pronounce *takfir* against fellow Muslims—in other words, to declare them outside the fold of Islam for some heresy.

But as the historian Bernard Lewis notes, "Islamic tradition gives recognition to the principle of justifiable revolt."[52] Takfir is also a recognized principle in Islamic tradition, with the limits on how often it can be used essentially subjective.[53] In other words, the actions of the Khawarij—and of their modern counterparts in ISIS—can be justified by generally accepted principles of Islamic law.

Thus it is difficult for Muslims to criticize the Islamic State and other jihad groups that fight against Muslim rulers they consider to be unjust. And thus the Islamic State continues to gain recruits, even after most Muslim organizations and spokesmen in the West have denounced it.

The Wahhabis

In the strictness of their Islamic observance, the Islamic State resembles the Wahhabis, who before the rise of ISIS were the world's best-known modern-day Muslim hard-liners. Although the Saudis don't refer to it by that name—for them it is just plain, unadulterated Islam—Wahhabi Islam is the official religion of the Kingdom of the Two Holy Places. That's another name for Saudi Arabia, which includes the two cities Muhammad called home, Mecca and Medina, and their two great mosques (the Two Holy Places). By virtue of this blessed location, the Saudis consider themselves to be the guardians not just of Muhammad's mosque but of his legacy—the guardians of Islam itself. The House of Saud has spent untold billions of dollars to spread the Wahhabi understanding of Islam around the world, and in many areas (notably East Africa and Central Asia) it has supplanted, or is in the process of supplanting, more relaxed forms of cultural Islam that had held sway in those places for centuries.

Those who place high hopes on the reform of Islam should note that Wahhabism *is* a reform movement—indeed, the quintessential reform movement in Islam. Muhammad ibn Abdul al-Wahhab was an eighteenth-century Muslim who proclaimed his intention to restore Islam's original purity by rejecting all innovation (*bid'a*) and basing his religious observance strictly on what the Qur'an and Muhammad taught.

Wahhab set out to extinguish all Islamic practices that he considered not to have come from either source: thus Wahhabi mosques lack minarets—the towers that the caller to prayer, the muezzin, climbs in order to chant the *azan*, the call to prayer. Wahhab also rejected the veneration of Muslim saints and prayers at their shrines, a practice that had become widespread by the eighteenth century. Wahhab pointed to hadiths in which Muhammad himself condemned this practice, calling it *shirk*, the combination of idolatry and polytheism that is the worst sin of all in Islam: associating partners with Allah in worship.

The Wahhabis were often just as brutal as the Islamic State is today. In an 1803 attack that could have come from today's headlines about ISIS, the Wahhabis entered Ta'if, a city near Mecca, massacred all the men, and enslaved all the women and children.[54]

Like the Khawarij, Wahhab declared all Muslims who disagreed with him to be unbelievers who could be lawfully killed as heretics and apostates. In 1744 Wahhab entered into an alliance with an Arab chieftain, Muhammad ibn Saud, and together they set out on jihad against those enemies, fighting against the Ottoman authorities, who Wahhab believed had lost all legitimacy by departing from the tenets of Islam.

Not long after Wahhab's death in 1792, the Wahhabis captured the Two Holy Places of Mecca and Medina and after that gradually expanded their domains until finally, in 1932, the Wahhabi sheikh ibn Saud captured Riyadh and established the Kingdom of Saudi Arabia.

Oil money has made Wahhabi ideals mainstream, even dominant, among Muslims worldwide. The Saudis have spent as much as $100 billion to spread Wahhabism worldwide.[55] However, other Muslims still make the same complaints against the Wahhabis as were made long ago against the Khawarij: they're Qur'anic rigorists, but nonetheless they misunderstand the noble book, and their piety is a false front: "While claiming to be adherents to 'authentic' Sunnah [Muslim tradition], these deviants are quick to label anyone who opposes their beliefs...as 'sufi,' [that is, akin to adherents of the mystical Sufi sect, elements of which many Muslims consider heretical] while exploiting the Muslims' love for Islam by overexaggerating the phrase 'Qur'an and Sunnah' in their senseless rhetoric."[56] The same criticisms are made about the new self-styled caliphate today.

Al-Qaeda is simply an especially virulent outgrowth of Wahhabism. And ISIS is just an especially virulent outgrowth of al-Qaeda.

The Case for ISIS's Bloody Tactics: How Zarqawi Laid the Intellectual and Theological Foundations of the Islamic State

Muslims in the West, the president of the United States, and our media regularly condemn the atrocities committed by ISIS as un-Islamic. And we have seen that the Islamic State's bloody deeds have made even al-Qaeda terrorists uncomfortable—though they seem to have found it difficult to articulate a principled case, grounded in Islamic texts and the accepted scholarly rulings of Islamic jurisprudence, against those bloodthirsty acts, instead falling back on tactical and prudential arguments.

ISIS, on the other hand, does not hesitate to justify its atrocities by Islamic law. The groundwork for that justification was laid in the course of the long-running controversy between al-Qaeda and the precursor organization of the Islamic State, which began not long after Zarqawi gave his allegiance (and that of the precursor organization, al-Qaeda in the Land of Two Rivers) to Osama bin Laden and ended in the 2014 break between the two groups. In the process of defending himself from criticism, Zarqawi ended up delineating and justifying many of the distinctive approaches of what would become the Islamic State.

For example, Zarqawi's group was criticized for killing Muslims as well as non-Muslims, in apparent defiance of the Qur'an's injunction, "never is it for a believer to kill a believer except by mistake" (4:92).

Responding to this criticism, on May 20, 2005, Zarqawi released an audiotape in which he presented a detailed defense of his operations. In the process, he set out what would turn out to be the Islamic State's eventual justification for many of its increasingly barbaric enormities.

OSTRICH ALERT

"Eliminating the ISIL threat.... will mean demolishing the distortion of one of the world's great peaceful religions."

—Secretary of State John Kerry[57]

Zarqawi argued not on prudential but on theological grounds: making copious reference to Islamic sources, he portrayed the murderous behavior of al-Qaeda in the Land of Two Rivers as legitimate jihad operations that every Muslim should endorse.

Zarqawi insisted that his group was behaving in a strictly Islamic manner: "the Mujahideen carry out their operations under strict adherence to the rules of engagement as set forth by Allah, His messenger, our prophet Muhammad, and his companions." His followers' Islam-approved methods followed from their overall goal as jihad warriors: "And why not? After all, the Mujahideen took to the battle fields only to establish the Deen [religion] of Allah (Islam), to make the word of Allah high above any others, and to gain the pleasure of Allah."

This statement is noteworthy in light of the fact that Western analysts universally ascribe the roots of jihad terror to poverty, lack of educational or economic opportunity—anything other than an endeavor to "establish the Deen of Allah" and "to make the word of Allah high above any others, and to gain the pleasure of Allah."[58]

Having thus situated his endeavors firmly within the Islamic religious imperative to wage war against non-Muslims, Zarqawi began his justification, by Islamic law, of killing Muslims as well as Americans. His intention, he said, was to "put forth and clarify the judgment and the rules of Allah's Sharia'ah (Islamic Jurisprudence) in connection with those incidents in which Muslims are killed as a result rather than the main target of Mujahideen operations."

It is noteworthy that at that point Zarqawi warned that he did "not intend to address the legality of martyrdom operations for it has been decided by more than one scholar already." That is, he was taking for granted that suicide attacks were permissible—most likely in light of the fact that the Qur'an guarantees a place in Paradise to those who "kill and are killed" for Allah (9:111).

Zarqawi also took for granted that Muslims had a responsibility before Allah to wage war against unbelievers. "There is no doubt," Zarqawi proclaimed, "that Allah commanded us to strike the Kuffar (unbelievers), kill them, and fight them by all means necessary to achieve the goal." He argued that any means at all were permissible in this endeavor:

> The servants of Allah who perform Jihad to elevate the word (laws) of Allah, are permitted to use any and all means necessary to strike the active unbeliever combatants for the purpose of killing them, snatch their souls from their body, cleanse the earth from their abomination, and lift their trial and persecution of the servants of Allah. The goal must be pursued even if the means to accomplish it affect both the intended active fighters and unintended passive ones such as

women, children and any other passive category specified by
our jurisprudence.

He was making the case, in other words, that operations such as 9/11
were fully sanctioned by Islamic law, even if women and children were
killed in them. And the same things would be true, he argued, even if Muslims were killed as collateral damage:

> This permissibility extends to situations in which Muslims may
> get killed if they happen to be with or near the intended enemy,
> and if it is not possible to avoid hitting them or separate them
> from the intended Kafirs. Although spilling sacred Muslim blood
> is a grave offense, it is not only permissible but it is mandated in
> order to prevent more serious adversity from happening, stalling
> or abandoning Jihad that is.

Zarqawi was killed over two years before Barack Obama became president, and eight years before President Obama declared: "ISIL is not
'Islamic.' No religion condones the killing of innocents, and the vast
majority of ISIL's victims have been Muslim."[59] Obama was assuming that
because its victims were Muslim, the Islamic State must not be Islamic;
however, ISIS's foremost founding figure had long before explained why
that was a false assumption.

Moreover, as far as Zarqawi was concerned, those who denied that it was
permissible to kill Muslims in jihad operations were enabling the victory of
the infidels over the Muslims, and the consequent disunity and subjugation
of the worldwide Muslim community:

> If one says that we must not allow the killing of Muslims under
> any circumstance, especially in light of modern war tactics, this

means nothing except stalling or permanently abandoning Jihad. This will lead to handing over the land and people to the unbelievers who are full of hate for Islam and Muslims. The unbelievers will have a free hand to humiliate and persecute Islam and Muslims and Muslims will be forced to live by Kafir rules and be treated like slaves. Many Muslims will be pressured or forced to give up their religion, Islam will be altered, modified, and replaced with another form that will be totally different from that which was revealed to the one who was sent with the sword, peace and prayer be upon him.

Wait, It Looks Like This Guy's Religion *Does* Condone the Killing of Innocents

	President Obama	Terror Master Zarqawi
On Killing Innocents	"No religion condones the killing of innocents"	"The goal must be pursued even if the means to accomplish it affect...women, children and any other passive category specified by our jurisprudence"
On Killing Muslims	"The vast majority of ISIL's victims have been Muslim"	"Although spilling sacred Muslim blood is a grave offense, it is not only permissible but it is mandated in order to prevent more serious adversity from happening, stalling or abandoning Jihad that is"

The "one who was sent with the sword" is, of course, the Muslim prophet Muhammad.

Zarqawi was harshly critical of Muslim scholars who rejected his jihad, referring to them as "the wicked scholars" who "have looked the other way and sold their Deen (religion) for a miserable price in this life." He predicted that one outcome of the conflict between al-Qaeda and the Americans in Iraq would be to separate "the true believers from the rest," and he fulminated against "the defeatists from our own skin" who "decided to stab the true Mujahideen [warriors of jihad] in the back and throw doubts about the permissibility of their operations."[60]

These people, he asserted, were nothing less than traitors to Islam itself, allying with unbelievers in defiance of the Qur'an's prohibition on such alliances (3:28, 5:51). They had, Zarqawi said, "in fact directly or indirectly helped the cross worshippers in their campaign against Mujahideen. The defeatists, the unfaithful, and the ill-intentioned people from our own skin, have criticized our operations against the enemies of Allah on the bases that some of these operations results in killing so called 'innocent civilians.'"[61]

These principles would become the hallmarks of the Islamic State: that any means were acceptable in fighting against and killing non-Muslims, which was an Islamic responsibility, and that it was acceptable to kill fellow Muslims in service of the goal of implementing Islamic law over the world.

It's All about the PR

Some senior al-Qaeda leaders, however, were skeptical. They believed that Zarqawi was too brutal and that his tactics were unwise: to implement Islamic law abruptly in areas of Saddam Hussein's Iraq where it had not been fully enforced in living memory would only alienate less fervent Muslims who might otherwise support the movement, as well as repulse the non-Muslim world to the degree that it might take more severe action against the jihadis than it otherwise would.

In response to Zarqawi's robust defense from Islamic law of the slaughter of innocents and fellow Muslims, Osama's lieutenant Ayman al-Zawahiri—the scholarly and bespectacled Cairo surgeon, a man of wealth and education, in contrast to Zarqawi's hardscrabble upbringing and education in the school of hard knocks—was reduced to arguing on prudential grounds that the kind of bloodthirsty jihad Zarqawi was waging would not make his group popular with the larger Muslim population.

In the same July 9, 2005, letter in which he had laid out al-Qaeda's four-step plan for reviving the caliphate, Zawahiri, who became the leader of al-Qaeda after bin Laden's death, praised Zarqawi's successes and very gently remonstrated with him for doing things that could turn public opinion against him.[62] Zawahiri is exceedingly polite and deferential in the letter, but cannot help allowing a hint of condescension to slip through now and again.

"I want to be the first to congratulate you," Zawahiri wrote, "for what God has blessed you with in terms of fighting battle in the heart of the Islamic world, which was formerly the field for major battles in Islam's history, and what is now the place for the greatest battle of Islam in this era, and what will happen, according to what appeared in the Hadiths of the Messenger of God about the epic battles between Islam and atheism." He praises Zarqawi in fulsome terms, writing that "God has blessed you and your brothers while many of the Muslim mujahedeen have longed for that blessing, and that is Jihad in the heart of the Islamic world. He has, in addition to that, granted you superiority over the idolatrous infidels, traitorous apostates, and those turncoat deviants."

Only then does he begin to upbraid Zarqawi gently for the ferocity of his jihad in Iraq. He warns:

Among the things which the feelings of the Muslim populace who love and support you will never find palatable—also—are the scenes of slaughtering the hostages. You shouldn't be deceived by the praise of some of the zealous young men and their description of you as the shaykh of the slaughterers, etc. They do not express the general view of the admirer and the supporter of the resistance in Iraq, and of you in particular by the favor and blessing of God.

Zawahiri anticipates Zarqawi's objection:

And your response, while true, might be: Why shouldn't we sow terror in the hearts of the Crusaders and their helpers? And isn't the destruction of the villages and the cities on the heads of their inhabitants more cruel than slaughtering? And aren't the cluster bombs and the seven ton bombs and the depleted uranium bombs crueler than slaughtering? And isn't killing by torture crueler than slaughtering? And isn't violating the honor of men and women more painful and more destructive than slaughtering?

These are Qur'anic references that Zawahiri knew Zarqawi would understand. The Qur'an directs Muslims to "make ready your strength to the utmost of your power, including steeds of war, to strike terror into the enemies of Allah" (8:60)—hence Zawahiri's anticipated question from Zarqawi, "Why shouldn't we sow terror in the hearts of the Crusaders and their helpers?"

Likewise, his refrain about various alleged Western atrocities being "crueler than slaughtering" is a reference to the Qur'an's declaration that "persecution is worse than slaughter" (2:191, 2:217). Islamic tradition explains that this statement from the Qur'an was revealed to Muhammad after he ordered a group of Muslims to raid one of the trading caravans of their enemies, the Quraysh, at Nakhla, a settlement near Mecca. In order not to lose their chance at the caravan altogether, the raiders struck during one of the sacred months of the Arabic calendar, during which violence was forbidden—violating the sacred month.

Muhammad, it is said, at first received them coldly—until Allah revealed to him the phrase, "persecution is worse than slaughter." The Muslims were persecuted by the Quraysh, or claimed they were, and so slaughtering them even in the sacred month was acceptable: the prohibition against fighting in the sacred month could be set aside for extenuating circumstances.

Zawahiri was thus anticipating that Zarqawi would object to his request to rein in his jihad by pointing out enemy atrocities and justifying his response with the Qur'anic phrase. And he stood by his statement that public opinion in this case would trump even the directive from the Muslim holy book, for their supporters, he said, did not comprehend this principle, and Zarqawi's actions would be vulnerable to "a campaign by the malicious, perfidious, and fallacious campaign by the deceptive and fabricated media. And we would spare the people from the effect of questions about the usefulness of our actions in the hearts and minds of the general opinion that is essentially sympathetic to us."

This was the core of the difference between al-Qaeda and what would become ISIS: al-Qaeda believed that the tactics practiced by Zarqawi, which he would pass on to the Islamic State, were counterproductive, arousing the horror and revulsion of the world, which could backfire by stirring the infidels to fury against the Muslims—an infuriated foe is harder to defeat than a complacent one.

Of course this was a bit rich coming from the masterminds of the single event most responsible for sparking the present round of the conflict between the West and the Islamic world: the September 11 attacks. Nothing aroused the anger of the world in the way that 9/11 did, and both al-Qaeda and the Islamic State read the Qur'an, which directs them to "strike terror into the hearts of the enemies of Allah" (8:60). As Zawahiri conceded, Zarqawi would be "justified" in objecting to his letter by pointing to this divine imperative. He could also have pointed to the fact that al-Qaeda and his group shared the same goals and the same beliefs, but differed only in tactics.

And on tactics, who turned out to be right? The problem with prudential arguments is that who's right depends on what actually happens next. You can never tell for sure who has the better end of the argument until you see how things turn out in practice. Zawahiri warned Zarqawi not to put too much stock in "the praise of some of the zealous young men and their description of you as the shaykh of the slaughterers." He thought that "the Muslim populace who love[d] and support[ed]" Zarqawi wouldn't ever find hostage-murder snuff videos "palatable." But as we'll see, Zarqawi and his successors in ISIS, aiming their PR campaign straight at the "zealous young men" demographic that Zawahiri discounted, were able to find a mass audience that would be inspired by those murders, so inspired that they would flock from all over the world in the tens of thousands to join ISIS's jihad— when they weren't undertaking jihad attacks at home in Europe and America. Ironically, bin Laden's organization apparently underestimated the appeal of the strictest Sharia and the most violent jihad—and overestimated the resolve of the United States to oppose it. So today, history seems to have passed al-Qaeda by, and ISIS is in the ascendant.

Zarqawi won the argument.

Chapter Two

ISIS COMES TO AMERICA

"I'll see you guys in New York," the Islamic State's future Caliph Ibrahim, Abu Bakr al-Baghdadi, supposedly said when he was released from Iraq's Camp Bucca.

Whether or not he said it, ISIS had designs on Gotham.

On October 23, 2014, in Queens, a man named Zale Thompson attacked four New York police officers with an eighteen-and-a-half-inch hatchet, wounding one in the head and another in the arm before he was shot dead. His father ascribed the attack to the racism that had apparently destroyed his son's life: "He wanted white people to pay for all that slavery and all that racism. I think he committed suicide—and he was taking one of y'all with him.... He just said, 'They have to pay for all their unfairness.' Unfairness for the way they treat black people."[1]

Did you know?

- Before Zale Thompson attacked NYPD officers with a hatchet, he did computer searches for "lone wolf" and how to say "death to America" in Arabic

- The month before the hatchet attack, the Islamic State issued a call to Muslims in the U.S. to attack the police

- Before the *Charlie Hebdo* massacre in France, an ISIS jihadi tweeted out "snail-eating people" with a weeping emoticon

NOBODY'S PERFECT

...

"If you're looking for 'perfect' Muslims who never make any mistakes in their Jihad, then you will be looking in vain! If the Zionists and the Crusaders had never invaded and colonized the Islamic lands after WW1, then there would be no need for Jihad! Which is better, to sit around and do nothing, or to Jihad fisabeelallah [for the sake of Allah]!"

—a September 2014 comment Thompson wrote on a YouTube video discussing the restoration of the caliphate[5]

But the police investigation of the attack uncovered a different motive. As one law enforcement official said, "This guy spent every waking moment on the Internet.... He Googled the words 'jihad against police.'"[2] He had also searched the internet for information for "lone wolf," "jihad," "jihad against the infidels," "fatwa against americans," and "death to America in Arabic."[3]

Thompson had also searched on the internet for information about two recent jihad attacks in Canada.[4]

Incitement to Murder

What exactly might Zale Thompson have seen in his relentless internet searches that could have inspired him to try to hack four members of the NYPD to death?

How about this: "You must strike the soldiers, patrons, and troops of the tawaghit [rebels against Allah]. Strike their police, security and intelligence members"?[6]

And, if he needed any further encouragement, how does this sound? "Knocking off a police, military or any other law-enforcement officer sends a chilling message to the so-called 'civilians' and fills their hearts with consternation."[7]

Those incitements to murder had been issued by the Islamic State in September of 2014, the very month before Thompson's hatchet attack. This encouragement to engage in violent jihad in America and the rest of the West were part of a continuing campaign on the part of ISIS to bring the war home to the "crusader" powers—by enlisting Muslims already present in the United States, Europe, and Australia to carry out the very kind of "lone wolf" attacks that Thompson had been searching for information about on his computer.

As one of the September 2014 Islamic State appeals calling Western Muslims to jihad noted, there are 2.6 million Muslims living in the United States today.[8] If ISIS can persuade even a small percentage of them to throw in their lot with the caliphate and commit acts of violence here, they could cause serious mayhem. ISIS would achieve the desired result: "you will pay the price as you walk on your streets, turning right and left, fearing the Muslims. You will not feel secure even in your bedrooms."[9]

Bringing the War Home to America

Just before ISIS proclaimed itself the caliphate in late June 2014, it had issued a warning to Americans that jihad attacks against U.S. embassies and American civilians would follow any American attack upon the terror group's holdings (grammar, spelling, and punctuation reproduced as in the original):

1. If the United States bomb Iraq, every American citizen is a legitimate target for us.
2. Every American doctor working in any country will be slaughtered if America attack Iraq.
3. Any company in Arab countries which employs Americans is a legitimate target for every Muslim.
4. If America attacks Iraq; every American embassy in the world will be exposed and attacked with car bombs.
5. American civilian blood is not more precious than the blood of the children and women of Iraq.
6. Is the blood of American civilians forbidden? The blood of the children of Fallujah permissible?

7. For every drop of blood shed by the Iraqis, Americans will shed a river of blood.

8. Every government that is willing to open its territory for U.S. aircrafts to launch attacks will bear the consequences.

9. Bin Laden says; dont consult anyone when killing Americans.[10]

By August 2014, Baghdadi's Islamic State had succeeded and grown to such an extent that then–Defense Secretary Chuck Hagel said that it was "as sophisticated and well-funded as any group we have seen. They are beyond just a terrorist group. They marry ideology, a sophistication of…military prowess. They are tremendously well-funded. This is beyond anything we've seen." What's more, he said that the Islamic State was "an imminent threat to every interest we have, whether it's in Iraq or anywhere else."[11]

"Anywhere else" included the United States. As Hagel was sounding his warning, Islamic State supporters posted photos of Islamic State symbols being held in front of the White House and other American sites, with the message: "We are in your state, we are in your cities, we are in your streets."[12]

That same month, VICE Media's Medyan Dairieh released a video report of his three weeks in the Islamic State–controlled city of Raqqa, Syria—the de facto capital of its new caliphate. Dairieh recorded ISIS spokesman Abu Mosa boasting and threatening: "I say to America that the Islamic Caliphate has been established. Don't be cowards and attack us with drones. Instead send your soldiers, the ones we humiliated in Iraq. We will humiliate them everywhere, God willing, and we will raise the flag of Allah in the White House."[13]

Calling the Muslims in the U.S. to Arms

On September 16, an Islamic State document entitled "To 2.6M Muslims in USA: A Call to Arms to Defend Islam and Avenge the Slaughter of

Muslims" called for Muslims in the West to wage "open source jihad" by mounting "lone wolf operations."

This is the appeal that pointed out, "Knocking off a police, military or any other law-enforcement officer sends a chilling message to the so-called 'civilians' and fills their hearts with consternation."[14] According to the FBI, which made this threat public on October 11, 2014—less than two weeks before Zale Thompson's hatchet attack on the NYPD—the "list of potential targets" also included "FBI personnel, government officials and media figures."[15]

"We Have Prepared for You What Will Pain You"

On September 21, 2014, Islamic State spokesman Abu Muhammad Adnani issued a lengthy and remarkable statement calling Muslims in the West to jihad. It is worth examining at length, as it reveals a great deal about the Islamic State's current mindset, as well as its goals for the future of the United States and the world.

The West, Adnani said, is not as strong as it seems to be: it is, rather, "a conceited and brash encampment of falsehood, which demonstrates itself to be powerful, and subduing, one that no conqueror can dominate nor any defender withstand. But the reality is they are fearful and terrified, humiliated and left with a weak plan, shaken and defeated, despite their uninhibited movement throughout the lands."[16]

By contrast, the believers are weak in earthly wealth and military might, but have the power of Allah on their side.

Adnani told the "soldiers of the Islamic State": "By Allah, He has healed the chests of the believers through the killing of the nusayriyyah (alawites) and rafidah (shiites) at your hands."[17] This was a reference to the Qur'an's promise that Allah will soothe the hearts (or "heal the chests" as Adnani put it, or "satisfy the breasts" in the translation below) of those who wage jihad against the unbelievers: "Fight them; Allah will punish them by your hands and will disgrace them and give you victory over them and satisfy the breasts of a believing people and remove the fury in the believers' hearts" (9:14–15).

Comparing the skepticism that greeted the Islamic State's declaration of the caliphate to the skepticism that initially greeted Muhammad, Adnani declared, "If the people belie you, reject your state and your call, and mock your caliphate, then know that your Prophet (blessings and peace be upon him) was belied. His call was rejected. He was mocked."[18] But, he said, Allah will grant the Islamic State victory because of its fidelity to him.

Then came the warning to the West: "O America, O allies of America, and O crusaders, know that the matter is more dangerous than you have imagined and greater than you have envisioned." Like many other jihadists, Adnani boasted that the Muslims will defeat the infidels because they love death more than the infidels love life, and since Paradise awaits them, they win either way.[19]

This makes for an invincible fighting force:

O crusaders, you have realized the threat of the Islamic State, but you have not become

NOT THAT THIS HAS ANYTHING TO DO WITH ISLAM

According to Adnani, "the followers of the messengers [the prophets]" have "lower numbers, meager equipment, and a weaker voice." Nonetheless, "their strength can never be subdued. Their authority can never be broken. They are firm in every battle. And they are forefront in every encounter, having neither fear nor dread. In the end, they will have the triumph and victory." Why? Because of "their faith in Allah, the Mighty, the Compeller. From Him is their strength, and through Him is their authority. He is sufficient for them, and upon Him they rely. They are certain of His aid. And they returned having attained His favor and bounty. They do not fear anyone save Him."

—September 21, 2014, letter from the Islamic State's Abū Muhammad al-'Adnānī ash-Shāmī[20]

aware of the cure, and you will not discover the cure because there is no cure. If you fight it, it becomes stronger and tougher. If you leave it alone, it grows and expands. If Obama has promised you with defeating the Islamic State, then Bush has also lied before him.[21]

Not only will the Islamic State not be defeated, he said, but it will conquer the West, beginning with Rome:

> We will conquer your Rome, break your crosses, and enslave your women, by the permission of Allah, the Exalted. This is His promise to us; He is glorified and He does not fail in His promise. If we do not reach that time, then our children and grandchildren will reach it, and they will sell your sons as slaves at the slave market.[22]

Adnani quoted the hadith that depicts Muhammad predicting that first Constantinople would be conquered by the Muslims (as it was in 1453), and then the Muslim conquest of Rome would follow. He also predicted a dark future for the U.S. and Europe:

> O Americans, and O Europeans, the Islamic State did not initiate a war against you, as your governments and media try to make you believe. It is you who started the transgression against us, and thus you deserve blame and you will pay a great price. You will pay the price when your economies collapse. You will pay

HEADS THEY WIN, TAILS WE LOSE

• • •

"You fight a people who can never be defeated. They either gain victory or are killed. And O crusaders, you are losers in both outcomes, because you are ignorant of the reality that none of us is killed but to resurrect the dead amongst us.... If [a jihadi] survives, he lives as a victor with freedom, might, honor, and authority. And if he is killed, he illuminates the path for those after him and goes on to his Lord as a joyful martyr."

—September 21, 2014, letter from the Islamic State's Abū Muhammad al-ʻAdnānī ash-Shāmī[23] the price when your sons are sent to wage war against us and they return to you as disabled amputees, or inside coffins, or mentally ill. You will pay the price as you are afraid of travelling to any land. Rather you will pay the price as you walk on your streets, turning right and left, fearing the Muslims. You will not feel secure even in your bedrooms. You will pay the price when this crusade of yours collapses, and thereafter we will strike you in your homeland, and you will never be able to harm anyone afterwards. You will pay the price, and we have prepared for you what will pain you.[24]

America and Europe were not his only targets. Adnani also called for attacks on Iraqi Shi'ites: "O Sunnis of Iraq, the time has come for you to learn from the lessons of the past, and to learn that nothing will work with the rafidah [Shi'ites] other than slicing their throats and striking their necks." He called for jihadis to target "the guards of the jews [sic], the soldiers of Sisi, the new Pharaoh of Egypt": "Rig the roads with explosives for them. Attack their bases. Raid their homes. Cut off their heads. Do not let them feel secure. Hunt them wherever they may be. Turn their worldly life into fear and fire. Remove their families from their homes and thereafter blowup [sic] their homes."[25]

Going by Adnani's statement, ISIS would not seem to have any concern about biting off more than it can chew. He also specifically mentioned Libya, Tunisia, and Yemen, as well as Europe, America, Australia, and Canada, Morocco, Algeria, Khorasan (Afghanistan), the Caucasus, and Iran. And in all these places, he urged jihad:

You must strike the soldiers, patrons, and troops of the tawaghit [rebels against Allah]. Strike their police, security, and intelligence members, as well as their treacherous agents. Destroy their beds. Embitter their lives for them and busy them with themselves.

If you can kill a disbelieving American or European—especially the spiteful and filthy French—or an Australian, or a Canadian, or any other disbeliever from the disbelievers waging war, including the citizens of the countries that entered into a coalition against the Islamic State, then rely upon Allah, and kill him in any manner or way however it may be.

Do not ask for anyone's advice and do not seek anyone's verdict. Kill the disbeliever whether he is civilian or military, for they have the same ruling. Both of them are disbelievers. Both of them are considered to be waging war [the civilian by belonging to a state waging war against the Muslims]. Both of their blood and wealth is legal for you to destroy, for blood does not become illegal or legal to spill by the clothes being worn. The civilian outfit does not make blood illegal to spill, and the military uniform does not make blood legal to spill.

The only things that make blood illegal and legal to spill are Islam and a covenant (peace treaty, dhimma, etc.). Blood becomes legal to spill through disbelief. So whoever is a Muslim, his blood and wealth are sanctified. And whoever is a disbeliever, his wealth is legal for a Muslim to take and his blood is legal to spill. His blood is like the blood of a dog; there is no sin for him in spilling it nor is there any blood money to be paid for doing such.[26]

Adnani, clearly not a big fan of Obama, taunted the American president for thinking that the Islamic State could be defeated with airstrikes:

And O Obama, O mule of the jews [sic]. You are vile. You are vile. You are vile. And you will be disappointed, Obama. Is this all you were capable of doing in this campaign of yours? Is this how far America has reached of incapacity and weakness? Are America and all its allies from amongst the crusaders and atheists unable to come down to the ground? Have you not realized—O crusaders—that proxy wars have not availed you nor will they ever avail you? Have you not realized, O mule of the jews [sic], that the battle cannot be decided from the air at all? Or do you think that you are smarter than Bush, your obeyed fool, when he brought the armies of the cross and placed them under the fire of the mujahidin on the ground? No, you are more foolish than him.[27]

Finally, Adnani closed his letter with an explanation that the Islamic State was fighting against the Kurds in Iraq and Syria not because of ethnic or tribal divisions, but because of Islam.

NOT THAT THIS HAS ANYTHING TO DO WITH ISLAM

"Our war with Kurds is a religious war. It is not a nationalistic war—we seek the refuge of Allah. We do not fight Kurds because they are Kurds. Rather we fight the disbelievers amongst them, the allies of the crusaders and jews [sic] in their war against the Muslims. As for the Muslim Kurds, then they are our people and brothers wherever they may be. We spill our blood to save their blood. The Muslim Kurds in the ranks of the Islamic State are many. They are the toughest of fighters against the disbelievers amongst their people."

—from the September 21, 2014, letter by the Islamic State's Abū Muhammad al-'Adnānī ash-Shāmī[28]

Brinsley: "Strike Terror into the Hearts of the Enemies of Allah"

Thirty-three days after Adnani's letter urging attacks on the police, absolving jihadis of any guilt for the blood of non-Muslims, and urging improvised attacks with any weapon that might be to hand, Zale Thompson used his hatchet on the New York City policemen. He wasn't the first Western Muslim to heed the call of ISIS here—and he wouldn't be the last.

On December 20, 2014, a Muslim named Ismaaiyl Abdullah Brinsley murdered NYPD Officers Rafael Ramos and Wenjian Liu as they ate lunch in their patrol car.

Brinsley had written that he was going to avenge the killings of Eric Garner and Michael Brown that caused so much racial strife in 2014. Much less noted in the media was the fact that Brinsley's Facebook page featured a photo of the Qur'an open to the eighth chapter, where Allah exhorts the believers to "strike terror into the hearts of the enemies of Allah" (8:60).[29] Brinsley also had worked for the Islamic Society of North America, an

DON'T BE AFRAID TO IMPROVISE!

"If you are not able to find an IED or a bullet, then single out the disbelieving American, Frenchman, or any of their allies. Smash his head with a rock, or slaughter him with a knife, or run him over with your car, or throw him down from a high place, or choke him, or poison him. Do not lack. Do not be contemptible. Let your slogan be, 'May I not be saved if the cross worshipper and taghut (ruler ruling by manmade laws) patron survives.' If you are unable to do so, then burn his home, car, or business. Or destroy his crops.

"If you are unable to do so, then spit in his face. If your self refuses to do so, while your brothers are being bombarded and killed, and while their blood and wealth everywhere is deemed lawful by their enemies, then review your religion. You are in a dangerous condition because the religion cannot be established without wala' [loyalty to believers] and bara' [disavowal of unbelievers]."

—September 21, 2014, letter from the Islamic State's Abū Muhammad al-'Adnānī ash-Shāmī[30]

organization with ties to Hamas and the Muslim Brotherhood, and went by the name Ismaaiyl Abdullah-Muhammad.[31]

Were his murders another example of a Muslim heeding the Islamic State's call to individual Muslims to attack police in Western countries? Authorities have remained tight-lipped, and there is no doubt that Brinsley was interested in avenging what he saw as the unjust deaths of Garner and Brown. But the Islamic State has sought to appropriate racial tensions in the U.S., and specifically anger about the killing of Michael Brown, for its own cause—tweeting out ISIS support for the Ferguson protestors and urging them to commit to jihad.[32] And the timing, as well as the photo of Qur'an 8:60 on Brinsley's Facebook page, was certainly suspicious. Brinsley may have thought, *What better way to strike terror into the hearts of the enemies of Allah than to kill a couple of infidel, racist police officers, just as the Islamic State has called for?* It would be refreshing if we had law enforcement and government officials willing to investigate such questions, but in this age of Obama, we do not.

Rouleau: "NO SURRENDER. IT'S EITHER VICTORY OR MARTYRDOM"

There was no such ambiguity about the motives of a Canadian convert to Islam, Martin Couture-Rouleau, who after his conversion called himself Ahmad Rouleau (on Facebook) and Abu Ibrahim AlCanadi (on Twitter).[33] On October 20, 2014, just a week after the Islamic State's call to Muslims in the West to pursue "[k]nocking off a police, military or any other law-enforcement officer" was made public by the FBI, Rouleau drove his 2000 Nissan Altima to a parking lot in St-Jean-sur-Richelieu, Quebec, about twenty-five miles southeast of Montreal. There he waited in his car for over two hours until he spotted Canadian Warrant Officer Patrice Vincent walking through the parking lot in his uniform. With Vincent was another Canadian soldier who was not in uniform.

Rouleau fired up his Altima and plowed into Vincent and his companion, killing Vincent and injuring the other soldier. Then he led police on a high-speed chase, ultimately crashing his car, charging out of it and lunging at a Canadian police officer, at which point he was shot dead.[34]

Unlike Brinsley, Rouleau left behind no question about his motives. One of his friends remarked on his fervent commitment to his new religion: "He thought it was true. He believed it all. He thought that of all the religions it was Islam that was the truest."[35] Said another: "It was a terrorist attack and Martin died like he wanted to. That's what happened.... He did this because he wanted to reach paradise and assure paradise for his family. He wanted to be a martyr."[36] According to the same friend, Canadian officials had stopped Rouleau while he was trying to leave Canada to join the Islamic State: "He became an extremist. He wanted to go fight jihad but they wouldn't let him do it. The caliphate called all the Muslims on earth to fight. He listened to what they had to say and he did his part here."[37]

Rouleau's Facebook page was full of Qur'an quotes and exhortations to jihad. One image featured the black flag of jihad with the legend, "WORK FOR KHILAFAH [caliphate]." Another also showed the black flag and proclaimed, "NO SURRENDER. IT'S EITHER VICTORY OR MARTYRDOM." Another quoted a prophecy, attributed to Muhammad in the hadith, that is popular among modern-day jihadis for its apocalyptic overtones and hint of the destruction of Israel: "(Armies carrying) black flags will come from Khurasan (Afghanistan). No power will be able to stop them and they will finally reach Jerusalem where they will erect their flags."[38]

Many of the Qur'an quotations on Rouleau's Facebook page simply exhorted skeptics to believe, but some took on a new significance in light of his hit-and-run jihad attack. One declared, "Those who believe fight in the cause of Allah, and those who disbelieve fight in the cause of Taghut [rebellion against Allah]. So fight against the allies of Satan. Indeed, the plot of Satan has ever been weak" (4:76).[39] The *New York Times* noted that "several of his postings there had extolled Islamic State violence, expressed anti-Semitic sentiments and denigrated Christianity," and that Canadian government officials had linked his attack to the Islamic State's call for violence against military men in the West.[40]

Zehaf-Bibeau: "There Can't Be World Peace until There's Only Muslims"

Just two days after Rouleau's hit-and-run jihad attack, another convert to Islam, Michael Zehaf-Bibeau, went to the Canadian War Memorial in Ottawa and shot dead Corporal Nathan Cirillo, who was on sentry duty there. He then entered the Parliament building, engaged in a shootout with security guards, and was killed.

Zehaf-Bibeau was a convert to Islam who had applied for a passport and told friends that he wanted to go to Libya.[41] The Royal Canadian Mounted Police (RCMP) said that he had intended to go to Syria, but his mother insisted that his real destination was Saudi Arabia. She wrote: "He ultimately wanted to go to Saudi Arabia and study Islam, study the Coran [sic]. He thought he would be happier in an islamic [sic] country where they would share his beliefs."[43]

NOT THAT THIS HAS ANYTHING TO DO WITH ISLAM

Like ISIS founder Zarqawi, Zehaf-Bibeau became devout in prison. He had once been a homeless crack addict, but he had turned his life around after converting to Islam. In his zeal, he began preaching his new religion to his coworkers. A coworker recalled, "He was always trying to convert me, (saying) 'You should read the Qur'an, bro,'" and said that Zehaf-Bibeau had told him, "There can't be world peace until there's only Muslims." Zehaf-Bibeau also "believed that there is this conspiracy that Jewish people were trying to suppress Muslim culture and they're trying to take over the world."[42]

During his attack at the Canadian War Memorial, a tourist took a photo of Zehaf-Bibeau wearing a scarf over his face and carrying a rifle. That photo soon afterward appeared on an Islamic State Twitter account. This didn't mean that Zehaf-Bibeau was acting on orders from the Islamic State, but it was a clear indication that its leaders approved of his actions and considered them to be a response to their call to kill Western military personnel.

We can't be sure that Zehaf-Bibeau killed a Canadian soldier because the Islamic State had called for precisely such attacks. But the timing, yet again, is noteworthy.

The Islamic State Strikes Muhammad Cartoonists . . . and Jews

On January 7, 2015, two Muslim brothers, Cherif and Said Kouachi, entered the Paris offices of the French satirical magazine *Charlie Hebdo* and, screaming "Allahu akbar," opened fire, killing eleven of the magazine's staff members. One shouted, "We have avenged the prophet Muhammad."[44] They were avenging the magazine's cartoons of Muhammad, which they considered blasphemous. Blasphemy carries the death penalty in Islamic law.

After the attack, a man called BFM-TV, a French TV network, claiming to be one of the jihadis and saying: "I, Cherif Kouachi, was sent by al Qaeda in Yemen. I had been there (to Yemen) and it's Sheikh Anwar Awlaki who financed me, may Allah have mercy on his soul."[45] "Al Qaeda in Yemen" is al-Qaeda in the Arabian Peninsula (AQAP), which, as we have seen, had declared its "solidarity" with the Islamic State on August 14, 2014, nearly five months before the massacre.[46] Said Kouachi trained with al-Qaeda in the Arabian Peninsula in Yemen in 2011, and Cherif Kouachi also spent some time in Yemen while his brother was there.[47] After the attack, a spokesman for al-Qaeda in the Arabian Peninsula said: "The leadership of AQAP directed the operation, and they have chosen their target carefully."[48]

Interestingly, some Islamic State operatives seemed to know about the attack before it took place. The day before the jihad massacre at *Charlie Hebdo*, a known Islamic State jihadist who called himself "Paladin of Jihad" on Twitter tweeted the words "snail-eating people" along with a weeping emoticon face. Then, two hours after the massacre, he tweeted: "You heard it here first. #SnailEaters ate lead. #DustNeverSettledDown."[49]

Islamic State supporters were thrilled with the massacre, taking to social media to exult over a video of one of the Kouachi brothers murdering a French policeman—"Watch how a brother kills a French policeman"—and to celebrate the murders as "heroic" and "joyous."[50]

The Kouachi brothers' attack at the *Charlie Hebdo* offices was coordinated with their associate Amedy Coulibaly's hostage-taking and massacre of four people at the Hyper Cacher kosher supermarket on the same day. When he entered the Hyper Cacher kosher supermarket, Coulibaly said, "I am Amedy Coulibaly, Malian and Muslim. I belong to the Islamic State."[51]

Coulibaly explained himself more fully in a video that the Islamic State released after the attack. He began by making it clear that he had carried out his attack for the Islamic State: "I am firstly addressing the caliph of the Muslims...the Caliph Ibrahim. I pledged allegiance to the Caliph as soon as the caliphate was declared."[52]

Then he explained how he and the Kouachi brothers had coordinated their attacks:

> The brothers of our team, divided in two, they did Charlie Hebdo, alhamdulillah [thanks be to Allah]. I also went out a bit against the police. So yeah, we did things a bit together, a bit separate, in order to have more impact.
>
> I helped in his project and gave him a few thousand euros so he could finish buying what he had to buy.

We managed to synchronise, to get out at the same time and not create problems because we are close and in the same affair....[53]

This cooperation is noteworthy because the Kouachi brothers had trained with al-Qaeda in the Arabian Peninsula and Coulibaly was an avowed supporter of the Islamic State. Al-Qaeda and ISIS are not the absolute antagonists and bitter rivals our media and government would like to think they are.

Coulibaly justified the attacks as completely legitimate under Islamic law:

What we are doing is totally legitimate, seeing what they are doing. Revenge on the prophet...mash'Allah.[54] It is fully deserved and has been for a long time.

If you attack the caliphate, if you attack the Islamic State, we attack you. You cannot attack and not get anything in return. So you victimise yourselves, as if you didn't understand what's going on, over a few deaths, so that you and your coalition, which you are almost at the head of now, you regularly bomb over there, you have invested forces, you kill civilians, you kill fighters, you kill...why? Because we apply the sharia? Even in our countries we are not allowed to apply the sharia now. You decide of what's happening on Earth? Is that it? No. We won't let this happen. We will fight, insha'Allah [Allah willing]. To elevate the word of Allah.[55]

Echoing the ISIS party line, Coulibaly exhorted fellow Muslims in the West to carry out similar attacks:

I am speaking to my Muslim brothers, everywhere and particularly in Western countries. And I ask them: What are you doing? What are you doing my brothers?

What do you do when there is a direct combat…What do you do when they insult the Prophet, repeatedly? What do you do when they harass us? What do you do when they slaughter entire populations? What do you do when in front of your house your brothers and sisters are held captive…? What do you do?

Since I got out [of prison], I moved a lot, I went to many different mosques in France a little bit, mostly in the region of Paris. They are full, mash'Allah. They are filled with men full of vigour, they are filled with young athletes, they are filled with healthy men. How come, with these thousands, millions of people, there aren't as many to defend Islam?[56]

He couched his justification for his murders in the same language of revenge that the caliphate had used in calling for such attacks. It was a vivid reminder that there are many young Muslims in the West who view the world the way the Islamic State does, and are prepared to murder as a result.

The National Guardsman: "Honestly We Would Love to Do Something like the Brother in Paris Did"

ISIS's call for jihad in the West has inspired a few successful terror killings. There is also a long list of other potential terrorists who have tried to heed the call of the Islamic State but failed.

Twenty-two-year-old Specialist Hasan Edmonds was an Army National Guardsman, but his true allegiance lay elsewhere: "I am already in the American kafir [unbeliever] army," he declared in January 2015, "and now I wish only to serve in the army of Allah alongside my true brothers."[57]

Edmonds began trying to devise ways to travel to the Islamic State. "I know several Muslims have been caught attempting the Turkey route," he said to a fellow plotter, "so tell me why not many Americans take the Egypt route. I am open to either way."[58] He added: "InshAllah [Allah willing] we will complete our task or be grants [sic] shahada [martyrdom] I look forward to the training."[59]

Hasan Edmonds was arrested at Chicago Midway International Airport on March 25, 2015; he had planned to go to Egypt and make his way from there into the Islamic State. His cousin, Yunus Edmonds, wanted to go as well, saying: "Number one on my list is Mosul." Specialist Edmonds was caught trying to leave the country for jihad overseas, but he and his cousin had also planned a jihad mass murder plot inside the United States: "If I find myself stuck here," said Yunus, "I intend to take advantage of being so close to the kuffar [unbeliever]."[60] Hasan agreed: "Honestly we would love to do something like the brother in Paris did."[61]

The "brother in Paris" was most likely Amedy Coulibaly—or possibly the transcript missed the terminal *s* and Hasan was referring to the Kouachi brothers.

The cousins concocted a plan: after Hasan traveled to the Islamic State, Yunus would wear his uniform and storm the Joliet Armory, where Hasan had trained for the National Guard.[62] Yunus, thinking big, said that he "anticipated a body count of 100 to 150." Hasan gave him a list of Joliet Armory officers and told him: "Kill the head."[63]

Yunus would have done so, but the fellow plotter to whom the cousins had divulged all their plans was actually an informant, and the plot was foiled.

The Army Recruit: "Getting Ready to Be Killed in Jihad Is a HUGE Adrenaline Rush!!"

Also attempting to carry out the Islamic State's call to kill U.S. military personnel was a U.S. Army recruit named John Thomas Booker Jr., also known as Mohammed Abdullah Hassan, who was arrested in April 2015 for a plot to set off a weapon of mass destruction in a jihad martyrdom suicide attack at Fort Riley in Kansas.[64]

Hassan had been the object of a manhunt a year before that, after he posted on Facebook (spelling and punctuation as in original):

> Oh those of the ummah [community] of the Prophet Muhammad(S). I will soon be leaving you forever so goodbye! I am going to wage jihad and hopes that i die. I want to be with my lord so bad that I cry but I will miss you guys I am not going to lie. I wish I could give you guys more but I am just a guy who is so very poor.
>
> I am telling you I am so broke that my pockets are sore:) I cannot wait to go the Prophet Muhammad's(S) door and prank Isa bin Maryam [Jesus Christ] and party so hard that it will rock Jannah to its core. Only Allah knows what the future has in store so that should make you fear Allah much much more.[65]

Shortly after writing that, Booker added that "getting ready to be killed in jihad is a HUGE adrenaline rush!!"[66]

He had planned to murder as many of his fellow soldiers as possible during basic training, intending to concentrate on murdering not just "privates," but "someone with power."[67]

FBI agents questioned him but decided that he didn't pose any danger, and that was that—and Hassan never did get into the Army. He did, however, maintain his dreams of jihad, and late in 2014 he began plotting to commit a jihad attack in service of the Islamic State. He began to formulate his plot against Fort Riley, while saying that he really wanted to attack "the White House right now."[68]

Booker had, however, been telling all this to an informant. His jihad would not come to fruition.

The "Real Bad Bitches"

On April 2, 2015, healthcare worker Noelle Velentzas and preschool teacher Asia Siddiqui, two Muslim women in Queens, were arrested for plotting jihad attacks in the U.S. At one point Velentzas had asked Siddiqui, "Why can't we be some real bad bitches?" They set out to accomplish that goal by plotting to build a jihad bomb and murder Americans for the Islamic State.[69] According to Loretta Lynch, then the U.S. attorney for the Eastern District of New York, "the defendants in this case carefully studied how to construct an explosive device to launch an attack on the homeland."[70]

Studying how earlier terrorist attacks had been carried out, Velentzas and Siddiqui began assembling the ingredients of the types of bombs that had been used in the 1993 World Trade Center jihad bombing, the 1995 bombing in Oklahoma City, and the 2013 Boston Marathon jihad bombing.[71]

Velentzas told Siddiqui that people should think of them both as "citizens of the Islamic State." But she didn't feel any need to make the trip all the way over there: a citizen of the Islamic State, she said, could "make history" by "pleasing Allah" right here in the United States.[72]

Velentzas and Siddiqui had wanted to be a part of the global jihad for a long time. Velentzas loved Osama bin Laden and even had a photo of him as the featured image on her cell phone. She once said, "Killing a police officer is easier than buying food, because sometimes one has to wait in line to buy food."[73] She said that to a man who she thought was a fellow Islamic State sympathizer but who turned out to be an undercover agent.

She also told him, "If we get arrested, the police will point their guns at us from the back and maybe from the front. If we can get even one of their weapons, we can shoot them. They will probably kill us but we will be martyrs automatically and receive Allah's blessing."[74] And she called the funeral of the policemen murdered by Ismaaiyl Abdullah Brinsley, with its huge assemblage of police officers, "an attractive potential target."[75] Time was short: "We are living…the last war, the big war before the end of day starts, in English they call it Armageddon, we are actually living in that time, it's not a joke, it starts in Syria."[76]

Siddiqui, for her part, was in regular touch with jihadis from al-Qaeda in the Arabian Peninsula. In 2009, she even contributed a poem to its magazine, which read in part that there was no "excuse to sit back and wait—for the skies rain martyrdom."[77]

Both of the "bad bitches" were active and respected members of the Masjid Al-Hamdulillah (the "Thanks be to Allah Mosque") in Brooklyn. The mosque's imam, Charles Aziz Bilal, confirmed that both women were members in good standing—and he was skeptical of the charges against them: "They have been here five years. I have not seen any signs of them being radicalized or promoting radical Islam, none of that stuff."[78] Velentzas, he said, was simply "a mother who took care of her daughter, normal. Very friendly, nothing political, nothing extremist."[79] There was no possibility, the imam insisted, that Velentzas and Siddiqui learned to be "bad bitches" who were "citizens of the Islamic State" at Masjid Al-Hamdulillah. "That's not what we promote here." If Velentzas and Siddiqui had really been involved in jihad terror activity, "they were doing it on the down low."[80]

But then he cast doubt on even that possibility by praising their families, which would certainly have known if Velentzas or Siddiqui had been involved in jihad plotting: "My observation of the families for the last five years," he declared, "has been impeccable—when it comes to character; when it comes to integrity—has been impeccable."[81] Of Velentzas and her family he said: "They have been an upright family. Very honest, very sincere, very dedicated family. They're family-oriented. They have children in the community, born in the mosque. Good religious people."[82]

What about those bomb ingredients? The imam insisted that the women had gathered them for innocent reasons: "You go to picnics, right? And what do you have on your [sic] to cook the meat and everything? You have propane tanks, right?"[83]

Velentzas's husband of six years, Abu Bakr, echoed this line of defense: "If anyone who had a pressure cooker in their house would be charged for it, a lot of people would be. It's like having a butter knife."[84] Like their imam, Velentzas's husband appeared in the media to be dismayed about the charges, saying of his wife: "I know nobody's perfect, but she is.... I want people to see her how I see her—as a mother, a wife, a friend, a confidant, a sister to the community, a daughter to the imam and the elders."

What, then, of the charges? "I don't believe any of it, period. We are all shocked, the whole community. That's not who she is."[85] So was she being framed by the authorities? "Yes, I would say yes they are lying."[86] For what reason, he did not explain. And of Siddiqui: "I can't say anything bad about her. She never showed anything to us like that. They were good friends— very good friends."[87]

Abu Bakr's credibility took a hit, however, when photos surfaced of him carrying the black flag of jihad at the Muslim Day Parade in New York City in 2007.[88]

Taqiyya: Lying for Islam

Those photos shed light on a recurring feature of these jihad plot cases. American Muslims often express shock and incomprehension when their family members, friends, and members of their mosques are arrested for plotting jihad attacks. No doubt some of them are genuinely clueless, but there is good reason to believe that others understand exactly why the jihadis in their lives are motivated to plot violence, share the same outlook themselves to one degree or another, and are engaging in deliberate deceit.

The fact is, deceiving non-Muslims isn't forbidden in Islam—in fact, in some circumstances it may be a religious duty for Muslims. This deceit is justified by Qur'an 3:28, a verse that warns believers not to take unbelievers as friends or helpers "except when taking precaution against them in prudence." This is the foundation of the idea that believers may legitimately deceive unbelievers when under pressure. The word used for "taking precaution" in the Arabic is *tuqĀtan*, from the verb *taqiyyatan*—hence the term *taqiyya*.

While many Muslim spokesmen today maintain that taqiyya is solely a Shi'ite doctrine, shunned by Sunnis, the great Islamic scholar Ignaz Goldziher has pointed out that while the doctrine of taqiyya was formulated by Shi'ites, "it is accepted as legitimate by other Muslims as well, on the authority of Qur'an 3:28."[89] The fourteenth-century Qur'an commentator Ibn Kathir, whose work is mainstream and still widely read, explains that in that Qur'an verse referred to "those believers who in some areas or times fear for their safety from the disbelievers." Muslims in such a situation were "allowed to show friendship to the disbelievers outwardly, but never inwardly." He quotes a companion of Muhammad saying, "We smile in the face of some people although our hearts curse them," and another maintaining that "the *Tuqyah* [taqiyya] is allowed until the Day of Resurrection."[90]

Christopher Lee Cornell: "You Know We See American Troops as Terrorists"

Another American convert to Islam, Christopher Lee Cornell (who has insisted that trial judges and others address him only by his Muslim name, Raheel Mahrus Ubaydah), was arrested in Ohio in January 15, 2015, after he bought two assault rifles and a healthy supply of ammunition. He had planned to place pipe bombs in the Capitol and shoot various U.S. government officials—including the president.

Cornell called a Cincinnati radio station after his arrest to profess his allegiance to the Islamic State and give vent to his plans and goals.[91] If he had not been arrested, he said, he would have taken a gun, and "I would have put it to Obama's head, I would have pulled the trigger, then I would unleash more bullets on the Senate and House of Representative members, and I would have attacked the Israeli embassy and various other buildings."[92] Why? Because of the "continued American aggression against our people and the fact that America, specifically President Obama, wants to wage war against Islamic State.... They might say I'm a terrorist, but you know we see American troops as terrorists as well, coming to our land, stealing our resources and killing our people, raping our women."[93]

Cornell called himself a "lone wolf," but he had pledged his fealty to the Islamic State, writing to an informant he thought was a fellow Muslim interested in jihad: "I believe that we should just wage jihad under our own orders and plan attacks and everything. I believe we should meet up and make our own group in alliance with the Islamic State here and plan operations ourselves."[94] He claimed that both the Islamic State and jihad mastermind Anwar al-Awlaki, who was killed by a U.S. drone in Yemen in September 2011, had approved of his plot: "we already got a thumbs up from the Brothers over there and Anwar al Awlaki before his martyrdom and many others."[95]

The fervent young convert also boasted to law enforcement officials that America is full of Islamic State supporters, all just biding their time and waiting for the right moment to strike: "We're here in Ohio, we're in every state. We're more organized than you think."[96]

Cornell requested a clock and a prayer mat so that he could continue his devout observance of Islam while in prison.[97] Prison officials, for their part, saw no incongruity in allowing the jihadi to steep himself in the beliefs and perspectives that had led him into treason and a plot to commit mass murder in the first place.

#CalamityWillBefallUS

There were many more threats to spill infidel blood in the United States and all over the West. The

TAQIYYA WATCH

The Islamic State is "distorting the whole message. So we have to respond to this by saying...what you are doing, killing innocent people, implementing so-called 'Sharia' or the so-called 'Islamic State', this is against everything that is coming from Islam."

—Islamic scholar Tariq Ramadan[98]

audacity and brutality of the Islamic State led Muslims (and even some non-Muslims) to sympathize with it, and even to issue threats in its name. And with ISIS calling repeatedly for lone wolf attacks in the West, the distinction between threats issued by actual Islamic State members and those who were not, but identified with it, was exceedingly fine.

Just before ISIS declared itself the caliphate, a group of jihadis from Great Britain who had joined the jihad in Syria produced a video in which they vowed that "the black flag of jihad" would soon wave over Downing Street. Another young British Muslim, Muhammad Hassan, threatened more attacks on the scale of 9/11 in the United States if the Americans moved against ISIS. Another, Junaid Hussain, took to Twitter to predict chaos in Britain: "Imagine if someone were to detonate a bomb at voting stations or ambushed the vans that carry the casted [sic] votes. It would mess the whole system up.... Watch out.... We'll come back and wreak havoc."[99]

A week before the declaration that the caliphate was restored, an American convert to Islam threatened the president on Twitter, writing, "Obama your days are numbered. You have nowhere to hide. Your family is first on our list. We will find you and remove your filthy heads!!" In another, he added that "soon" ISIS would "encompass the entire world."[100]

And on June 25, 2014, four days before the announcement of the restoration of the caliphate, ISIS supporters began a Twitter campaign featuring the hashtag #CalamityWillBefallUS. In the next four days, this hashtag was used almost twenty-four thousand times, with a large number of tweets featuring threats against the United States.[101]

Credible Threats

In October 2014, the Islamic State's online magazine *Dabiq* featured on its cover a photoshopped picture of the black flag of jihad flying over St. Peter's Square in the Vatican.[102]

While many plots have been foiled, supporters of the Islamic State have succeeded in killing enough people in Western countries that it's not safe to dismiss their threats as fantasies. When the Politico website misreported the words of Republican Representative Michele Bachmann of Minnesota to give the impression that she was calling for the United States to go to war against the Islamic State, this aroused the ire of ISIS to such an extent that they issued threats to Bachmann; federal officials took them seriously enough to place her under twenty-four hour guard.[103]

There was good reason to place such a guard around Bachmann, and to be alert to the general possibility of Islamic State violence in Europe and the United States. Adding to the very realistic concerns about potential terrorist recruits already at home in Western countries, a veteran Turkish smuggler claimed in November 2014 that he had sent "more than ten" Islamic State jihadis into Europe. His claim couldn't be proven, but it was eminently plausible: he said he charged $2,500 for every person he brought out of the Islamic State and into Europe through Turkey, and that the jihadis he had helped get to Europe were pretending to be refugees.

But according to the smuggler they are actually jihadis biding their time: "They are waiting for their orders. Just wait. You will see.... The Western world thinks there is no ISIS in their countries—that all the jihadis have gone to fight and die in Syria." He recalled that one of the Islamic State jihadis he helped get to Europe told him about Muslims from Europe who had been killed in Syria, "We are sending our fighters to take their places." He told the smuggler, "We want you to bring our brothers too." The smuggler noted that it was easy for them to go to Europe. "They can come to any smuggler and say they are refugees."[104]

In December 2014, Aaron Wieder, an orthodox Jew and member of the Rockland County Legislature in New York State, was opening his mail when he came upon a strange and jarring image: a photograph of an Islamic State beheading with his own face pasted over that of the victim. The photo was captioned simply "Aaron Wieder," with "Harun" (Arabic for Aaron), written in Arabic script above it. The Arabic writing suggests that the person who was making the threat was not just someone who saw the Islamic State beheadings on the news and thought they were cool. It could have been just someone who thought that the Islamic State's gleeful evil was worthy of emulation and who happened to know some Arabic—or it could have been an actual Islamic State operative in the U.S.

Said Wieder, "I opened the letter and I was completely shocked. I literally had shivers running down my spine." Rockland County Sheriff Louis Falco remarked, "We're taking this very seriously as a threat and will be working with our partners in law enforcement and the FBI to try to track down who sent this."[105]

In March of 2015, a group calling itself the Islamic State Hacking Division helped out Muslims in the U.S. who were thirsty for infidel blood by publishing online the names, addresses, photographs, and units of a hundred members of the United States Air Force, Navy, and Marines.

The Hacking Division proclaimed:

These Kuffar that drop bombs over Syria, Iraq, Yemen, Khurasan [Afghanistan] and Somalia are from the same lands that you reside in, so when will you take action? Know that it is wajib [an Islamic religious duty] for you to kill these kuffar [unbelievers]! and now we have made it easy for you by giving you addresses, all you need to do is take the final step, so what are you

OSTRICH ALERT

One British official dismissed concerns about the possibility that there could be Islamic jihadis among the refugees that European states were accepting from Syria. "We're talking about millions of people that need help. We should not get to the stage where we start to fear Syrian refugees as a terrorist threat in Europe."[106] In other words, they may in fact be a threat, but it is not politically acceptable to say so.

waiting for? Kill them in their own lands, behead them in their own homes, stab them to death as they walk their streets thinking they are safe.

We have made it easy for you by giving you addresses, all you need to do is take the final step, so what are you waiting for?

You crusaders that fight the Islamic State, we say to you: "Die in your rage!"[107]

The Islamic State published the photos of these members of the U.S. military in the hope that there would be Muslims in the U.S. who would heed their call to kill them.

#WeWillBurnAmerica

Combining its penchant for threats with its social media acumen, in April 2015 the Islamic State released a video and simultaneously a hashtag, both with the same theme: "We Will Burn America," vowing yet again to mount a major jihad attack, on the scale of 9/11, inside the United States (spelling and grammar as in the original):

America thinks its safe because of the geographical location
Thus you see it invades the Muslim lands, and it thinks that the
  army of the Jihad wont reach in their lands
But the dream of the Americans to have safety became a mirage
Today there is no safety for any American on the globe
The Mujahedeen before although they had less resources
Attacked New York and bombed the twin towers in September
  Eleven attacks
That blessed incursion was a fatal blow
All praise is due to Allah, the American economy was shaken
In such way Americans lived,

> And By Allahs willing the fear will spread among them again
> soon
> Here its America now losing billions still to make sure their
> country is safe
> But today, its time for payback,
> By the grace of Allah, today the Mujahedeen are much more
> stronger and they have more resource than before
> Thus they are able to burn United States Again[108]

With supporters of the Islamic State already having struck in the U.S., and several of its operatives and sympathizers arrested for plotting attacks in America, this threat could not be dismissed.

Chapter Three

IRRESISTIBLE ISIS

While a disturbing number of Muslims in America and Europe are heeding the call to make their jihad at home, a much larger number are flocking to the Islamic State.

ISIS is so appealing to many young Muslims that by the end of May 2015, nearly thirty thousand from one hundred countries had joined it in Iraq and Syria, with five thousand joining its Libyan wing.[1] These numbers included as many as 150 Muslims from the United States.[2]

The foreign jihadis in the Islamic State are a gleam in the eye of any Director of Diversity and Inclusion worth his (or her, or their, etc.) salt. They include a former Catholic altar boy from Belgium, a rapper from Tunisia, three teenage girls and nine physicians from Britain, and even former military men from the United States.[3]

Did you know?

- Over twenty thousand jihadis from more than ninety different countries have flocked to join the Islamic State
- ISIS posts a hundred thousand pieces of propaganda to the internet every day, including bloodthirsty recruiting materials, but also jihadi fitness programs and computer games
- According to a Rand Corporation expert, terrorists are "more rather than less educated than the general population"

EQUAL OPPORTUNITY EMPLOYER

John Horgan of the Center for Terrorism and Security Studies at the University of Massachusetts-Lowell has said that the Islamic State "is an equal opportunity organization. It has everything from the sadistic psychopath to the humanitarian to the idealistic driven."[4]

Though possibly it has a little more to offer to the sadistic psychopath.

A significant and growing number of these foreign jihadis are coming from Europe. As of April 2015, there were at least 1,430 Muslims from France waging jihad in the Islamic State—almost half of the European Muslims who had gone to the caliphate. French Prime Minister Manuel Valls said in an early 2015 interview that three thousand Muslims from Europe were already in the Islamic State, and estimated that that number would reach five thousand by mid-summer and ten thousand by the end of 2015.[5]

In February 2015 Nicholas Rasmussen, director of the National Counterterrorism Center, put the total of Muslims from the West in the Islamic State at thirty-four hundred and noted: "The rate of foreign fighter travel to Syria is unprecedented. It exceeds the rate of travelers who went to Afghanistan and Pakistan, Iraq, Yemen or Somalia at any point in the last 20 years."[6] This is the lure of the caliphate.

The estimates of both Valls and Rasmussen could be low. In August 2014, Khalid Mahmood, a Muslim Parliamentarian in Britain, estimated that as many as fifteen hundred young Muslims from Britain had gone to the Islamic State—more than twice the number of Muslims in the British military.[7] Three months later he revised that estimate up to two thousand—which if true would make the total number of Muslims from the West in the Islamic State much higher than Valls's estimate, since Muslims have gone to the Islamic State in large numbers not just from Britain and France, but from all over continental Europe.[8] Intelligence officials from outside Britain estimated in April 2015 that there were sixteen hundred Muslims from Britain in the Islamic State.[9]

"BORN N RAISED IN YOUR LANDS, & NOW HERE THIRSTY FOR UR BLOOD"

In March 2015, a Muslim woman from Australia named Zehra Duman posted on Twitter photographs of a group of women wearing niqabs covering their faces and holding machine guns while standing under the Islamic State's black flag of jihad and next to a white BMW. Duman boasted of the "five star jihad" she was enjoying in the Islamic State, and bragged: "Can't mess with my clique. From the land down under, to the land of Khilafah [caliphate]. Thats the Aussie spirit." She also added a threat: "US + Australia, how does it feel that all 5 of us were born n raised in your lands, & now here thirsty for ur blood?"[10]

ISIS on Social Media: They R Callin U 2 #Jihad

Many analysts have attributed the attractiveness of the Islamic State to young Muslims in the West to ISIS's sophisticated social media campaigns. The UK's *Daily Mail* reported in September 2014 that "ISIS has shown remarkable sophistication with its online presence. When the group released its video showing the execution of journalist James Foley, it was simultaneously posted on dozens of online forums, Twitter accounts [and] other social media sites. A slew of Twitter and Facebook accounts spread the group's message by posting pictures of the brutal executions and torture that ISIS terrorist bestow [sic] on their enemies—all while staying a step ahead of Silicon Valley's attempts to shut them down."[11]

Said State Department spokeswoman Jen Psaki: "There's no question what we're combating with ISIL's propaganda machine is something we have not seen before. It's something we need to do a lot more work on. We are seeing 90,000, I think, tweets a day that we're combating."[12] Even more than that: "Islamic State sympathisers," the *Australian* reported in March

2015, "produce about 100,000 pieces of online propaganda every day, including fitness programs for jihadis, smartphone apps and ideological computer games."[13]

The Islamic State is proud of its social media acumen. An ISIS supporter wrote on his Twitter page in June 2014: "Praise be to Allah, who gave Twitter to the mujahideen so that they may share their joys and not have listen to [sic] the BBC."[14] Not having to listen to the BBC is indeed a consummation devoutly to be wished, but the Islamic State's alternative offered little to those who were not young, Muslim, and angry.

For that targeted demographic, however, they offered plenty. The Center for Terrorism and Security Studies' Horgan noted that the Islamic State has "become so adept at social media that they are reaching out to disaffected individuals on a global scale."[15] According to CNN, this campaign specifically targets young people in their native online habitats: "UK surveillance chief Robert Hannigan has said ISIS and other extremist groups use platforms like Twitter, Facebook and WhatsApp to reach their target audience in a language it understands. Their methods include exploiting popular hashtags to disseminate their message."[16]

According to an October 2014 report in the German publication *Spiegel* about their media effectiveness, the Islamic State jihadis "even market themselves to kids, manipulating popular video games such as *Grand Theft Auto V* so that Islamic State fighters and the group's black flag make an appearance." Life in the Islamic State is portrayed as superior to life in the West:

> In short videos from the series "Mujatweets," an apparently German fighter talks about his supposedly wonderful life in the Caliphate. Such scenes, depicting the multicultural Islamic State brotherhood, are clearly meant for Muslims in the West. "Look here," the message is, "everyone is equal here!" The images

suggest that jihad has no borders; that it brings people together and makes them happy. Other blogs include women gushing about family life in wartime and the honor of being the widow of a martyr.

"Their propaganda is unusually slick," said FBI Director James B. Comey in November 2014. "They are broadcasting their poison in something like 23 languages."[17] Nazir Afzal, the United Kingdom's former Chief Crown Prosecutor, agreed: "What is happening with ISIL, ISIS, Deash [sic]—they are very evil people, but they are very good at propaganda, they are good at marketing."[18]

It's All about the Islam

The Western analysts who note the Islamic State's propaganda skill generally fail to observe the obvious fact that the substance of all this slick propaganda is wholly and solely Islam. The Islamic State bases its appeal on Islamic teachings, and its propaganda demonstrates an intimate knowledge of Islamic tradition—an appealing feature to the young and devout. The Islamic State's professionally designed, lavishly illustrated online magazine, for example, is called *Dabiq*, after the name of a town in Syria where a hadith records Muhammad as predicting that an apocalyptic battle between the Romans—that is, the Christians—and the Muslims will take place.

The Islamic State is thus positioning itself as the harbinger of the end times—of the final and decisive battle between the Muslims and the enemies of Allah, from which the Muslims will emerge victorious, after which peace—the peace of total Sharia adherence—will prevail all over the earth.

It's this religious content that appeals to young Muslims far more than the slick and highly professional presentation—the deep knowledge of Islam, the fanatical loyalty to it, and the unapologetic claim of the Islamic

State to be the fulfillment of the desires of so many Muslim hearts for so long. Not only does it embody the restoration of the caliphate; it is also a harbinger of the end times.

As we have seen, al-Qaeda's Zawahiri warned ISIS founder Zarqawi not to build his strategy on public atrocities even if they could be justified by a rigorist application of Islamic principles, and not to let his head be turned by the plaudits of the "zealous young men" demographic that those atrocities and that rigorism appealed to most strongly. The al-Qaeda position was that jihadis should stick with tactics more "palatable" to the Muslim population in general, not rush to implement harsh elements of Sharia that could turn off supporters. But the phenomenal success of the ISIS media campaign is a testimony to the power of the unapologetic, full-bore Islam that Zarqawi and his successors have insisted on.

Western analysts in the Obama years, however, who have been trained to ignore and downplay the Islamic aspects of the Islamic State's appeal, are compelled to find other sources for the group's appeal. Thus they fasten on the gloss and slickness of the Islamic State's media approach, mistaking the medium for the message.

It may seem strange that a group that has become notorious, hated, and feared for its videos of beheadings and of the burning alive of a captive would be noted for its media savvy. Would the Islamic State win over even more young Muslims to its cause if it weren't so bloodthirsty and so exhibitionistic about its savagery and violence? Its propagandists obviously don't think so; they appear to believe that it is preferable to use contemporary means of communication to "strike terror into the hearts of the enemies of Allah" (Qur'an 8:60)—that doing so will appeal to young Muslims who know what the Qur'an says but don't see other Muslims acting upon it to their satisfaction.

The authorities of the Islamic State clearly believe that devout Muslims want to see these gruesome videos because they're documentations of how

PREACHING TO THE CHOIR

Maybe it's easier for our media to think the Islamic State media are clever because ISIS takes care to echo their own biases. In late 2014, the Islamic State's slick propaganda included a multi-episode "news" program hosted by British hostage John Cantlie, a photographer and a friend of Prince William and Prince Harry, who articulated (willingly or not) the Islamic State's view of the contemporary global situation. Cantlie's analysis coincided perfectly with the Left's preoccupation with the wrongheadedness of American military interventions, and with the lack of good sense and prudence in carrying them out—as the many Westerners now working for ISIS had to have known it would.[19]

Cantlie mocked "Obama's under-construction army" against the Islamic State, pointing out (quite correctly) that the "moderate" Free Syrian Army that Obama had hoped would lead the charge on the ground against the Islamic State was an "undisciplined, corrupt and largely ineffective fighting force." The British hostage called Obama's response to the Islamic State "disappointingly predictable" (his colleagues in the Western media might have phrased it as "lacking in nuance"), caricaturing the American administration's position as "America is good, the Islamic State is bad" and ridiculing Obama's apparent belief that the Islamic State would be defeated and eradicated "using aircraft and a motley collection of fighters on the ground."[20]

ISIS is obeying Islamic law to the letter. Islamic State supporter Abu Bakr al-Janabi explains: "The beheading, execution in public are messages to ISIS enemies, but also part of Sharia law and shows that they implement it fully."[21]

Al-Janabi added that the common perception that the Islamic State was made up of grim, humorless, bloodthirsty fanatics was false: "We are friendly! Unless you are an enemy, of course, I mean, just because people are in ISIS doesn't mean that they go around on a killing rampage. They are humans, they laugh they joke, they goof with each other."[22]

Not Just Media Savvy, but Technically Skilled

In January 2015, at the precise time when Barack Obama was speaking to the nation about cyber security, Islamic State hackers took over the Pentagon's Middle East Twitter account. The hackers also took over the United States Central Command's YouTube page, posting jihad videos there, and they added links on the United States Central Command's Twitter page to "confidential data from your mobile devices," and boasted, "ISIS is already here, we are in your PCs, in each military base. With Allah's permission we are in CENTCOM now."[23]

Two months later, as we have seen, the "Islamic State Hacking Division" (ISHD) published the names, photographs, and home addresses of a hundred members of the U.S. military, gleefully boasting:

> O Kuffar in America, O You who worship the cross, O You Crusaders that fight the Islamic State, we say to you, "DIE IN YOUR RAGE!", die in your rage because with the grace of Allah, The Islamic State Hacking Division (ISHD) has hacked several military servers, databases and emails and with all this access we have successfully obtained personal information related to military personnel in the United States Air Force, NAVY & Army ... With the huge amount of data we have from various different servers and databases, we have decided to leak 100 addresses so that our brothers residing in America can deal with you.

Then came the obligatory Qur'an quotes:

> O you who believe! Fight those of the disbelievers who are near to you and let them find in you harshness, and know that Allah is with the righteous ... (9:123).

Fight them; Allah will punish them by your hands and will disgrace them and give you victory over them and satisfy the breasts of a believing people ... (9:14).

And then the direct call to murder:

O Brothers in America, know that the jihad against the crusaders is not limited to the lands of the Khilafah, it is a world-wide jihad and their war is not just a war against the Islamic State, it is a war against Islam. These Kuffar that drop bombs over Syria, Iraq, Yemen, Khurasan and Somalia are from the same lands that you reside in, so when will you take action? Know that it is wajib [a religious duty] for you to kill these kuffar! and now we have made it easy for you by giving you addresses, all you need to do is take the final step, so what are you waiting for? kill them in their own lands, behead them in their own homes, stab them to death as they walk their streets thinking that they are safe, and remember that the Prophet Muhammad (s.a.w.) said: "A disbeliever and a believer who killed him will never be gathered together in hell." – Sahih Muslim – Hadith No: 4661[24]

Apparently the ISHD's claim to have obtained the addresses from hacking "several military servers, databases and emails" was just propaganda. In actuality the information seems to have been garnered from publicly available sources online.[25] But the fact that ISIS was able to hack into accounts owned by the U.S. military—and that someone claiming to be from ISIS also managed to break into the Facebook and Twitter accounts of the wife of a Marine who had served five deployments in Iraq and Afghanistan—was a disturbing indicator of Americans' vulnerability to ISIS cyber attacks. The Marine wife, Liz Snell, whose social media accounts were hacked in February 2015, seems to have been targeted because she had been interviewed for a story about the January hacks into the Pentagon and CENTCOM accounts. The hacker warned Snell—from her own Twitter account—"You think you're safe but the IS is already here, #CyberCaliphate got into your PC and smartphone."[26]

Why Join ISIS? To Win Friends and Massacre People

Western analysts differ on what makes ISIS so attractive to Muslims the world over, but one thing they're sure about: whatever it is, it has nothing to do with Islam. Max Abrahms, a terrorism expert at Northeastern University, summed up the prevailing view when he said, "If you ask terrorists why they joined an organization after they have been in it, they will pair it with the official line of the group. But in reality they don't join the group for that reason." He said that Islamic State jihadis "would probably fail the most basic test on Islam."[27]

So why do they join it? Here are some of the "anything but Islam" explanations Western "experts" have offered for why young Muslims join the Islamic State:

- **Poor education**: the failure of "Arab education systems" in fostering an "us-versus-them mentality along ethnic, ideological, and sectarian lines, making youth vulnerable to external influence";
- **Joblessness and poverty**: "a lack of economic opportunities and weakened welfare systems";
- **Anger at oppression**: "bad governance" that "has created an entrenched feeling of injustice"; plus the "brutal clampdown" on the "Arab Awakenings";
- **Let down by Uncle Sam**: a lack of trust in the West.[28]

- **To redress injustice**: ISIS recruits feel "a sense of disparagement and discrimination, a not uncommon experience of many immigrants. And it can come from a sense that one's brethren in faith are being humiliated and disgraced around the world."[29]

- **The thrills, the chills**: ISIS recruits simply wanted to "belong to something special. They want to find something meaningful for their life. Some are thrill seeking, some are seeking redemption."[30] The Islamic State "provides these deluded young men and women with an adventurous trip."[31]

- **To make friends**: "The general picture provided by foreign fighters of their lives in Syria suggests camaraderie, good morale and purposeful activity, all mixed in with a sense of understated heroism, designed to attract their friends as well as to boost their own self-esteem."[32]

- **To help the downtrodden**: ISIS recruits "erroneously believe they are going out to help people. And they don't think ISIS is doing anything wrong because they think ISIS is helping people in their sort of warped thinking."[33]

- **Girls and guns**: "Sex is the most primitive assertion of one's significance; it's a means to perpetuate one's name—and genes—into the future. Islamic State strategically uses it as a reward for aggression."[34]

These were not mutually exclusive, and there was a measure of truth to many of them. Certainly it was thrilling to be caught up in the excitement of the formative days of the caliphate. Islamic State jihadi Abu Sumayyah said of life in the Islamic State, "Something is always going on—always bombings. By the time it gets to midday, you are in the midst of the fighting. Or totally peaceful day, shower, play some football, play with the lads, football. So many Americans, so many Canadians, so many British guys—guys from all over the place, China, Indonesia."[35]

Abu Sumayyah also offers some support for the idea that the Islamic State gained recruits because of Muslims' grievances against the West: "Mainly my main inspiration to come to Syria was George Bush, Tony Blair, and the presidents of the West and their foreign policy towards Islam—Egypt, Kashmir, Sinai, Yemen, Afghanistan. Guantanamo Bay. Abu Ghraib."[36]

When asked why they had joined the Islamic State, however, its recruits return again and again to the appeal of the caliphate.

Restoring the Glory Days

Abu Sumayyah also explained that a key element of what drew him to the Islamic State was the fact that it was a state: "ISIS was a state, not a group—it was an actual state. It runs the affairs of people, like any other state—American, British, French—ISIS is running as a state. It provides food for the poor—like shelter, clothing, charity, clean roads. It does everything a normal state does. Postal services. Everything the people need. This is what attracted me about ISIS. No other groups—al-Nusra, El-Aqsa Brigade, is doing that."[37]

As far as Sumayyah and others who joined the Islamic State were concerned, Muslims had not had such a state since March 3, 1924. The Islamic State was a chance to restore the bygone glories of past caliphates and to reverse the catastrophe that the abolition of the caliphate had wrought upon the Muslim ummah.

"I was in a hotel, and I saw the declaration on television," recounted Musa Cerantonio, an Australian convert to Islam who has frequently exhorted Muslims to work for the restoration of the caliphate. "And I was just amazed, and I'm like, *Why am I stuck here in this bloody room?*"[38]

He is still stuck: Australian authorities confiscated Cerantonio's passport to prevent him from traveling to join the Islamic State.[39]

BUT THAT WAS WHEN THEY
RULED THE WORLD

A year before the Islamic State declared its caliphate, in June 2013, Mohammed Malkawi of the pro-caliphate organization Hizb ut-Tahrir expressed common sentiments among jihadis when he blamed the abolition of the caliphate on a conspiracy of infidels: "After Islam had reached the peak of glory and the Muslims were masters of the world, there came a time when the infidels conspired against the Muslims, who were in a deep slumber. Britain conspired against them, along with Arab and Turkish collaborators and traitors, and ended the Islamic Caliphate and its glory."[40]

But with ISIS's proclamation of the caliphate on June 29, 2014, it was finally time to recover that glory.

A young Muslim in the Chicago area, Mohammed Hamzah Khan, nineteen, along with his sister, who was seventeen, and their brother (sixteen), got farther, but like Cerantonio, didn't make it. On October 4, 2014, they sneaked out of their home early in the morning and made their way to O'Hare International Airport, intending to travel to the Islamic State. Hamzah Khan left a note for his parents that combined piety with grievance (an extremely common combination among Muslims who are inclined toward the Islamic State and other jihad groups: "An Islamic State has been established and it is thus obligatory upon every able-bodied male and female to migrate there," he declared. "Muslims have been crushed under foot for too long.... This nation is openly against Islam and Muslims.... I do not want my progeny to be raised in a filthy environment like this."[41]

Khan's sister contributed her own note: "Death is inevitable, and all of the times we enjoyed will not matter as we lay [sic] on our death beds. Death is an appointment, and we cannot delay or postpone, and what we did to prepare for our death is what will matter."[42] In other words, death while in the process of serving Allah should be one's highest aspiration.

The three Khan teens were arrested at the airport, their search for the pure Islamic land and a death worthy of Allah postponed for the time.[43]

In reporting on the Khans' aborted flight, the *Washington Post* gave ample space to their parents to make their case that they had not raised the three children in an "extremist" atmosphere, but were just ordinary, albeit conservative Americans whose offspring had inexplicably gotten "radicalized." However, the *Post* story unwittingly provided a glimpse into the world of a devout Muslim upbringing in the United States, in which a young person who has learned hatred and contempt for infidel civilization can easily decide that (in the words of the Muslim Brotherhood motto) death for the sake of Allah is his highest aspiration.

The would-be Islamic State jihadis' mother, Zarine Khan "has worked for many years as a teacher at a local Islamic school," and "the Khans tried to shield their children from unwanted influences. They had a TV when the children were younger, but they had no cable service. The TV was used solely for showing DVDs—mainly cartoons and educational JumpStart programs from the public library."[45]

Given the Islamic outlook it's obvious the family had, those DVDs most likely also included Islamic teaching tools. The *Post* also tells us that "the children studied at a local Islamic school, which offered a standard U.S. curriculum of English, math and science—but also classes on Islam.... All three Khan children also became Hafiz, which means they completely memorized the Koran in Arabic."[46]

TAQIYYA WATCH

"The vast majority of Muslim clerics say the group cherry picks what it wants from Islam's holy book, the Quran, and from accounts of Muhammad's actions and sayings, known as the Hadith. It then misinterprets many of these, while ignoring everything in the texts that contradicts those hand-picked selections, these experts say."

—Associated Press, March 2, 2015[44]

FROM DELTA AIR LINES TO THE JIHAD

Again and again, those who find the Islamic State's call impossible to resist turn out to be the most devout young Muslims. Abdirahmaan Muhumed, a Muslim from Minneapolis who had once had a job cleaning Delta Air Lines airplanes at Minneapolis airport, made his way to ISIS only to become one of the first U.S. residents to die in the Islamic State's jihad.[47] He explained: "A Muslim has to stand up for [what's] right. I give up this worldly life for Allah." Muhumed said that if some thought of him as a terrorist, he was "happy with it," and prayed that Allah would "make my mom strong for the decision that I made."[48] Muhumed, a twenty-nine-year-old father of nine children, was killed while fighting for the Islamic State in late August 2014.[49]

Lack of Opportunity Drove Them to It?
Middle Class Kids, Medical School
Acceptees Flock to ISIS

Noting that many young Somali Muslims from the Twin Cities had made their way to Iraq and Syria to join the Islamic State, Mohamud Noor of the Confederation of Somali Community in Minnesota made a significant statement: "Most of [those who left] don't have the resources to even buy a ticket to go to Chicago. So that means there is [sic] some influential individuals who are taking advantage of our youth."[50] Not just influencing them, apparently, but paying for the trips of these poor young people.

Are Muslims being driven to join the Islamic State by the prospect of financial gain? John Kerry, Obama administration spokesperson Marie Harf, and many others have declared repeatedly that poverty is driving people to terrorism, and that giving them economic opportunities is what will end the appeal of terrorist groups. In line with this, Mohamud Noor explained why former Delta employee Abdirahmaan Muhumed threw in his lot with

ISIS: "He had so many challenges, lack of opportunities in life. Those are the things that have driven him to be who he is."[51]

Yet many Islamic State jihadis had plenty of opportunities in life. A Muslim in Britain, Nasser Muthana, had been accepted into four medical schools, but turned them all down to travel to the Islamic State—because, he said, "jihad is obligatory."[52] Another Muslim from Britain, Muhammad Hamidur Rahman, who like Muthana was killed fighting for the Islamic State, came from a prosperous middle class background—but according to his father, he "said he wanted to become a shaheed [martyr] for the sake of Allah."[53]

Andre Poulin: "Mujahedeen Are Regular People"

The idea that poverty drives young Muslims to terrorism was directly contradicted by the story of a middle class youth from Canada named Andre Poulin, who after his conversion to Islam began calling himself Abu Muslim. In a video that became an Islamic State recruitment tool, Poulin emphatically ruled out the idea that he was driven to join the Islamic State because of "challenges" or "lack of opportunities in life." Abu Muslim declared: "It's not like I was some social outcast, wasn't like I was some anarchist or somebody who just wants to destroy the world and kill everybody. No, I was a regular person. And, mujahedeen are regular people, too."[54]

Poulin, who was in his twenties when he made the video, explained: "Before I come here to Syria, I had money, I had family, I had good friends, I had colleagues. You know I worked as a street janitor—I made over $2,000 a month at this job. It was a very good job, a very good job. And even though I wasn't rich beyond my wildest imaginations, you know I was making it. It was good, and you know I always had family to support me, and I had friends to support me."[55]

What, then, was lacking? Life, he said, was not "religiously fulfilling." He asked his fellow Muslims in Canada and elsewhere in the West how they could think that they were pleasing Allah while paying taxes to a government that used them "to assist the war on Islam."[56]

Poulin appealed to Muslims in the West to join him: "We need the engineers, we need doctors, we need professionals. Every person can contribute something to the Islamic State."[57] But they didn't have to make the journey if it were difficult: he said that Muslims should all aid the Islamic State in some way. "If you cannot fight, then you can give money. And if you cannot give money, then you can assist in technology. And if you can't assist in technology, you can use some other skills." He promised that if they did come with their families to the Islamic State, "your families will live here in safety just like back home."[58]

FBI Director Comey has noted that the Islamic State is trying to lure "both fighters and people who would be the spouses…to their warped world."[59] The lusty young jihadis of the Islamic State especially want to draw potential spouses to their domains. Aqsa Mahmood, a young Muslim woman who was born and raised in Scotland and then made her way to the Islamic State, tried to recruit other young Muslim girls from the West with the promise, paradoxically enough, of stability and prosperity: the recruits would get, she promised, "a house with free electricity and water provided to you due to the Khilafah and no rent included. Sounds great, right?"[60]

Belying this talk of safety and security, however, the Islamic State recruitment video featuring Andre Poulin ends with footage of his bloody corpse and praise for him as a martyr of Islam.[61] Apparently the slick ISIS propagandists have decided that the lure of martyrdom is superior to the appeal of safety, in line with the Qur'an's declaration: "Not equal are believers who sit home and receive no hurt and those who fight in Allah's cause with their wealth and lives. Allah has granted a grade higher to those who fight with their possessions and bodies to those who sit home. Those who fight he has distinguished with a special reward" (4:95).

INTERFAITH DIALOGUE

. . .

A convert to Islam from Britain, Sally Jones, made her way to the Islamic State and took to Twitter to threaten her former coreligionists: "You Christians all need beheading with a nice blunt knife and stuck on the railings at Raqqa. Come here. I'll do it for you!"[62]

Jake Bilardi: "With My Martyrdom Operation Drawing Closer, I Want to Tell You My Story"

The case of Jake Bilardi (who after converting to Islam adopted the name Abdullah al-Australi—that is, "the Australian slave of Allah"), a young Australian convert to Islam who was killed in a jihad suicide attack in the Islamic State in March 2015, is also instructive. Far from being underprivileged or lacking in opportunities, Bilardi described his middle class upbringing in "affluent Melbourne" as "very comfortable."

The trajectory of Bilardi's life is also disquieting evidence that the hard-line Leftist slant of public school education, not just in the United States but all over the West, is not only endangering the future of the free world, but even serving as a recruitment tool for the global jihad.

Jake Bilardi was a conscientious young man who had co-founded a children's charitable organization, Soccer for Hope, to get soccer balls to poor children in Uganda.[63] But his education led him onto a path that his elders who admired him for his social conscience would never have expected. Shortly before his death, he wrote a lengthy blog post explaining the evolution of his thinking, his embrace of Islam, and his decision to become not only a jihadist but a suicide bomber.[64] Bilardi's post begins with a direct denial of the poverty-causes-terrorism claim and a forthright declaration that he soon plans to carry out a "martyrdom operation"—that is, to kill himself while murdering infidels:

> With my martyrdom operation drawing closer, I want to tell you my story, how I came from being an Atheist school student in

affluent Melbourne to a soldier of the Khilafah preparing to sacrifice my life for Islam in Ramadi, Iraq....

My life in Melbourne's working-class suburbs was, despite having its ups and downs just like everyone else, very comfortable. I found myself excelling in my studies, just as my siblings had, and had dreamed of becoming a political journalist....

Bilardi explained that he had a fascination with Islamic culture and Muslim countries from an early age, and when he started hearing about the war on terror he was skeptical of the mainstream narrative: "I saw the foreign troops burning villages, raping local women and girls, rounding up innocent young men as suspected terrorists and sending them overseas for torture, gunning down women, children and the elderly in the streets and indiscriminately firing missiles from their jets. Who was I to believe was the terrorist?"

Bilardi praised Abu Musab al-Zarqawi and retailed a great deal of jihadist polemic about alleged American atrocities in Iraq and Afghanistan and supposed Israeli enormities against the Palestinians, echoing the usual Leftist justifications for supporting the Palestinian jihad against Israeli civilians, saying with unintentional irony that "the true problem was, not Israel, nor Israelis but the religious ideology that governed them":

I began to support the violent resistance in the Gaza Strip, recognising that it was this resistance that kept small pockets of Palestine from the hands of the Jews, even if it does mean that they are frequently hit with airstrikes. Also, the presence of a base to attack Israel from the west was always a sign of hope, especially considering the current aggressive advance of the Islamic State from the East and as well as the bayah [pledge of allegiance] to the Khilafah by the mujahideen in Egypt's Sinai

Peninsula potentially allowing for attacks from all directions to liberate Palestine.

In this way, Bilardi said, he "transitioned from being a reluctant-supporter of Islamic militant groups in different lands to become certain that violent global revolution was the answer to the world's ills."

Education for Treason

The young jihadi's thinking offers an intriguing study of how the Leftist, anti-American perspective that dominates public school textbooks today warps young minds:

> In the course of my research I decided to delve deeper into the blood-stained history of the world. I learnt for the first time in great detail, the scale of the atrocities committed against the native population of the Americas by both the British and Spanish colonialist forces. About how both nations attempted to completely wipe out the natives in order to build their own respective civilisations, slaughtering millions of innocent people, intentionally spreading disease amongst them and raping the native women in an effort to breed-out the present race. I also learned more about the similar systematic genocide in my own country, Australia, the stories they choose to leave out when you're in history class at school.

Of course they don't really leave such stories out; they are practically all that is taught nowadays, particularly when it comes to Islam and the Crusades:

> I learnt about how the Crusaders rampaged across Europe and the Middle East, seeking to eliminate Islam from the region and restore the rule of the Catholic Church.

In reality, the Crusaders never had any intention of eliminating Islam from the region and made no attempt to do so.

Jake Bilardi went on to repeat a great deal more Leftist agitprop—sounding for all the world like a typical public school student of the early twenty-first century who has swallowed uncritically the worldview of his teachers. This hatred of America and the West meshed nicely in his mind with denial about the Islamic State's atrocities—really the jihadis are the victims of an oppressive and unjust West:

> Whenever America goes to war now, they claim it is simply humanitarian intervention. Take their recent airstrikes against the Islamic State, they hyped-up the story of the Yazidis trapped on Mount Sinjar, making unsubstantiated claims of genocide before admitting the situation was greatly exaggerated and it was not much of an issue. But this correction came after the first missile had been fired and therefore, they were already in, so … 'Well, we can't pull out now' … Now as a result, every day the Americans are firing missiles at innocent Muslims in both Iraq and Sham.

"It was also through these two successive American-led campaigns to impose the Democratic system upon the world," said Bilardi, "that I woke up to the reality of what this ideology was, nothing but a system of lies and deception." He came to harbor "complete hatred and opposition to the entire system Australia and the majority of the world was based upon," and determined that "violent global revolution was necessary to eliminate this system of governance and that it [sic] I would likely be killed in this struggle." But violent revolution in the service of what? "What would replace," he asked, the rotten Western system of democracy? "Socialism? Communism?? Nazism??? I was never quite sure."

Bilardi's hatred of the U.S. and its interventionism coincided with what he was reading in the Qur'an, which he had picked up because of his admiration for the mujahideen:

> As I read through the Qur'an, I couldn't help but make strong associations between the speech of Allah (azza wa'jal) and the chaotic scenes around the world today. For example, Allah (azza wa'jal) says, "And when it is said to them: 'Make not mischief on the Earth', they say: 'We are only peace-makers.' Verily! They are the ones who make mischief, but they perceive it not." [Surat al-Baqarah 2:11–12]. Is this not the reality of the kuffar today? Who claim to be helping to free the people while doing nothing but increasing their suffering.

NOT THAT THIS HAS ANYTHING TO DO WITH ISLAM

"As the Messenger of Allah, Muhammad ibn Abdullah (peace and blessings be upon him) said: 'The head of the matter is Islam, its pillar is the prayer and its peak is jihad.' I now for the first time truly understood why there were Islamic armies from Mali to China, from Chechnya to Indonesia, it was an obligation upon every able Muslim to fight, an obligation that a person who dies without having fulfilled, he dies upon a branch of hypocrisy as stated by Prophet Muhammad (peace and blessings be upon him)."

—Australian teenager Jake Bilardi explains why he became an ISIS suicide bomber

Thus he finally "began to truly understand what I had focused on studying for more than five years, the motivation of the mujahideen: The doctrine of jihad and it's [sic] superiority in Islam." John Kerry might be surprised to learn that the young suicide bomber says nothing at this juncture about poverty or a lack of economic opportunity.

Now he understood "the concept of jihad, it's

[sic] benefits, it's [sic] importance and the rewards for taking part in military operations to raise Islam in the land." And the more he learned, "the more I desired to join the mujahideen."

Bilardi had originally agreed with "the assessment of the mischief-makers that the Islamic State were from the khawarij," the seventh-century rigorists who fought, as we have seen, against all other Muslims, and that accordingly it was "a duty upon others to slaughter the mujahideen of the Islamic State." However, the more he had online discussions with Muslims who had joined the Islamic State, the more he began to come around to their point of view. He acknowledged forthrightly that in this matter, might made right: "As the Islamic State began to expand, seizing the cities of Raqqah, Fallujah, Mosul, Tikrit and others, Allah (azza wa'jal) Himself exposed the lies of the liars and humiliated the enemies of the State, a clear sign that they were upon the truth."

As he came to admire and approve ISIS, he was also "growing tired of the corruption and filthiness of Australian society and yearned to live under the Islamic State with the Muslims." But failing, at first, to find any way to get there, he decided instead to wage jihad right at home, launching "a string of bombings across Melbourne, targeting foreign consulates and political/military

NOT THAT THIS HAS ANYTHING TO DO WITH ISLAM

"Slowly but surely, I would come to love the [Islamic] State, recognising that they are the only people in the region establishing the Islamic system of governance, providing services for the people and most importantly they possess a sound aqeedah [creed] and manhaj [methodology for discovering the truth] that has led to their correct and effective implementation of the Sharia."

—Australian convert Jake Bilardi explains how he originally fell in love with ISIS targets as well as grenade and knife attacks on shopping centres and cafes and culminating with myself detonating a belt of explosives amongst the kuffar."

Bilardi realized, however, that if he tried to assemble all the necessary material for such an attack, he would attract the attention of the authorities. And then, unexpectedly and in a way he declines to explain so as to refrain from "revealing any sensitive information," he found a way to get to the Islamic State. Once there, "I felt a joy I had never experienced before, the first time my eyes spotted the banner of tawheed [Islamic monotheism] fluttering above the city, everything felt surreal, I was finally in the Khilafah.... I guess I was always destined to stand here as a soldier in the army of Shaykh Abu Musab al-Zarqawi (May Allah have mercy upon him) considering the great respect I had for him even before I entered Islam. May Allah accept him among the best of shuhadah [martyrs] and allow me to sit with him in the highest ranks of Jannah [Paradise]."[65]

Once happily in the caliphate, al-Australi issued a series of threats to his infidel homeland: "What we have in store for you dogs will make 9/11 look like child's play.... Martin place was just the beginning for you dogs."[66] Martin Place in Sydney was the site of a jihad terror attack in December 2014. A Muslim who went by the name Man Haron Monis and declared that he was a supporter of the Islamic State took customers and employees hostage at the Lindt Chocolat Café there; two people were killed.[67] As far as Abdullah al-Australi was concerned, that was just an appetizer.

However, it will not be he who makes good on these threats. Although it has been impossible to identify him conclusively, Jake Bilardi, who says that he found truth, happiness, and peace as Abdullah al-Australi, apparently killed himself in a jihad-martyrdom suicide attack in the Islamic State in March 2015.[68]

Shannon Maureen Conley:
"One of the Brightest Kids"

The transition of the young charity founder Jake Bilardi into a traitor who gleefully predicted blood and death for his own nation and people has been repeated again and again by Muslims who succumbed to the lure of the Islamic State.

Shannon Maureen Conley was "one of the brightest kids" at Arvada West High School in Arvada, Colorado, according to Arvada West Principal Rob Bishop.[69] But that was before she converted to Islam, adopted the name Halima, and began describing herself as a "slave to Allah."[70] Her parents were not initially all that concerned—and anyone who might have warned them had long since been demonized as a "racist" and "bigot."

Wearing traditional Muslim garb, Halima started to show up regularly at Arvada's Faith Bible Church. Asked by church leaders if she was interested in converting to Christianity, she responded that she was a Muslim and was only there to do "research."[71] She began taking notes during church classes and worship services, explaining that she was hoping to "alarm" church members and adding: "If they think I'm a terrorist, I'll give them something to think I am."[72] When church members asked her about her notes, she responded, "Why is the church worried about a terrorist attack?"[73] Authorities later asked her why she was frequenting the church; she replied, "I hate those people."[74]

Halima Conley made contact online with Islamic jihadists, and joined the U.S. Army Explorers, which gives young people a taste of what it is like to be in the U.S. military. She explained that she didn't join up out of patriotism or interest in a military career, but because she hoped to learn American military tactics that she could then explain to the jihad terrorists of the Islamic State.[75]

Eventually Conley made online contact with a Tunisian Muslim who persuaded her to travel to the Islamic State to meet and marry him, as well as to wage jihad herself.[76] "Jihad must be waged to protect Muslim nations," she later explained, saying that she hoped, once she reached the Islamic State, that she "would be defending Muslims on the Muslim homeland against people who are trying to kill them." When asked if she would engage in jihad fighting herself, she answered: "If it was absolutely necessary, then yes. I wouldn't like it…but I would do it." However, she said her Islamic State fiancé was "the man, he should be doing the fighting."[77]

Conley was arrested at the Denver International Airport as she made the attempt to go meet him in person for the first time.[78] She later pleaded guilty to aiding a foreign terrorist organization and was sentenced to four years in prison.[79] Her arrest, guilty plea, and sentencing did nothing to dim her Islamic fervor; as she prepared to enter prison, she changed her name yet again to Amatullah—"servant of Allah."[80]

"Jihad Shannon," as she came to be known, was widely written off as a confused young girl whose head had been turned by the much older Tunisian who courted her online—she was nineteen, he was thirty-two.[81] But Shannon/Halima/Amatullah was by no means the only convert to take conversion to Islam as a call to commit treason and join the Islamic State, and it was not so easy to write off some of the others as confused youths befuddled by romance.

Pugh and Edmonds: From the U.S. Military to the Islamic State

Tairod Nathan Webster Pugh served in the United States Air Force from 1986 to 1990. He was an avionics instrument specialist, trained to repair and maintain airplane engines.[82] In 1998 he converted to Islam, and by September 11, 2001, when he was working for American Airlines as an airplane mechanic, he had turned against the country of his birth, in whose military he had served, so completely that he alarmed his coworkers with his open hatred for America and support for Osama bin Laden.[83]

By January 2015, Pugh had been living outside the United States for years, and he had his eye on a new place to live: the Islamic State. He tried to enter the Islamic State through Turkey, but Turkish officials wouldn't let him into the country. Pugh had flown to Turkey from Egypt, and upon his return to that country he was sent back to the United States. FBI agents seized his laptop and discovered that he had conducted internet searches for "borders controlled by Islamic state" and "kobani border crossing." Kobani is a town on the Syrian border with Turkey that the Islamic State had tried and failed to seize from Bashar Assad's forces.[84]

We've already seen how U.S. Army National Guard Specialist Hasan Edmonds was arrested on March 25, 2015, at Chicago's Midway Airport for planning to join the Islamic State.[85] The plan he and his cousin, Jonas "Yunus" Edmonds, who was arrested as well, had put together involved Yunus storming the Joliet Armory, where Hasan had trained, with hand grenades and rifles—in a jihad attack emulating that of Major Nidal Malik Hasan at Fort Hood in November 2009. Nidal Hasan murdered thirteen people and injured thirty-two.[86]

Half the World

"More than half the world's countries are now producing jihadists to fill the ranks of violent sunni terrorist organisations in the Middle East." In May 2015 the *Financial Times* reported those findings from the United Nations Security Council's Special Permanent Committee for Monitoring Violent Islamism. The UN put the total number of jihadis who have flocked from around the world to join al-Qaeda and ISIS at twenty-five thousand. And that number is going up rapidly, as is the number of different countries from which they are originating. Meanwhile, ISIS is doing a much better job of assimilating foreigners than al-Qaeda did in Afghanistan. "'Those who eat together and bond together can bomb together,' [the report] notes: unlike in Afghanistan, where foreign fighters tended to stick together in their own ethnic groups, in Syria and Iraq jihadists are far more closely integrated into more developed and sophisticated networks."

Mehdi Masroor Biswas, a twenty-four-year-old manufacturing executive at ITC Foods, a massive packaged foods conglomerate in India, was almost one of them. His friends and family were stunned when police swooped down on Biswas's apartment in North Bangalore and arrested him on December 13, 2014.

Biswas, as it turned out, was leading a double life. By day he worked at ITC Foods, but by night he would take to Twitter as @shamiwitness (Syrian witness), a propagandist for the Islamic State.

Police said that Biswas was "very emotionally invested in the cause of Islam"—so much so that "the @shamiwitness account seemed to have become his main cause in life. He was so consumed by it that he did not have much of a life beyond his work and the Internet. He was however probably only a major sympathiser of the Islamic State and did not take any concrete measures to join the outfit."

Bangalore police commissioner M. N. Reddi stated that Biswas "was not directly involved with the Islamic State but he was also not a mere sympathizer." A police spokesman added, "He was particularly close to English-speaking terrorists of ISIS and became a source of incitement and information for the new recruits trying to join ISIS. Through his social media propaganda he abetted ISIS in its agenda to wage war against the Asiatic powers."[87]

"Our son is a devout Muslim," said Biswas's father. "He had learnt the Quran Sharif [Noble Quran] by heart, and would often give me and my wife lessons from the Holy Book."[88]

He seems to have taken many of those lessons to heart himself.

Jihadis Wanted

The Islamic State has recruited openly in the West on at least one occasion: in August 2014, the Islamic State's supporters in central London handed out leaflets proclaiming the restoration of the caliphate. The leaflet announced:

KHILAFAH ESTABLISHED

THE DAWN OF A NEW ERA HAS BEGUN

The darkness of following manmade law and the abandonment of the Shariah of Allah led to the destruction of the Khilafah (Islamic State) in the year 1924.

Since that year, for over 90 years we have been living in a constant state of ignorance. Our lands separated, resources stolen, Ummah [worldwide Muslim community] disunited, honour humiliated and the laws of Shirk [polytheism] established over us.

After many attempts and great sacrifices from the Ummah of Islam throughout the world, the Muslims with the help of Allah have announced the re-establishment of the Khilafah and appointed an imam as a Khaleef (Muslim leader).

As Muslims around the world we all have many great responsibilities towards the success and spread of the Khilafah across the world.

1. **Pledge** our Bayah [allegiance] to the Khaleef.
2. **Obey** the Khaleef according to the Shariah.
3. **Advise** the Khaleef if he does anything wrong.
4. **Dua**—Make dua to Allah to help and guide the Khaleef.
5. **Migrate**—Those that can migrate and resettle should migrate.
6. **Educate** Muslims and non-Muslims about the Khilafah.
7. **Expose** any lies and fabrications made against the Islamic state.

"...And if they seek help of you for the religion then you must help..." (Qur'an 8:72)[89]

In February 2015, Michael Steinbach, chief of the FBI's counterterrorist division, said that the Islamic State was recruiting young Muslims in America, and that it was very difficult to track such efforts: "I'm worried about individuals that we don't know about that have training. We know what we know. But there is a number that's greater than that that we don't know."

According to Steinbach, in America today, "there are individuals that have been in communication with groups like ISIL who have a desire to conduct an attack," including Muslims as young as fifteen years old: Steinbach said that he "can't speak with 100% certainty that individuals of that age group have not gotten over there successfully." These teen Muslims, he said, were often encouraged by their parents: "There are individuals out there who are inspired by the message of terrorist groups and they encourage family members, including their children, to follow that path."[90]

They do so because it is the path of jihad. The path of Islam.

It's the Meaning, Stupid

But American officials continued to be tone deaf to the jihadis' religious motivations and committed to the poverty explanation—to the point of absurdity. In February 2015 State Department spokesperson Marie Harf said,

> We're killing a lot of them, and we're going to keep killing more of them. So are the Egyptians, so are the Jordanians—they're in this fight with us. But we cannot win this war by killing them. We cannot kill our way out of this war. We need in the medium to longer term to go after the root causes that leads people to join these groups, whether it's a lack of opportunity for jobs—

At that point Harf was interrupted by MSNBC's Chris Matthews, who said: "We're not going to be able to stop that in our lifetime or 50 lifetimes. There's always going to be poor people. There's always going to be poor Muslims, and as long as there are poor Muslims, the trumpet's blowing and they'll join. We can't stop that, can we?"

Harf responded: "We can work with countries around the world to help improve their governance. We can help them build their economies so they can have job opportunities for these people."[91]

Harf was roundly ridiculed for these remarks, but what she said was just a particularly unconvincing statement of the same line that many other U.S. officials have been pushing over the years. In October 2014, Harf's boss, Secretary of State John Kerry, had given essentially the same analysis of the rise of the Islamic State. "The extremism that we see," he said, "the radical exploitation of religion which is translated into violence, has no basis in any of the real religions. There's nothing Islamic about what ISIL/Daesh stands for, or is doing to people." ("Daesh" is an insulting name for the Islamic State derived from the Arabic acronym for ISIS and loosely resembling the Arabic words for someone who "crushes something under foot" or "sows discord.")[92]

Instead, it was all about the poor envying the rich: "We're living at a point in time where there are just more young people demanding what they see the rest of the world having than at any time in modern history." They don't have it because of . . . global warming: "And that brings us to something like climate change, which is profoundly having an impact in various parts of the world, where droughts are occurring not at a 100-year level but at a 500-year level in places that they haven't occurred, floods of massive proportions, diminishment of water for crops and agriculture at a time where we need to be talking about sustainable food. In many places we see the desert increasingly creeping into East Africa. We're seeing herders and farmers pushed into deadly conflict as a result. We're seeing the Himalayan glaciers

FIGHT THE JIHAD—SHRINK YOUR CARBON FOOTPRINT

"Understand, climate change did not cause the conflicts we see around the world, yet what we also know is that severe drought helped to create the instability in Nigeria that was exploited by the terrorist group Boko Haram [which pledged allegiance to the Islamic State in March of 2015][93].... It's now believed that drought, crop failures, and high food prices helped fuel the early unrest in Syria, which descended into civil war in the heart of the Middle East."

—President Obama explains how climate change contributes to jihad conflicts around the world in his 2015 commencement address at the U.S. Coast Guard Academy[94]

receding, which will affect the water that is critical to rice and to other agriculture on both sides of the Himalayas. These are our challenges."

So as far as Kerry was concerned, jihad terrorism was all about poverty—poverty brought about by global warming. If that poverty were alleviated, presumably jihad terror would evanesce worldwide.

The secretary of state also blamed Israel: "As I went around and met with people in the course of our discussions about the ISIL coalition, the truth is we—there wasn't a leader I met with in the region who didn't raise with me spontaneously the need to try to get peace between Israel and the Palestinians, because it was a cause of recruitment and of street anger and agitation that they felt—and I see a lot of heads nodding—they had to respond to. And people need to understand the connection of that. It has something to do with humiliation and denial and absence of dignity."[95]

The idea that poverty causes terrorism (of which the idea that the jihadis just need jobs is one variant) is, in fact, U.S. government policy: the United States spent billions building schools, hospitals, and roads in Afghanistan under the assumption that once Afghans were well educated and had access to modern services and amenities they would not turn to jihad.

And in October 2013, the idea that poverty is responsible for terrorism was cemented even more firmly as a cornerstone of U.S. policy at a meeting of the Global

Counterterrorism Forum (GCTF), when Secretary of State John Kerry and Turkish Foreign Minister (and soon to be Prime Minister) Ahmet Davutoglu launched what they called the "Global Fund for Community Engagement and Resilience," which was intended to counter "violent extremism" essentially by giving potential jihad terrorists economic assistance.[96]

Kerry spoke about the importance of "providing more economic opportunities for marginalized youth at risk of recruitment" into jihad groups.[97] The GCTF devoted $200 million to this project, a core element of Barack Obama's "countering violent extremism" (CVE) program.[98]

Kerry said this money would be used for "challenging the narrative of violence that is used to justify the slaughtering of innocent people."[99] How? By giving young would-be jihadis jobs: "Getting this right isn't just about

ISLAMIC STATE SUPPORTERS AT BROOKLYN COLLEGE

An indication of how popular the Islamic State is among young middle class Muslims in the United States came on April 22, 2015, when human rights activist Pamela Geller spoke to an extremely hostile, mostly Muslim crowd at Brooklyn College. The Muslim college students heckled and hectored Geller throughout her talk and took to Twitter and other social media to boast about how they were disrupting her address. One Muslim student posted a picture of a group of attendees, several of whom were holding up one finger in the gesture of adherence to Islamic monotheism that has come to be associated with support for the Islamic State. And when Geller referred in her speech to the rapid growth of the Islamic State, one of the Muslim students in the audience called out "Alhamdulillah"—thanks be to Allah. None of the other Muslim students in the crowd rebuked or contradicted the one who had thanked Allah for the growth of the Islamic State.[100]

taking terrorists off the street. It's about providing more economic opportunities for marginalized youth at risk of recruitment. In country after country, you look at the demographics—Egypt, the West Bank—60 percent of the young people either under the age of 30 or under the age of 25, 50 percent under the age of 21, 40 percent under the age of 18, all of them wanting jobs, opportunity, education, and a future."[101]

This initiative is foredoomed. In reality, study after study has shown that jihadists are not poor and bereft of economic opportunities, but generally wealthier and better educated than their peers. A 2009 Rand Corporation report, for example, found that "terrorists are not particularly impoverished, uneducated, or afflicted by mental disease. Demographically, their most important characteristic is normalcy (within their environment). Terrorist leaders actually tend to come from relatively privileged backgrounds."[102] Rand's Darcy Noricks noted that "terrorists turn out to be more rather than less educated than the general population." [103]

The *Economist* reported in 2010:

> Social scientists have collected a large amount of data on the socioeconomic background of terrorists. According to a 2008 survey of such studies by Alan Krueger of Princeton University, they have found little evidence that the typical terrorist is unusually poor or badly schooled.[104]

A National Bureau of Economic Research study likewise found that "the risk of terrorism is not significantly higher for poorer countries."[105]

But none of this has sunk in among the political elites. In his inaugural address as caliph, Abu Bakr al-Baghdadi said of the unity of Muslims from all over the world in the caliphate, "If kings were to taste this blessing, they would abandon their kingdoms and fight over this grace."[106] That in a nutshell explains why Harf and Kerry are wrong, and why the "Global Fund for Community Engagement and Resilience" is a gargantuan boondoggle. It doesn't take into account the fact that human beings have souls, and that they long to do something that matters—to be part of some great cause.

The Muslims who have flocked to the Islamic State from all over the world have done so because they long to be warriors for the restoration of the great caliphate, the center of the unity of the Muslims worldwide, the tip of the spear of worldwide jihad against the infidel—just as young men have always flocked to join great causes throughout history. ISIS gives their lives meaning and purpose. This movement to join the global jihad is not about poverty or lack of economic opportunity; it is about living a life that means something.

There is absolutely no chance that these young men will trade being a noble mujahid, waging jihad for the sake of Allah, for a chance to greet people entering Walmart or to spend their days saying, "Would you like fries with that?" Kerry spoke about "humiliation" and "absence of dignity" that supposedly drives Palestinians to the jihad, with no apparent appreciation of how his plan was asking the warriors of Allah to forsake Allah's battlegrounds for what, in comparison, is exactly that: humiliation and the absence of dignity.

Chapter Four

HOW THEY DID IT—
AND WHO'S TRYING TO
STOP THEM

The Islamic State is the wealthiest and most successful terror group in the history of the world. If it is able to maintain control over its territory for an extended period, it will provide a modern-day example of how a gang of warriors and thugs is able to make the transition from warfare and violent intimidation to stability and governance.

Throughout history, others have made this transition—from the Germanic tribes that harassed the Western Roman Empire to the Ottomans who harried the Eastern Roman Empire and ultimately extinguished it altogether. And let's not forget the Palestine Liberation Organization, which, if Barack Obama gets his way, is about to make the final step from terror organization to respected national government.

The Islamic State is attempting to make that transition now. Whether or not it will succeed remains to be seen, but it has already gotten farther along

Did you know?

- ISIS uses WhatsApp and Kik to facilitate donations from sympathizers
- The Islamic State received $20 million in ransom payments in 2014
- In March 2015, the Islamic State bulldozed the 3,300-year-old city of Nimrud
- The Islamic State caliph has called the destruction of the Pyramids a "religious duty"

the way than any other jihad terror group in modern times, aside from the Palestinians.

How Was the Islamic State Able to Gain Control over a Nation-Sized Expanse of Land?

The Islamic State's foremost achievement, what sets it apart from other jihad terror groups, is that it has managed to conquer and hold territory. The National Movement for the Liberation of Azawad (MNLA), an al-Qaeda–linked group, declared an independent state of Azawad in Malian territory in April 2012, but this "state" soon collapsed into infighting, and in February 2013, the MNLA withdrew its declaration of independence. The Islamic State isn't likely either to succumb to infighting or give up its pretensions anytime soon; nor does there appear to be a power on hand with the will to take decisive action to destroy it.

In seizing control of large areas of Syria and Iraq, the Islamic State was following in the footsteps of the first great Arab conquests, and its attainments are similar to those of the early Arab conquerors.

Early in the seventh century, the two great powers of the day, the Byzantine Eastern Roman Empire and the Sassanid Persian Empire, fought a series of bloody and costly wars. In 611, the Persians under the Emperor Khosrau (called Chosroes by the Byzantines) began a remarkably successful offensive, routing Byzantine forces in the Caucasus, Mesopotamia, Anatolia, Egypt, and elsewhere. In 613 the Persians took Chalcedon, right across the Bosporus from the Byzantine capital of Constantinople.

The Byzantine Emperor Heraclius sued for peace and paid huge sums in tribute to the Persians, while quietly rebuilding his army. In the early 620s he began an enormously successful counteroffensive against the Persians, defeating them almost everywhere his armies had been defeated a decade before and in 628 taking the war to the gates of Ctesiphon, the Persian capital.

Heraclius was thus able to restore the glory of the Byzantine Empire and send the Persian one into a spiral of decline. This victory, however, came at an enormous cost. By the early 630s, the Byzantines didn't have troops in sufficient numbers to properly man their garrisons in Syria, Palestine, and Egypt. Their control over these areas was more a matter of political convention and history than present-day reality; they were ripe for conquest by any group with the will and means to take them. The Persians had the will, but no longer the means, and in previous decades, that would have been enough to secure Byzantine control over these regions until the Christian empire was able to reassert a more active presence. At this point, however, the newly united and energized Arabs were ready to exploit the Byzantines' weakness. They moved quickly to take advantage of the power vacuum to embark upon their own series of conquests, laying the foundation for what has been known ever since as the heart of the Islamic world.

The parallels with the rise of the Islamic State are striking. The Iraq war that saw the removal of Saddam Hussein from power and the installation of a weak Shi'ite regime in Baghdad left much of Iraq in chaos. The Baghdad regime was essentially a client of Shi'ite Iran, but much of the Sunni areas of the country was never in its control, and significant numbers of Sunnis deeply resented the Shia-dominated regime.

Meanwhile, the "Arab Spring" uprisings heralded pro-Sharia revolts against relatively secular regimes in Tunisia, Egypt, Libya, and ultimately Syria; while the Western mainstream media celebrated these as pro-Western, pro-democracy popular uprisings, the only regard many of the protesters had for democracy was as a means to an end: to install Islamist governments all over the region with the blessing of the United States.

When Assad stood much firmer than his counterparts Ben Ali in Tunisia and Mubarak in Egypt had, Syria was engulfed in a great civil war, with Iran backing its client Alawite regime in Damascus while Sunnis all over the rest of the country aligned with various jihad groups that were determined to remove Assad and install an Islamic regime in Syria. Barack Obama's precipitous and ill-considered withdrawal of American troops from Iraq (as precipitous and ill-considered as it was to put them there in the first place) left a vacuum that Sunni groups could and would exploit.

The Islamic State, being the most ruthless, best equipped, and most fanatically dedicated to Islamic principles of all these jihad groups, was able to take advantage of Sunni discontent in both Syria and Iraq, and the weakness of the central governments of both, to take the most effective advantage of the power vacuum and proclaim its caliphate.

The Spoils of War

It helped that the Islamic State was able to gain control of several reliable—and immense—sources of wealth and ultimately to become the richest jihad terror group the world has ever known. The Islamic State looted nearly $500 million from the banks in the city of Mosul alone.[1]

It has also obtained an astonishing amount of war materiel in the same way. The Islamic State's conquests include millions of dollars' worth of American munitions and fighting equipment taken from the Iraqi Army. Just at Mosul, ISIS is reported to have taken twenty-three hundred Humvees.[2] And at the fall of Ramadi, the capital of Anbar Province, in May 2015, the Pentagon admitted that Iraqi troops abandoned "a half-dozen tanks, a similar number of artillery pieces, a larger number of armoured personnel carriers and about 100 wheeled vehicles like Humvees" to the Islamic State.[3] Video of a Ramadi police station from an ISIS jihadi showed "box after box of American mortar shells and bullets that appeared shiny and new. Several Humvees, apparently not long out of the packing crates, sat abandoned nearby. 'This is how we get our weapons,' the narrator said in Arabic. 'The Iraqi officials beg the Americans for weapons, and then they leave them here for us.'"[4]

David Cohen, the Undersecretary of the Treasury for Terrorism and Financial Intelligence, said on October 23, 2014, that the Islamic State had "amassed wealth at an unprecedented pace and its revenue sources have a different composition from those of many other terrorist organizations."[5] He noted that the Islamic State "obtains the vast majority of its revenues from local criminal and terrorist activities."[6]

And there is also the oil.

A Million Dollars a Day: ISIS Awash in Oil

The resurgent global jihad of the twentieth and twenty-first centuries has always been powered by oil. In the mid-twentieth century, the Saudis began spending their oil billions to spread the virulent Wahhabi understanding of Islam throughout the Islamic world, confronting head-on the relatively benign and peaceful forms of cultural Islam that had become dominant in areas of Central Asia, East Africa, and elsewhere.

The foremost child of this ideological campaign has been the Islamic State, a caliphate declared in line with the rigorist version of Islam that the Saudis have spent billions to spread, right on the Saudis' doorstep and, in a neat bit of poetic justice, denying the legitimacy of the House of Saud. Still, one thing that the Saudis' ideological children have in common with their despised parents is their use of oil revenues in the cause of Islam and jihad.

Theodore Karasik, research director at the Dubai-based think tank INEGMA, explained in July 2014 that the Assad regime was unprepared for the Islamic State's concentrated assault on Syria's oil fields: "These fields were probably under guard, but not in a robust nature that could take overwhelming force from groups like ISIS. They are trying to establish a state, and these types of revenues are important for the state's formation because it makes up a significant chunk of their revenue." Karasik explained that seizing oil fields was "part of an ongoing plan" that the Islamic State had "to develop their own economic system."

And the plan worked. Karasik noted that "officials from the Iraqi oil industry have said that ISIS reaps $1 million per day in Iraq in oil profits." If the Islamic State took all the oil fields upon which it had designs, "the total would be $100 million per month for both Iraq and Syria combined." The jihadis sell the oil at prices that so far undercut OPEC that many cannot resist buying it on the black market: "They sell it for $30 a barrel because it's a black market. It's not pegged to international standards for oil prices, which are over $100 a barrel. The oil is bought through Turkey from Syria, and it's sold to black market traders who function throughout the Levant."[7]

Our "Ally" Turkey

Turkey is ostensibly an ally of the United States and a fellow NATO member. It is key, however, to the Islamic State's black market trade in oil. Barack Obama and John Kerry have failed in repeated efforts to persuade the Turkish government to move against this black market in oil.[8]

The Pentagon has even spotted oil tanker trucks moving Islamic State oil in Turkish territory—but has hesitated to strike them, for fear of further weakening what is not much more than a paper alliance at this point.

The fact that Turkey is still considered an ally against the Islamic State manifests the crying need for a thoroughgoing reevaluation and realignment of U.S. foreign policy, which is still based on old Cold War models, procedures, and alliances that not only do not apply to the struggle against the global jihad and against the Islamic State in particular, but are actively counterproductive.

In September 2014, Turkish President Recep Tayyip Erdogan refused to sign a pledge committing the nations of the Persian Gulf region to fighting the Islamic State, even though that pledge was so toothless as to specify that the participating nations were only committing to fighting ISIS to the extent that each deemed "appropriate."

Forty-nine Turkish diplomats were being held hostage in the Islamic State, Turkish authorities explained, and declaring that Turkey was going to fight against ISIS would endanger them. The possibility that refusing to sign up to fight the Islamic State might present an appearance of weakness that ISIS could exploit by kidnapping even more Turkish diplomats was not considered.[9]

In any case, black market oil, a key element of the Islamic State's wealth, continues to be transported through Turkey, with our friends and allies the Turks doing absolutely nothing to stop it.

According to Undersecretary Cohen, "Our best understanding is that [ISIS] has tapped into a long-standing and deeply rooted black market connecting traders in and around the area." He assured the world that the United States was working with "our partners in the region to choke off cross-border smuggling routes and to identify those involved in smuggling networks."[10]

Despite the lack of Turkish cooperation, these endeavors have been successful at least to some degree. Speaking in February 2015, a week after the Islamic State failed to take the Syrian town of Kobani after a four-month siege, Pentagon spokesperson Rear Admiral John Kirby announced, "We know that oil revenue is no longer the lead source of their [ISIS's] income in dollars." He explained that this was because the Islamic State had suffered losses on the battlefield: "They are changing. They are largely in a

COVETING THE CALIPHATE?

. . . .

Turkey was the home of the last caliphate, the Ottoman Empire, and Turkish President Erdogan has frequently been accused of "neo-Ottoman" tendencies—that is, of wanting to restore the caliphate. It is conceivable, therefore, that Erdogan sees the Islamic State less as an enemy than an opportunity: he may envision it defeating his other enemies, such as the Kurds and Assad's Alawite regime in Damascus, at which point he can move in and reap its benefits, transferring the seat of its caliphate to Istanbul, and perhaps even installing himself as the caliph. Far-fetched? Sure. But so are every day's headlines nowadays. And these ambitions would help explain why Erdogan has been mysteriously reluctant to oppose the Islamic State.

defensive posture. They aren't taking new ground. So, they are losing ground. They are more worried now about their lines of communications and supply routes."

Kirby sounded a confident note: "This is a different group than it was seven months ago. I'm not saying they're not still dangerous. I'm not saying they're not still barbaric, but they're different. Their character, their conduct, their behavior is different. And that's a sign of progress."

The Islamic State was unable to rely as much upon oil sales as it had been, he explained, because it had "lost literally hundreds and hundreds of vehicles that they can't replace. They've got to steal whatever they want to get, and there's a finite number."

Upon what, then, was the Islamic State relying as its primary source of income?

Said Kirby: "A lot of donations."[11]

Well-Heeled Donors

A *lot* of donations. The Islamic State received $40 million in donations in 2013 and 2014—not only from rich individual donors, but even from government sources in Saudi Arabia, Qatar, and Kuwait. Qatar and Kuwait, according to Lori Plotkin Boghardt of the Washington Institute for Near East Policy, "continue to stick out as two trouble spots when it comes to counterterrorist financing enforcement." Boghardt noted that "the U.S. government continues to be concerned about spotty, to say the least, Kuwaiti and Qatari enforcement of their counterterrorist financing laws," and attributed this spotty enforcement to the fact that "cracking down on some ISIS financiers is politically complicated for these countries' leaderships"—because the financiers are men of power and political influence there.[12]

What motivates these shadowy donors? There can be only one answer: Islam. The oil-rich Middle East is full of fantastically wealthy men who read the same Qur'an that is read in the Islamic State, and they are ready to use their wealth to aid the jihad for the sake of Allah worldwide. They don't see the Islamic State as a twisting and hijacking of the peaceful tenets of their religion—that kind of talk is for Western consumption. Quietly, and with the full force of their pocketbooks, they demonstrate that—on the contrary—they see ISIS as a true and faithful embodiment of Islamic teaching.

These donors get money into the Islamic State by means of old smugglers' routes that have been used for generations, and which are supported by well-established systems ensuring kickbacks to government and law enforcement officials who obligingly turn a blind eye.[13] They also, in line with the Islamic State's technical savvy, make skillful use of modern means to launder money. *Newsweek* reported in November 2014 that donations are often "laundered through unregistered charities in the form of 'humanitarian aid,' with terrorists coordinating geographical drop-off points for payments using cellphone applications such as WhatsApp and Kik. Not only can WhatsApp be used around the world but, crucially, it incorporates a GPS mapping tool that makes it easier for terrorists to communicate their exact locations to each other. Kik offers the added benefit of allowing terrorists to register a username without providing a phone number that could identify them. Affiliated ISIS Twitter accounts openly publish their Kik usernames."[14]

Kidnapping and Ransoming Infidels

The Islamic State demanded $100,000,000 for the release of journalist James Foley.[15] When payment was not forthcoming, Foley was beheaded. Later, the Islamic State demanded $200,000,000 from the Japanese government for the life of hostage Haruna Yukawa. When the deadline passed with no response from Japanese Prime Minister Shinzo Abe, the Islamic State beheaded Yukawa and released an audiotape purporting to feature their surviving Japanese hostage, Kenji Goto. The speaker said, "They no longer want money. You bring them their sister from the Jordanian regime, and I will be released immediately. Me for her. Don't let these be my last words you ever hear. Don't let Abe also kill me."[16]

"Their sister from the Jordanian regime" was Sajida Mubarak al-Rishawi, a Muslim woman who was at that time imprisoned in Jordan after a failed jihad suicide bombing attempt in 2005. When the Jordanian government failed to release her, the Islamic State beheaded Goto.

In both cases, the Islamic State did not get the ransom money it demanded; however, on other occasions—which have received little to no publicity because of the embarrassment of those paying the ransoms—its ransom demands have been more successful. The Treasury Department estimates that in 2014 alone the Islamic State took in $20 million in ransom payments.[18]

These payments were for hostages who never received the media attention accorded to Foley, the Japanese hostages, and the other high-profile prisoners of the Islamic State. One Syrian Christian whom the Islamic State held captive for five months recounted that throughout his captivity he was kept chained to a wall blindfolded and was frequently beaten and infrequently fed. There were, he said, around one hundred captives of the Islamic State in the place where he was being kept; most were Christian. ISIS jihadis once told one of them, "We know everything about you. We know where your family lives, what their names are." Another was forced to call his family during a torture session so that his screams would frighten them into paying the ransom. The jihadis told another, whose family was slow in paying, "We will make you call your family and tell them it's their fault you are going to die."

> **OSTRICH ALERT**
>
> "Extremism and Islam are completely different things."
> —Japanese Prime Minister Shinzo Abe[17]

Among those guarding him, the Syrian Christian recalled, were Muslims from France, Belgium, Germany, Russia, Britain, and Saudi Arabia. Eventually his family paid $80,000 to the Islamic State, and he was released.[19] Ransoms make up as much as 20 percent of the Islamic State's revenue.

All in all, the Islamic State is estimated to take in around $6 million a day.[20]

How the U.S. Paved the Way

In March 2015, Barack Obama offered a succinct explanation for how the Islamic State came to be: it was George W. Bush's fault. "ISIL," said Obama, "is a direct outgrowth of al Qaeda in Iraq, which grew out of our invasion, which is an example of unintended consequences, which is why we should generally aim before we shoot."[23]

Obama was derided for playing politics yet again in an area where partisanship should have had no place, and for blaming his predecessor for the umpteenth time. Yet in this particular instance, Obama was actually partially right—though only in a way that showed up his own failures and mistakes all the more vividly.

NOT THAT THIS HAS ANYTHING TO DO WITH ISLAM

A manual of Islamic law stipulates that "when an adult male is taken captive, the caliph considers the interests…(of Islam and the Muslims) and decides between the prisoner's death, slavery, release without paying anything, or ransoming himself in exchange for money or for a Muslim captive held by the enemy."[21]

Revered Islamic jurist Mawardi, agrees: "As for the captives, the amir has the choice of taking the most beneficial action of four possibilities: the first, to put them to death by cutting their necks; the second, to enslave them and apply the laws of slavery regarding their sale or manumission; the third, to ransom them in exchange for goods or prisoners; and fourth, to show favor to them and pardon them."[22]

George W. Bush invaded Iraq in 2003 with the confident hope that once Saddam Hussein was toppled the Iraqi people would welcome the Americans as liberators and establish a Western, secular republic that would become a beacon of freedom and the vanguard of the new Middle East.

Saddam Hussein was duly toppled, but the Americans were not universally welcomed as liberators. Soon American troops were being called "occupiers." The new Iraqi constitution that was eventually adopted was an American production—but it enshrined Islamic law as the highest law of the land instead of instituting truly republican principles and guaranteeing people equality of rights before the law, freedom of speech, and other essential elements of a genuine functioning republic. Sharia is a political as well as a religious system, and it is authoritarian, not allowing for equality of rights for women or non-Muslims, or for the freedom of speech that any genuinely free society must have.

The elections that were eventually held were less exercises in Jeffersonian principles than in tribalism, with Sunnis, Shi'ites, and Kurds voting strictly along tribal and sectarian lines. Shi'ites constitute 60 to 70 percent of Iraq's population, and so the Shi'ites won the elections. Sunnis, who had ruled Iraq for decades under Saddam Hussein, felt angry and disenfranchised when a Shi'ite regime was established in Baghdad. And soon Sunni jihadist groups began to capitalize upon that anger and gain recruits from among the large body of young Sunnis in Iraq who hated the United States and the Baghdad government—and were ready to wage jihad against both.

That much can indeed be laid at the feet of George W. Bush. He and his advisers misjudged the nature of Islam and of Islamic law: their constitution for Iraq, with its adherence to Sharia, directly contradicted their desire to establish Iraq as a Western-style republic. They were wrong to assume that the lure of democracy would be stronger than the pull of government constituted according to Islamic law. Ultimately, in encouraging Sharia rule in Iraq, Bush encouraged the forces that led to the rise of the Islamic State.

However, in criticizing Bush for his Iraq policies, Obama was also incriminating himself. We have seen how, in his speech at Fort Bragg on December 14, 2011, Obama called his withdrawal of American troops from Iraq a "moment of success" and added: "Now, Iraq is not a perfect place. It has many challenges ahead. But we're leaving behind a sovereign, stable and self-reliant Iraq, with a representative government that was elected by its people."[24]

None of this was true. Iraq was neither sovereign, nor stable, nor self-reliant, and Obama gave ISIS a golden opportunity by withdrawing American troops before any of those things actually was true. Obama created a vacuum, and the Islamic State filled it.

Destroying Civilization

Once in power, the Islamic State set about "purifying" the land.

An apocryphal story holds that the caliph Umar, the second successor of Muhammad, ordered the famous Library of Alexandria to be burned to the ground. The books in it were not needed: "they will either contradict the Qur'an, in which case they are heresy, or they will agree with it, so they are superfluous."

Although this almost certainly never happened, the words ascribed to Umar are illustrative of a tendency within Islam that manifested itself on February 22, 2015, when jihadis from the Islamic State ransacked the Mosul Public Library, burning over eight thousand rare and irreplaceable books and manuscripts, including an ancient Arab astrolabe and books from the Ottoman period.[25]

The Islamic State has also destroyed numerous ancient Assyrian artifacts in the Nineveh Museum in Mosul.[26] It released videos showing jihadis taking sledgehammers and drills to priceless artifacts such as an Assyrian winged bull statue dating from the ninth century BC.[27]

In March 2015, the Islamic State bulldozed the thirty-three-hundred-year-old city of Nimrud and the two-thousand-year-old city of Hatra and blew up a tenth-century Chaldean Catholic Church north of Mosul.[28] It sold Christian icons and other artifacts from the looted churches and turned some of the destroyed churches themselves into torture chambers.[29]

The Islamic State has also destroyed cemeteries—some of them Christian, in which they destroyed the crosses on tombstones, in line with the Islamic hatred of the cross—in order to prevent "veneration of the dead."[30]

The world watched agog as ISIS gave it this new confirmation of the Muslim group's gleeful contempt for civilization and embrace of barbarism. But once again, the Islamic State is simply acting in accord with its stated principles. In April 2015, the Islamic State published photos of jihadis smashing tombstones and destroying the crosses upon them, along with a statement of the fourth

NOT THAT THIS HAS ANYTHING TO DO WITH ISLAM

"'These books promote infidelity and call for disobeying Allah. So they will be burned,' a bearded militant in traditional Afghani two-piece clothing told residents, according to one man living nearby who spoke to The Associated Press. The man, who spoke on condition of anonymity because he feared retaliation, said the Islamic State group official made his impromptu address as others stuffed books into empty flour bags."

—Associated Press report from the sacking of the Mosul Public Library by ISIS[31]

"Muslims, these artefacts behind me are idols for people from ancient times who worshipped them instead of God.... The so-called Assyrians, Akkadians and other peoples had gods for the rain, for farming, for war ... and they tried to get closer to them with offerings. The prophet removed and buried the idols in Mecca with his blessed hands.... Even if they are worth billions of dollars, we don't care."

—the ISIS video explains the destruction of archaeological and artistic treasures at the Ninevah Museum in Mosul[32]

caliph, Ali ibn Abi Talib: "I am dispatching you with what the Prophet dispatched me: That you not leave an elevated grave without levelling it, nor an image without erasing it."[33]

Many have scoffed at the Islamic State's claim that they're simply removing temptations to idolatry. Who, after all, would be tempted to worship a three-thousand-year-old Assyrian statue of a bull? And there is more to the Islamic State's actions than just that. Besides removing supposed temptations to idolatry, Islamic jihadists want to ruin the artifacts of non-Muslim civilizations because doing so testifies to the truth of Islam, as the Qur'an suggests that ruins are a sign of Allah's punishment of those who rejected his truth: "Many were the Ways of Life that have passed away before you: travel through the earth, and see what was the end of those who rejected Truth" (Qur'an 3:137).

THE ISLAMIC ETHIC AND THE SPIRIT OF VANDALISM

This dynamic in which ISIS jihadis are inspired to turn archaeological treasures into broken shards is a chilling Islamic variation on the *Protestant Ethic and the Spirit of Capitalism* effect that Max Weber claimed to have discovered. Like Dutch Calvinists in the seventeenth century working hard to succeed in business to prove to themselves that they were among the elect—and creating capitalism in the process—the jihadis of the twenty-first century Islamic State smash the priceless art of pre-Islamic civilizations to reassure themselves that the Qur'an is the truth, Allah is triumphant, and they are his instruments, responsible for creating ruins so as to show his wrath and his judgment. For the Qur'an exhorts believers to fight unbelievers as the tools of Allah's chastisement: "Fight them; Allah will punish them by your hands and will disgrace them and give you victory over them and satisfy the breasts of a believing people" (9:14). They don't seem likely to create anything of value in the process.

In other words, travel through the earth and see the ruins of non-Islamic civilizations, and realize that it is Allah who has destroyed them for their idolatry.

The duty to reduce ancient cities to ruins is related to the Islamic idea that pre-Islamic civilizations, and non-Islamic civilizations, are all *jahili-yya*—the society of unbelievers, which is worthless. Consequently, any art, literature, or architecture produced by any non-Islamic culture has no value whatsoever: it is all simply a manifestation of that pre-Islamic ignorance and barbarism.

Nobel laureate V. S. Naipaul encountered this attitude in his travels through Muslim countries. For many Muslims, he observed in *Among the Believers*, "The time before Islam is a time of blackness: that is part of Muslim theology. History has to serve theology." Obviously this cuts against the idea of tourism of ancient sites and non-Muslim religious installations. Naipaul recounted that some Pakistani Muslims, far from valuing the nation's renowned archaeological site at Mohenjo Daro, saw its ruins as a teaching opportunity for Islam, recommending that Qur'an 3:137 ("Many were the ways of life that passed away before you....") be posted there as a

PUBLIC ENTERTAINMENT, ISIS-STYLE

In May 2015, as part of an offensive that left them in control of more than half Syria's territory, Islamic State forces took over the ancient city of Palmyra, a UNESCO Heritage Site containing irreplaceable buildings from the Roman Empire.[34] ISIS jihadis issued a video explaining that they would be destroying the "polytheistic" statues in Palmyra but leaving the buildings intact[35]—perhaps because they had found a use for them: they summoned the local population to the ancient Roman amphitheatre to watch the public executions of twenty men they said were supporters of the Syrian government.[36]

teaching tool, to warn the stupefied onlookers that they were witnessing not the artifacts of a once-great civilization but the visual proof of the awesome judgment of Allah.

The implications are clear. The Islamic State's caliph has said that the destruction of the Sphinx and the Pyramids is a "religious duty."[37] If he thinks that way about the Sphinx and the Pyramids, it is not hard to guess his opinion of the Vatican, and the Louvre, and the Cathedral of Notre Dame. Even if the Islamic State never makes good on its threat to enter and conquer Europe, admirers of ISIS and its caliph among Muslims

TWO-ALARM
OSTRICH ALERT

"Although the Diocese condemned the act of sacrilege against the Madonna statue, it also followed the Pope's lead by absolving Islam of any responsibility for what happened. In the words of Monsignor Paolo Giulietti, the auxiliary bishop of Città della Pieve, near Perugia: 'For Islam, the figure of Mary is very important: she is the mother of the Prophet Jesus conceived in virginity, and the Blessed Virgin is the most holy woman. Muslims pray at the Marian shrines in the Middle East. We cannot see in this act of vandalism—which as I said is wrong in every way—an episode of religious hatred. It is important not to feed mutual suspicion, especially at this time.'"

—Catholic officials respond to a January 2015 incident in which five Muslims smashed the statue of the Virgin Mary and then urinated on the pieces[38]

"Mumbling phrases of the Koran in Arabic, a Moroccan threw to the ground and severely damaged five statues of artistic value and other furniture and religious objects in a church in Trentino.... The Moroccan is a longtime resident in Trentino, and since last summer has lived in Cles. According to the police, his actions are connected to mental problems, and not to religious fanaticism. The man has for several months shown signs of anxiety, and already last month disturbed a religious function in the same parish church of Cles."

—Italian police respond to a similar incident two weeks earlier[39]

NOT THAT THIS HAS ANYTHING TO DO WITH ISLAM

As they destroyed the ancient Assyrian statues in the Nineveh Museum in Mosul, one of the jihadis explained that they were just imitating Muhammad: "The Prophet ordered us to get rid of statues and relics, and his companions did the same when they conquered countries after him."[40]

living in the West could menace the very patrimony of Western civilization and render the works of Michelangelo and Leonardo da Vinci lost artifacts that are known only from old photographs in history books. There have already been incidents of Muslims destroying religious statues in Italy.

Infidels Will Shoulder the Blame

It is highly likely that in a few centuries (or sooner), Muslims in the areas where the Islamic State destroyed ancient artifacts in the early twenty-first century will be blaming non-Muslims for the damage, and this altered version will go into the history books. This is what has happened with the Sphinx's nose, which was destroyed not by Napoleon's troops in target practice (as goes the oft-repeated story), but by the Muslim precursors of the Islamic State.

In a rare moment of candor, *Russia Today* noted in late March 2015:

> Attacks on the Sphinx date back centuries. Despite many legends surrounding the monument's missing nose—with harm from Napoleon's cannon being among the most popular myths—historians believe it was actually destroyed by Sufi Muslim Muhammad Sa'im al-Dahr in the 14th century, after he learned that some peasants worshipped the Sphinx.[41]

Many of the incidents of Muslim destruction of artifacts are ascribed to infidels, in keeping with the general tendency of Islamic supremacists to blame everyone but themselves for their own wrongdoing. In *Balkan Ghosts: A Journey through History*, Robert D. Kaplan repeats uncritically what he probably heard from local Muslims—or from Christians fearful of what might befall them if they said that Muslims were responsible: that the icons in the local churches had had their eyes scraped off because the superstitious local Christians had taken them to mix in health potions: "According to a peasant belief, the plaster and dye used to depict a saint's eyes can cure blindness."[42]

It is, however, virtually inconceivable that Orthodox believers, even the most ignorant and superstitious, would desecrate their own icons in this way. It is much more likely that the icons had no eyes because Islamic authorities considered it obligatory that they deface the images in order to ruin them as representations of the human form.[43] And that's why the nose of the Sphinx was gone long before Napoleon's troops ever had target practice.

There are men who build, and there are destroyers. The Judeo-Christian West has always loved life and celebrated creativity. By contrast, these Muslims of the Islamic State, acting on principles of Islam, are the enemies of life and creativity; they love death and destruction. As many Islamic jihadists have boasted, "We will win because we love death more than you love life."

That they love death is obvious. We can all take heart, however, from the fact that their claim that destruction will ultimately triumph completely over creation and civilization is, at best, dubious.

The Resistance: Enemies of the Islamic State

Who hates the Islamic State? Short answer: everyone.

But some groups in the region hate it more than others, and are actually doing something about it. The Islamic State's principal enemies:

BARBARIANS AT WORK: PRICELESS ARTIFACTS AND MONUMENTS OF CIVILIZATION THAT THE ISLAMIC STATE HAS DAMAGED OR DESTROYED

A partial list—and more are being added all the time

Ancient Assyrian:

1. **Khorsabad**: 2,700-year-old Assyrian city full of huge statues of winged bulls with human heads.[44]

2. **Assyrian gateway lion statues** from the Arslan Tash archaeological site in northern Syria. At least one of the lion statues was 2,800 years old.[45]

3. **The winged bulls at Nineveh**, near Mosul: 2,700 years old.[46]

4. **Nimrud**: 3,300-year-old Assyrian city containing numerous Assyrian statues and other artifacts.[47]

5. **Mosul Museum**: Iraq's second-largest museum, containing numerous Assyrian artifacts.[48]

6. **Hatra**: 2,300-year-old Assyrian city near Mosul, containing ancient temple artifacts and more.[49]

7. **Mari**: 3,000-year-old city near the border of Syria and Iraq.[50]

8. **Tell Ajaja and Tell Brak**: 3,000-year-old sites containing numerous Assyrian statues and other artifacts.[51]

The Islamic State has also been busy destroying sacred places of Jews, Christians, and Muslims it considers deviant:

Christian:

1. **The Church of the Immaculate Virgin** in Mosul, one of the oldest Christian churches in the city.[52]

2. **The Church of the Virgin Mary** in the al-Arabi area of Mosul.[53]

3. **The St. George Catholic Monastery, also known as the St. Markourkas Church** in Mosul, dating from the tenth century.[54]

4. **The Armenian Genocide Memorial Church** in Der Zor, Syria.[55]

5. **The Green Church** in Tikrit, Iraq.[56]

6. **The Mar Benham Monastery** south of Mosul, which dated to the fourth century.[57]

7. **St. Sargis Assyrian Church**, Tel Tamar, Syria.[58]

Muslim:

1. **The tomb of the prophet Jonah (Yunus)** in Mosul: This 2,800-year-old site was said to house the remains of the Biblical prophet Jonah, and was converted into a mosque, honoring the Qur'an's version of Jonah (Yunus), centuries ago.[59] The tomb of the prophet Daniel was likewise destroyed.[60]

2. **The Prophet Jirjis Mosque** in Mosul, dating from the fourteenth century.[61]

3. **The Khudr Mosque** in Mosul, which dated from the twelfth century.[62]

4. **The tomb of Meqam Shiekh Aqil al Manbaj** and at least three other Sufi and Sunni shrines in Syria.[63]

5. **A Shi'ite mosque in Jalawla, Iraq**, where ISIS also murdered the muezzin, and at least five other Shi'ite mosques.[64]

6. **The Shi'ite shrine of Fathi al-Ka'en** and another Shi'ite shrine in the Iraqi villages of Sharikhan and al-Qubbah.[65]

7. **The Tomb of the Girl**, a shrine near Mosul that, according to legend, honored a beautiful young girl who died of a broken heart.[66]

8. **The Al-Arbain Mosque** in Tikrit, which was said to contain the tombs of warriors from the early days of Islam.[67]

- *The Kurds.* Kurdistan lies within Turkey, Syria, Iraq, and Iran, and the Kurds have been trying to establish an independent state since before World War I. Each of those countries has done whatever it could to prevent attainment of that goal, and now the Islamic State poses an additional obstacle. The Kurds today have fielded one of the most significant military forces (the Peshmerga, which means "those who face death") arrayed against the Islamic State, and they successfully broke the ISIS siege of the Syrian town of Kobani in January 2015—despite the initial unwillingness of the Turks to provide the slightest assistance, due to their own animosity toward the Kurds.[68] The Turks blockaded the city, which lies on the Syria/Turkey border, and wouldn't allow Kurdish troops from elsewhere to cross Turkish territory to enter it—until finally they relented under heavy pressure from the United States.[69]

- *The Iranians.* Iran now has a client regime in Baghdad and another in Damascus. It also controls the jihad terror group Hizballah, which is a major force in Lebanese politics, and funds the Sunni jihad group Hamas in Gaza. This gives Iran a significant sphere of influence all across the Middle East, and a claim to be the leader of the Islamic world, despite its allegiance to the Shia Islam shared by only a minority of Muslims. But in between its presence in Lebanon and Syria and its regime in Baghdad stands the Islamic State, vowing to subjugate the entire world under its caliphate and kill or convert the Shia to Sunni Islam. The Iranians have thus far undertaken only limited operations against the Islamic State, but if ISIS continues to grow and expand, that could easily change.

- *Shi'ites in Iraq.* The Islamic State is a Sunni group that has made its contempt and hatred for Shi'ites abundantly clear. Because of the weak Shi'ite government in Baghdad, the Islamic State is able to target Shi'ite civilians as well as soldiers. An Islamic State spokesman explained in July 2014 that before ISIS attacks Israel, which it fully intends to do, it needs to take care of the Shi'ites and Muslims who prefer secular government (or any government other than their own): "The greatest answer to this question is in the Qur'an, where Allah speaks about the nearby enemy—those Muslims who have become infidels—as they are more dangerous than those which were already infidels."[70]

- *The Sunni Muslims in and around the city of Ramadi.* The Islamic State would count among those "Muslims who have become infidels" the Sunni Arabs of Anbar Province who held out against ISIS attempts to take the provincial capital of Ramadi from early 2014 to May of 2015, when the city finally fell to ISIS. Despite being Sunni, the residents of Ramadi appear to prefer the Shi'ite government of Baghdad to the Islamic State. Their resistance to ISIS represented the remnants of the 2006 "Anbar Awakening," in which local Sunni tribes formed an alliance against the al-Qaeda in Iraq (AQI) jihadis[71] who had been terrorizing the local population with the rigorist adherence to Sharia and the atrocities for which they would later—under their new name of ISIS—become infamous worldwide. The stakes were high: Ramadi is less than seventy miles from Baghdad. In November 2014 Anbar Province governor Ahmed al-Dulaimi said, "If we lose Anbar, that means we will lose Iraq."[72] The Islamic State's May 2015 conquest of Ramadi inspired more than forty thousand refugees to flee the city before the Baghdad government closed a key bridge—that's on top of the one hundred thirty thousand who had already fled during the fighting in April.[73] Apparently the local population has not forgotten life under AQI, and they don't want to have to live under the rule of ISIS.

- *The Saudis.* The Saudis spent billions to propagate their virulent, violent form of Islam around the world. They covered the earth with Islamic proselytizing material that declared that the only legitimate government on earth was an Islamic caliphate. Now a caliphate is on their doorstep, declaring that the House of Saud itself is as illegitimate as every other government on earth. They are reaping what they have so assiduously sown.

- *The Christians*. The Islamic State has decimated ancient Christian communities across Iraq and Syria. When it captured northern Iraq, the Islamic State drove thirty thousand Christians from the Nineveh plain where they had lived since not long after the time of Christ.[74] In August 2014, the Chaldean Catholic Archbishop of Mosul, Amel Shimoun Nona, predicted that the same thing would eventually happen to Christians in the West: "Our sufferings today are the prelude of those you, Europeans and Western Christians, will also suffer in the near future. I lost my diocese. The physical setting of my apostolate has been occupied by Islamic radicals who want us converted or dead." The archbishop explained that the West was making a grave error by assuming that Islam was a religion of peace that taught the equal dignity of all human beings:

    Please, try to understand us. Your liberal and democratic principles are worth nothing here. You must consider again our reality in the Middle East, because you are welcoming in your countries an ever growing number of Muslims. Also you are in danger. You must take strong and courageous decisions, even at the cost of contradicting your principles. You think all men are equal, but that is not true: Islam does not say that all men are equal. Your values are not their values. If you do not understand this soon enough, you will become the victims of the enemy you have welcomed in your home.[75]

In early 2015 the Christians of Iraq began to fight back, forming a Christian militia of four thousand men.[76] And while Western governments contented themselves with cosmetic gestures, some individuals in the West took notice as well. A U.S. Army veteran named Sean Rowe founded an organization called Veterans Against ISIS, hoping to attract veterans to join active combat against the Islamic State.

Others joined existing groups. Marine Corps vet Louis Park joined an Iraqi Christian militia, explaining: "I know that if [ISIS] is allowed to stay here, we will see violence in the United States as well. So I'm protecting my homeland too. I'm not being paid at all. I'm being fed and I'm being clothed and everything, but any gear that I need, I'm paying out of pocket. This is all money that I saved for this effort myself, because I believe in the cause a lot, so I'm willing to finance everything."[77] Brett Royales, an Army veteran who also joined the Iraqi Christians fighting against the Islamic State, invoked his Army training: "I've been given a skill set. I've honored it over the years. I can't sit home and watch what's going on here—the atrocities, crucifixions, rapes, sex slaves, people being driven out from their towns. It's unacceptable to me, so I'm here to do what I can to get people back in their homes and protect their way of life."[78]

Chapter Five

INSIDE THE ISLAMIC STATE

P erhaps because of its destruction of ancient artifacts (not to mention its reign of terror), the Islamic State has not exactly become a thriving tourist hub. Even as Muslims from all over the world are traveling to join it, many who have found themselves within its domains through no choice of their own have fled, even if it meant leaving behind everything they owned and the only life they knew.

A look at daily life in the Islamic State makes it abundantly clear why so many people have chosen to flee rather than to stay and try to adapt to the new overlords—even in areas where Bashar Assad and Saddam Hussein had been notorious for their tyranny.

Did you know?

- ISIS condemns smoking as slow-motion suicide and has punished it with death
- The Islamic State has opened a consumer protection office
- ISIS has developed an elaborate secret service to control the population
- Four hundred Syrian children have joined "Cubs of the Caliphate," the Islamic State's answer to the Hitler Youth

Planning a Vacation to the Islamic State? Be Sure to Abide by the Rules

Millions of people still live in the Islamic State, of course, as they do not have the wherewithal to flee even if they want to. Others are unwilling to leave their homeland no matter what regime comes into power—after all, regimes come and regimes go, and the next change may be for the better. Whatever may keep people there, the Islamic State has been very specific about how they must behave. After all, they consider themselves to be in the process of building the ideal Islamic polity, and that depends on an absolute adherence to Islamic law. Breaking the law in the Islamic State can get you lashed or even beheaded, so if you're planning a relaxing vacation in the caliphate, be sure you abide by the local laws:

- Women must cover their entire body except face and hands. (According to some reports, they must cover their faces as well.)[1]
- Women may not wear makeup or sit in a chair.[2]
- Women may not leave the house without a male accompanying them.[3]
- Men may not cut their hair, put gel in it, or wear it in a "modern style." Barber shops have been shut down (as have beauty salons for women).[4]
- You may not refer to the ruling group as *"Daesh."*[5]
- Only women may sell clothing to women.[6]
- Men may not wear low-hanging jeans (*they've got a point there—ed.*).[7]
- Taxi drivers who overcharge are guilty of theft; they could have a hand amputated, or worse.[8]
- Thieves will have their hands amputated (as per Qur'an 5:38). Blackmailers will face killing or crucifixion (as per Qur'an 5:33).[9]

- Drugs, alcohol, and cigarettes are forbidden.[10]
- No political parties or armed groups are allowed other than the Islamic State.[11]
- Those who leave Islam are to be killed.[12]
- Sharia is the sole law of the land.[13]
- Graves and shrines are forbidden, and are to be destroyed.[14]
- Those wearing soccer jerseys will receive eighty lashes.[15]

There are other rules as well. In December 2014 ISIS was reported to have used "the 'biter,'" "a bear trap-like device" with spikes, on the breast of a woman who was guilty of "breastfeeding in public" in Raqqa.[16] In April 2015 near Tikrit, Iraq, Saddam Hussein's hometown, in April 2015, the Islamic State beheaded a man for "witchcraft."[17] (ISIS authorities did not explain what exactly that meant.) The next month a UN official announced that a young woman in the Islamic State had been burned alive for "refusing to take part in [an] 'extreme sex act.'"[18] A deserter from the Islamic State has recounted that Islamic State prisons in Raqqa are filled with people who were not sufficiently reverent during prayers or who have uttered the name of Allah in a way that Islamic State authorities deemed blasphemous. Their Islamic State captors torture them with sticks and cattle prods, and occasionally even burn prisoners to death.[19]

Special Rules for Christians

Most of the Christians in the Islamic State's domains fled or were killed; "all who are left there now are a few handicapped or sickly Christians," remarked a nun from Mosul in June 2014, and the situation has only deteriorated since then.[20]

Nonetheless, those who remain have to submit to the rule of Sharia. The Islamic State's rules mandating the subjugation of Christians are straight out of traditional Islamic law.

NOT THAT THIS HAS ANYTHING TO DO WITH ISLAM

· ·

"Fight those who do not believe in Allah, nor in the latter day, nor do they prohibit what Allah and His Apostle have prohibited, nor follow the religion of truth, out of those who have been given the Book, until they pay the tax in acknowledgement of superiority and they are in a state of subjection."

—Qur'an quotation (9:29) from the preamble to a list of seven rules for Christians issued by the Islamic State in December 2014[21]

In Sharia, Christians are allowed to live in an Islamic state as "dhimmis" (protected people) only if they submit to a regime of severe restrictions designed to mark their subordinate place in society and defuse any challenge that Christianity might pose to Islam. If Christians disobey these rules, they are no longer "protected," and the relationship between them and the Islamic authorities reverts to a state of violent hostility.

Thus in the Islamic State Christians are forbidden to:

- Make any public display of their religion (all Christian worship has to take place behind closed doors);[22]
- Ring church bells;[23]
- Display the cross in public, including in markets and other areas where Christians might come into contact with Muslims;[24]
- Pray so loudly that Muslims could chance to hear their prayers;[25]
- Build new churches or repair old ones;[26]
- Make fun of Muslims or Islam;[27]
- Try to prevent anyone from converting from Christianity to Islam.[28]

The rules also specify that Christians were not to bear arms and that treachery against the Islamic State is punishable by death.[29]

None of these rules is optional. The Islamic State has explained that if Christians reject them, "they are subject to being legitimate targets, and nothing will remain between them and ISIS other than the sword."[30] Of course, one would be hard pressed to find infractions that do not bring the Islamic State's righteous sword upon the hapless offender.

The Islamic State issued new threats to Christians in an April 2015 video, shortly after releasing the footage depicting its beheading of twenty-eight Ethiopian Christians. Islamic State spokesman Sheik Abu Malik Anas An-Nashwan declared,

> We say to Christians everywhere, the Islamic State will expand, with Allah's permission. And it will reach you even if you are in fortified strongholds. So whoever enters Islam will have security, and whoever accepts the Dhimmah contract will have security. But whoever refuses will see nothing from us but the edge of a spear. The men will be killed and the children will be enslaved, and their wealth will be taken as booty. This is the judgment of Allah and His Messenger.

The Dhimmah is the contract of protection in Islamic law, whereby Christians and other non-Muslims accept second-class status and institutionalized

EVERYBODY'S DOING IT

This regime for oppressing Christians was no harsh throwback to the seventh century or misunderstanding and misapplication of Islamic law. These rules are principles of Islamic law accepted to this day by millions of Muslims who live outside the Islamic State. A manual of Islamic law endorsed by Al-Azhar University in Cairo as a reliable guide to the "practice and faith of the orthodox Sunni community" stipulates that dhimmi Jews and Christians under the "protection" of any Islamic state— are "forbidden to openly display wine or pork...to ring church bells or display crosses...recite the Torah or Evangel aloud, or make public display of their funerals and feastdays."[31]

discrimination in return for the right to continue to live as non-Muslims within the Islamic state.

ISIS spokesman An-Nashwan laments the fact that Muslims today are not collecting the jizya, the tax specified for non-Muslims in Qur'an 9:29: "In the recent past, these rites were absent from the condition of the Muslim Nation. Rather, these rites were the hostages of jurisprudence books and theoretical legal discussions."

The Islamic State spokesman followed that by quoting the medieval Muslim scholar Ibn Taymiyya: "Whoever does not consider the Jews and Christians to be disbelievers and does not hate them is not a Muslim." Then he quoted a saying attributed to Muhammad himself: "If you meet Jews or Christians, do not greet them in peace."

The video even shows a Christian accepting his subjugated status: "By Allah, we are happy. We've seen security under the Islamic State."[32]

Security in exchange for submission.

Daily Life in the Caliphate: The Islamic State of Fear

Patrick Cockburn wrote in the *Independent* in March 2015:

> It is one of the strangest states ever created. The Islamic State wants to force all humanity to believe in its vision of a religious and social utopia existing in the first days of Islam. Women are to be treated as chattels, forbidden to leave the house unless they are accompanied by a male relative. People deemed to be pagans, like the Yazidis, can be bought and sold as slaves. Punishments such as beheadings, amputations and flogging become the norm. All those not pledging allegiance to the caliphate declared by its leader, Abu Bakr al-Baghdadi, on 29 June last year are considered enemies.[33]

Strange to those of us accustomed to the recognition of universal human rights and the humanitarian penal code of the Judeo-Christian West, perhaps. But none of this was any departure from Islamic law as it had been codified for centuries. In fact, many of the punishments that drew the attention of a horrified world when ISIS carried them out had been applied by other Sharia-compliant governments for decades.

In the Islamic State's de facto capital of Raqqa, Syria, a city of three hundred thousand people, twenty-four-hour Sharia patrols, one for men and one for women, make sure that everyone who ventures onto the street at any time is conforming to the strictures of Islamic law.

They are little different from the religious police that terrify the citizenry in Saudi Arabia and Iran, but this new Sharia regime represents a significant change from the relatively secular rule of Bashar Assad. Abu Saif, an observer on the scene in Raqqa, noted, "People have started growing their beards, people have started praying on time, and during prayer times all the shops close. All this might come across as small details for some people, but this is a whole lifestyle change for civilians."[34]

The Islamic State also deploys a uniformed military police, primarily to track down jihadis who have fled from the front lines and send them back to the battle.[36]

Schools remain open, but the curriculum has been significantly altered to reflect the Islamic State's priorities. According to Abu Saif, "Schools and universities

EXECUTIONERS WANTED

• • •

In May of 2015, the *New York Times* reported, "Job seekers in Saudi Arabia who have a strong constitution and endorse strict Islamic Law might consider new opportunities carrying out public beheadings and amputating the hands of convicted thieves." The Kingdom was advertising eight executioner positions because of an uptick in beheadings and "a scarcity of qualified swordsmen in some parts of the country." The *Times* did report that the amputations of thieves' hands are "rarely carried out"—not because that punishment isn't clearly established in Sharia and thus in the laws of Saudi Arabia, but because "judges consider it distasteful."[35] The judges in the Islamic State aren't so squeamish.

are a big disaster, they have changed the curriculum a lot. They forbade law studies, philosophy, and other social studies, which they consider infidel studies and 'outside the Shariah of Allah.'"[37]

Smoking Kills

The Islamic State authorities take a dim view of smoking because they regard it as a slow-motion form of suicide, which is forbidden in the Qur'an: "And do not kill yourselves" (4:29).

The way the Islamic State has dealt with smoking epitomizes how it deals with everything it opposes: with threats and increasing brutality. In Mosul in November 2014, the Islamic State decreed that any shop owners found to have sold cigarettes would be fined $580 and given two weeks in jail and eighty lashes. Cigarette importers would get a $3,300 fine, plus four months in jail, and also eighty lashes. Those simply caught smoking would be fined $16.[38]

In its de facto capital of Raqqa, the rules were even more draconian. If a shop was found to be selling cigarettes, it was closed down. Islamic State jihadis took pliers to the fingers of one man who was caught smoking on the street. Abu Mohammed Hussam of the anti-ISIS group Raqqa is Being Slaughtered Silently (RBSS) explained that the Islamic State has a series of punishments for serial smokers: "The first time he will be arrested and flogged (40 lashes). If he smokes again, he will be whipped and imprisoned. On the third occasion, he will be taken to a camp in the countryside and fined a large sum of money."[40]

NOT THAT THIS HAS ANYTHING TO DO WITH ISLAM

"Every smoker," ISIS has declared, "should be aware that with every cigarette he smokes in a state of trance and vanity is disobeying God."[39]

What if someone were caught smoking a fourth time? A deputy emir for the Islamic State's police force in the Syrian province of Deir al-Zor, who also served as an ISIS executioner, was himself found beheaded in January 2015. There was a cigarette stuck between the lips of his severed head. Written on the body was "This is evil, O Sheikh."[41]

Abu Bakr al-Janabi, an Islamic State supporter who helps spread ISIS propaganda online, praised the Islamic State's efforts to get people to quit smoking: "It took time for ISIS until they implemented the law, but after having lectures about it and so on, there is no objection—with exception to those who smoke. It's a little hard for them to suddenly quit smoking. But ISIS have been very good at helping them quit."[42]

Indeed. What could be a more effective deterrent to smoking than the prospect of being beheaded for it? Surgeon General, take note!

Reign of Terror

The Islamic State brings bloodshed and brutality wherever it goes. In April 2015, it seized and occupied the Yarmouk camp for Palestinian refugees, four miles from the center of Damascus. One man who escaped recalled the Islamic State's casual and even gleeful bloodlust: "I saw severed heads. They killed children in front of their parents. We were terrorized. We had heard of their cruelty from the television, but when we saw it ourselves...I can tell you, their reputation is well-deserved."

A teenage boy who also got away remembered more horrors: "In Palestine Street, I saw two members of Daesh playing with a severed head as if it was a football."[43]

In October 2014, ISIS executed a seventeen-year-old boy for apostasy and then crucified the dead body, leaving it on display as a warning to others.[44] In one frenzied two-day period of January 2015, Islamic State jihadis hurled a gay man off a tower, stoned a woman to death for adultery, and crucified no fewer than seventeen young men.[45] The Islamic State drew crowds to such events, holding grisly executions in public even as children watched.[46] On other occasions it published photographs of stonings and other Sharia punishments on social media.[47]

All this was likely calculated to "strike terror into the hearts of the enemies of Allah" (Qur'an 8:60). But the gruesome executions also appear to be serving as entertainment for his friends. It seems that some within the Islamic State's domains have grown accustomed to the bloodlust and begun to enjoy the spectacle—or perhaps they fear to show anything but enthusiasm for the executions, under the watchful eye of the Sharia police. In February 2015, the Islamic State set up giant screens around Raqqa to show its burning alive of Jordanian pilot Muath al-Kaseasbeh; throngs watched and cheered the poor man's horrific death.[48]

The Islamic State has developed an elaborate and sophisticated secret service structure, worthy of a nascent totalitarian state that intends to assert total control over its citizens, and to watch them closely to ensure they toe the line. This spy network enables ISIS not only to enforce Sharia penalties, but to assert total control of an area. When conquering a new town or city, Islamic State operatives have been instructed to:

- List the powerful families.
- Name the powerful individuals in these families.
- Find out their sources of income.
- Name names and the sizes of (rebel) brigades in the village.
- Find out the names of their leaders, who controls the brigades, and their political orientation.
- Find out their illegal activities (according to Sharia law), which could be used to blackmail them if necessary.[49]

All this and more is used to assert total control over the new area, and solidify that control quickly and decisively.

It Really *Is* a State—It Even Has a Consumer Protection Office

Even amidst all this coercion, terror, and bloodlust, however, the Islamic State is trying to set up a viable state. "With the departments they have established, they really have created a state. One cannot deny that, for instance, they opened a consumer protection office. If one has a restaurant and they came to check it out, and the meat was bad, or it was exposed to dirt or sunlight, they would take expired material and dispose of it as a sanitary action. They follow up on these issues completely with the departments they have created." So reported Abu Saif, an opponent of the Islamic State in Raqqa.[50]

And it was true: the Islamic State moved quickly to establish genuine governance. It was initially organized with a command structure that indicated its intention to govern in a manner that at least in some ways resembles the manner in which a conventional state is governed. As of October 2014, the Islamic State leadership included the following officials (some of the offices appear to be what we might style "in waiting"—the ISIS governor of Baghdad, for example, like a member of Britain's "shadow cabinet" standing ready to take power—except that while Labour is hoping to win the next election, ISIS is planning to conquer the Iraqi capital by force of arms):

- **Caliph**: Abu Bakr al-Baghdadi
- **Deputy to the Caliph, Overseer of the Iraqi Provinces**: Abu Muslim al-Turkmani[51] (killed in December 2014)[52]
- **Deputy to the Caliph, Overseer of the Syrian Provinces**: Abu Ali al-Anbari[53]
- **War Minister**: Abu Suleiman[54]
- **Senior Military Commander**: Abu Wahib[55]
- **Director of Military Operations in Syria**: Umar al-Shisani[56]
- **Finance Minister**: Abu Salah[57]

- **Minister of General Coordination**: Abu Hajar al-Assafi[58]
- **Minister of General Management**: Abu Abd al-Kadir[59]
- **Minister for Social Services**: Abu Saji[60]
- **Minister of General Security**: Abu Louay (a.k.a. Abu Ali)[61]
- **Governor of Baghdad**: Abu Maysara[62]
- **Governor of Anbar and Chief of the Military Council**: Abu Abdul Salem (Abu Mohammed al-Sweidawi)[63]
- **Governor of the "Border Provinces"**: Abu Jurnas[64]
- **Governor of the South and Central Euphrates**: Abu Fatima (Ahmed Mohsen Khalal al-Juhayshi)[65]
- **Governor of Kirkuk**: Abu Fatima (Naima Abd al-Naif al-Jouburi)[66]
- **Governor of Raqqa**: Abu Luqman[67]
- **Governor of Aleppo**: Abu Atheer al-Absi[68]
- **Governor of Deir ez Zour**: Haji Abd al-Nasir[69]
- **Governor of Homs**: Abu Shuayb al-Masri[70]
- **Governor of Salaheddin**: Abu Nabil[71]
- **Chief Spokesman**: Abu Muhammad al-Adnani (Taha Sobhi Falaha)[72]
- **Chief of Media Operations**: Ahmad Abousamra[73]

Then there were a few positions that we don't see in the cabinets of Western leaders—at least not yet:

- **Minister for Foreign Fighters and Suicide Bombers**: Abu Kassem[74]
- **Sharia Official**: Abu Hummam al-Athari[75]
- **Coordinator for the Affairs of Martyrs and Women**: Abu Suja[76]
- **Minister for Explosives**: Abu Kifah[77]

- **Minister for Weapons**: Abu Sima[78]
- **Minister of Prisoners**: Abu Mohammed (Bashar Ismail al-Hamdani)[79]

ISIScare

Mujahidah bint Usama (Jihad Warrior the Daughter of Osama) was a doctor in Britain before she traveled to the Islamic State. Once there, she posted on her Twitter feed a photo of herself wearing a niqab, the Islamic veil that covers the face, and a white lab coat and holding a severed head as two children stand by. Her caption: "Dream Job.. A Terrorist Doc," along with a smiley face and two hearts.[80]

Other medical professionals followed her. In March 2015, nine Muslim medical students from Britain went to the Islamic State to work in hospitals there. Turkish politician Mehmet Ali Ediboglu, who met with their families when they went to Turkey to try to persuade their children to return, remarked, "Let's not forget about the fact that they are doctors; they went there to help, not to fight. So this case is a little bit different."[81] A little, but not much. Surely a British doctor who traveled to Nazi Germany to work in a German hospital in 1943 would have been recognized as a traitor.

In any case, the Islamic State still hadn't achieved universal access to healthcare. In mid-April 2015 it executed ten doctors in northern Iraq for refusing to treat its jihadis.[82] And two weeks later, the Islamic State issued a video announcing the formation of the Islamic State Health Service.[83] The clip featured a Muslim pediatrician from Australia, Dr. Tareq Kamleh (now known as Abu Yusuf), standing in a hospital and holding a newborn baby. He called upon Muslim doctors to travel to the Islamic State: "Please consider coming, please don't delay." Providing medical services in the Islamic State was his "jihad for Islam," the good doctor said.[84]

On April 26, 2015, just days after Kamleh's video appeared, a photo of a newborn baby with a handgun and a grenade placed next to him, along with what was claimed to be the Islamic State's first official birth certificate, began circulating on Twitter.[85]

Cubs of the Caliphate

When that lad gets older, he may join the Islamic State's answer to the Hitler Youth, "Cubs of the Caliphate." Between January and late March 2015, the ISIS youth organization enrolled at least four hundred Syrian children under the age of eighteen, giving them training in how to fire weapons as well as an intensive indoctrination into the Islamic State worldview. An ISIS video released in March showed one of these boys shooting and killing an accused spy.

The caliphate has called upon Muslim parents around the world to send their children to the Islamic State for jihad training.[86] The Cubs of the Caliphate program makes it likely that even if the Islamic State is defeated and eradicated, its aftershocks will be felt around the world for years to come.

ISIS: Bringing Mass-Murdering Totalitarian Government Back into Fashion

The Islamic State's confident and emphatic proclamations that it is the foremost exponent of the Islamic faith, and its primary earthly authority, have not kept it from the infighting and internal strife that plague most organizations—and particularly those of a strongly authoritarian bent.

"Daesh tries to portray itself as one thing, but beneath the surface there's a lot of dirt," said a critic of the group inside its capital of Raqqa, Syria. There were fights within the group, he claimed, over money and power.[87] Jamie Dettmer of the Daily Beast reported in February 2015 that there were "quarrels over a range of issues—from divvying up of the spoils of war to competition over women and, yes, the handling of foreign hostages."[88]

After ISIS besieged but then failed to capture the town of Kobani on the Syrian border with Turkey, other tensions emerged as well. One refugee who fled from the Islamic State said: "The prolonged battle for Kobani caused a lot of tensions—fighters accused each other of treachery and eventually turned on each other."[89] A Free Syrian Army member noted: "There is a lot of mutual suspicion among the commanders. We tried to exchange some information with an ISIS commander recently and within days he was executed."[90]

The anti-ISIS Syrian group "Raqqa is Being Slaughtered Silently" has reported that the Islamic State is just as brutal with dissenters as antecedent totalitarian states such as the Soviet Union and Nazi Germany. After the Islamic State burned alive Jordanian pilot Muath al-Kaseasbeh, "an ISIS cleric in Aleppo province who dared to criticize the immolation of al Kasasbeh has been removed from his post by the 'caliphate' leadership and will be put on trial by the group. The Saudi-born imam had said those responsible for the video-recorded murder are the ones who should be put on trial."[91]

Also like the Soviet Union and other totalitarian states, the Islamic State has made it difficult for those who have joined it to change their minds and go home. The Syrian Observatory for Human Rights reported in December 2014 that in a two-month span ISIS had killed at least 116 foreign jihadis who had tried to leave the caliphate for home, and added, "We believe that the real number of people that had been killed by IS is higher than the number documented."[92] In March 2015 came another report, that the Islamic State had killed nine of its own jihadis who had tried to abandon the caliphate.[93]

And over a six-month period the Islamic State's reign of terror claimed the lives of at least 1,878 people—including over 1,175 civilians, 930 of whom were members of a tribe that had fought the ISIS jihadis for control of two oilfields. It also executed over 500 soldiers of Bashar Assad's regime, and nearly 100 who were fighting against Assad but as members of groups other than the Islamic State.[94]

Who's Who in ISIS:
The Caliph

The Islamic State's Caliph Ibrahim is more commonly known as Abu Bakr al-Baghdadi, but that is a *nom de guerre*. His real name, insofar as any of the information that has been reported about him is accurate, is Ibrahim Awad Ibrahim al-Badri. According to many accounts, he hails from a family that has produced numerous Muslim clerics, and he himself has a Ph.D. in Islamic law from the Islamic University in Baghdad.[95]

While all that we know about him is questionable, some of the reports contain interesting details. The most vivid impression that Baghdadi apparently left on those who knew him in his early life in his native city of Samarra was of a quiet, bookish boy just the opposite of Zarqawi, the thuggish ISIS founder. A neighbor recalled that he was "so quiet you could hardly hear his voice. He was peaceful. He didn't like to chat a lot."[96] The future caliph was deeply committed to Islam from the beginning: "He always had religious or other books attached on the back of his bike, and I never saw him in trousers and shirt, like most of the other guys in Samarra. He had a light beard, and he never hung out in cafés. He had his small circle from his mosque." Another former neighbor recalled, "He was from a poor but well-mannered family. He was someone very introverted... go the mosque [sic], study, read books, that's it." A third remembered that he "was, like most of his family, a devoted Muslim."[97]

From 1994 to 2004, while the worldwide jihad was heating up, Baghdadi lived quietly in a room at a mosque in Baghdad, occasionally leading prayers when the imam was away.[98]

A former neighbor recalled that despite his devout commitment to Islam he was a quiet man who wasn't even stirred to open action when American troops entered Iraq: "He didn't show any hostility to the Americans. He wasn't like the hot blooded ones. He must have been a quiet planner."[99]

One of Baghdadi's classmates at the Islamic University remembered him as "quiet, and retiring. He spent time alone." The classmate eventually joined the jihad against the Americans, and didn't find Baghdadi among its leaders: "I used to know all the leaders personally. Zarqawi was closer than a brother to me. But I didn't know Baghdadi. He was insignificant. He used to lead prayer in a mosque near my area. No one really noticed him."[100]

This shy, quiet Muslim cleric did, however, eventually join the jihad against the U.S. forces, and he was imprisoned by the Americans.[101] It was on his release from Camp Bucca that he is said to have issued his famous veiled threat, "I'll see you guys in New York."[102]

The future caliph's support for the idea of the caliphate was based on a straightforward idea of fairness. One Islamic State supporter has explained: "In short, for Sheikh Baghdadi, each religion has its state except Islam, and it should have a state and it should be imposed. It is very simple."[103] A warrior for the rival al-Qaeda group Jabhat al-Nusra remarked, "He is becoming very popular among jihadis. They see him as someone who is fighting the war of Islam.... He has received letters expressing loyalty from Afghanistan and Pakistan as well. Sheikh Zawahri is trying but I think it is too late."[104]

With all the reports of dissension with the Islamic State, there have not been any reports of serious challenges to the authority of the caliph Ibrahim. There has been no hint of a power struggle like the one that went on between Ali ibn Abi Talib and Muawiya in the early days of Islam, and no rival claimants or pretenders to the caliph's throne.

A power struggle could be going on behind the scenes, of course, and locked up as tightly as al-Baghdadi himself, who has only been seen once in public since he proclaimed his caliphate in June 2014.

Since then, al-Baghdadi's serious injury and even death have been reported more than once: "Iraqi Isis Leader Abu Bakr al-Baghdadi 'Severely Injured and Flees to Syria,'" read the International Business Times headline just six days after the proclamation of the caliphate.[105] And then Al Arabiya reported four months later that al-Baghdadi had been seriously wounded in an airstrike on November 8, 2014.[106] There was widespread speculation at that time that the caliph was dead. General Nicholas Houghton, the Chief of the Defence Staff of the British Armed Forces, said the next day: "I can't absolutely confirm that Baghdadi has been killed. Probably it will take some days to have absolute confirmation."[107]

We're still waiting. Just a few days after the airstrike, the caliph released an audiotape full of bravado and threats. "America and its allies are terrified, weak, and powerless," he bragged, and denounced the familiar bogeymen: the Jews and the "apostate" and "treacherous" Muslim leaders who rejected his authority.

"Oh soldiers of the Islamic State, continue to harvest the [enemy] soldiers," al-Baghdadi exhorted. "Erupt volcanoes of jihad everywhere.

DON'T WORRY, THE CALIPH IS SAFE AND SOUND— THE JIHAD WILL SOON REACH ROME

"Be assured, O Muslims, for your state is good and in the best condition. Its march will not stop and it will continue to expand, by Allah's permission. The march of the mujahidin [Muslim holy warriors] will continue until they reach Rome. And soon, the Jews and Crusaders will be forced to come down to the ground and send their ground forces to their deaths and destruction."

—the caliph reassuring ISIS supporters after the November 2014 airstrike that gave rise to speculation he had been killed[108]

Light the earth with fire under all the tyrants and their soldiers and supporters."

Since then, silence. The caliph has become as spectral and surrounded by myth as Orwell's Big Brother, or Osama bin Laden in his secret Pakistani redoubt. But the brutality of the caliphate he leads is an all too solid reality.

The Shadow Caliph

On April 21, 2015, it was reported yet again that the caliph had been seriously wounded in an airstrike.[109] The Pentagon, however, immediately denied the report, saying that the caliph was not in the car that had been hit.[110] Ignoring this denial, Iraqi government adviser Hisham al Hashimi stated that al-Baghdadi's de facto replacement was a former protégé of Osama bin Laden, Abu Alaa Afri: "After Baghdadi's wounding," al Hashimi said, "he has begun to head up Daesh with the help of officials responsible for other portfolios. He will be the leader of Daesh if Baghdadi dies."[111] On April 27, reporter Kareem Shaheen of the UK's *Guardian* said: "Sources tell us Baghdadi is still alive, but still unable to move due to spinal injury sustained in the March air strike."[112] That same day, Radio Iran reported that the caliph was dead.[113]

The conflicting reports made it impossible to tell what al-Baghdadi's condition really was, but there was no reason to doubt that Afri was an important figure inside the Islamic State. Al Hashimi, the Iraqi government adviser, claimed that Afri was more important to the Islamic State's leadership than the caliph himself: "Yes—more important, and smarter, and with better relationships. He is a good public speaker and strong charisma [sic]. All the leaders of Daesh find that he has much jihadi wisdom, and good capability at leadership and administration."[114]

Al Hashimi added that Afri had been a physics teacher and "has dozens of publications and religious (shariah) studies of his own."[115] He was also apparently Osama bin Laden's choice to lead al-Qaeda in Iraq in 2010 and is thought to support reconciliation between al-Qaeda and the Islamic State. In May 2015, the Iraq military claimed that Afri himself had been killed in an airstrike, but the Pentagon would not confirm the claim,[116] and the video of the airstrike released by the Iraqis was apparently from a different location from the one they claimed.[117]

The Executioner

In sharp contrast to the elusive caliph, the Islamic State's principal killer is highly visible, although his identity wasn't discovered until his international notoriety was already well established. The man whose knife sawed into the throats of James Foley, Steven Sotloff, David Haines, Alan Henning, Peter Kassig, Haruna Yukawa, Kenji Goto, and others while the Islamic State cameras rolled always wore a balaclava over his face, and never announced who he was. He speaks with a pronounced English accent and is known as "Jihadi John" after John Lennon of the Beatles, he and three other British Muslims in ISIS—"Paul," "George," and "Ringo"—having been nicknamed after the Fab Four by hostages they held in the Islamic State.[119]

Jihadi John's "bandmates," however, have remained obscure, while the prominence of "John" in Islamic State beheading videos inspired an all-out effort to discover his identity. "Jihadi John" turned out to be Mohammed Emwazi, a former London resident in his mid-twenties. Emwazi was born in Kuwait and moved with his family to London in 1994, where he lived a quiet middle class existence and attended a Greenwich mosque. He graduated from the University of Westminster with a degree in computer programming.[120]

THE BLUE MEANIES TAKE IRAQ

"It's bullshit. What they are doing out there is against everything The Beatles stood for.... If we stood for anything we never stood for that. The four of us absolutely stood for peace and love. But we are not in control."

—Ringo Starr commenting on Jihadi John, Paul, George, and Ringo[118]

Once it became clear that Emwazi had not suffered from poverty, the root cause to which a Muslim's turn to jihad terror is typically attributed, the mainstream media began casting Emwazi as a victim of Britain's overzealous security services. Emwazi and two of his friends had flown to Tanzania in August 2009; they said they just wanted to go on safari, but authorities in Dar es Salaam refused him admission. In September 2009 he went to his native Kuwait; ten months later he returned to Britain and then was refused a visa to go back to Kuwait. "I had a job waiting for me and marriage to get started," Emwazi recounted. "I feel like a prisoner, only not in a cage, in London, a person imprisoned and controlled by security service men, stopping me from living my new life in my birthplace and country, Kuwait."[121]

This was the cause of Emwazi's "radicalization," claimed Asim Qureshi of Cage, a far-Left group in Britain that agitates for the release of Guantanamo detainees and other jihadists. Qureshi complained, "When we treat people as if they are outsiders they will inevitably feel like outsiders—our entire national security strategy for the last 13 years has only increased alienation. A narrative of injustice has taken root."[122]

Perhaps—but does this "narrative of injustice" and alienation-producing national security strategy really apply to Tanzania? None of those who claimed that Emwazi had been "radicalized" by his supposedly unfair treatment at the hands of British security officials explained why it was not only the British who had denied Emwazi a visa to go to Kuwait, but also Tanzanian officials who had refused to let him into that country. Emwazi aroused the suspicion of security officials in not one but two nations long before he became "Jihadi John."

What's more, if British authorities were so venomously Islamophobic that they spent their time and resources harassing innocent young Muslims like poor Mohammed Emwazi, why were they so inattentive that they allowed Emwazi to make his way to the Islamic State?

Then again, one doesn't need a visa to go there.

The Computer Wizard

Ahmad Abousamra grew up in Stoughton, Massachusetts, a toney suburb of Boston. His father, Dr. Abdul Abousamra, was for two decades an endocrinologist at Massachusetts General Hospital and is now a professor of medicine, physiology, and molecular genetics in the School of Medicine at Wayne State University in Detroit.

Young Ahmad attended top schools: Xaverian Brothers High School, where he made the honor roll, and then Northeastern University, where he made the Dean's List and graduated with a technology degree.[123] But he was deeply committed to Islam from an early age, and finally in 2004, when he was twenty-two, he went to Iraq and joined al-Qaeda in Iraq's "media wing"—foreshadowing the key role he would play ten years later in establishing the Islamic State's widely touted social media presence. He also went to Pakistan and Yemen to try to get jihad terror training.[124]

Returning to the United States two years later, Abousamra was questioned, was released without being charged with anything, and fled to Syria.[125] In 2009, he was implicated in a jihad plot to gun down Americans in shopping malls and murder U.S. officials and was finally charged with terrorist activity.[126]

Special Agent Heidi Williams of Boston's Joint Terrorism Task Force (JTTF) said that Abousamra and his fellow Boston jihadi Tarek Mehanna were inspired by 9/11, and "they celebrated it."[127]

Ahmad Abousamra made the FBI's Most Wanted List, with a $50,000 reward on his head.[128] Until the spring of 2015, he was believed to be in the Islamic State, where he oversaw ISIS's sophisticated social media campaigns.

Williams said of Abousamra and his co-conspirator Tarek Mehanna, the son of a professor at the Massachusetts College of Pharmacy and Health Sciences: "Both men were self-radicalized and used the Internet to educate themselves. They came to it independently, but once they found each other, they encouraged each other's beliefs."[129]

"Self-radicalized"? Did Ahmad Abousamra turn away from the tolerant and peaceful Islam that he had learned at home? Possibly. However, it is noteworthy that his father Dr. Abdul Abousamra (or Abou-Samra, as he now styles it), in addition to his distinguished medical career, also served as the longtime president of the Islamic Center of New England and vice president of the Boston branch of the Muslim American Society.[131]

NOT THAT THIS HAS ANYTHING TO DO WITH ISLAM

"Abousamra expressed his belief that suicide bombings were permissible.... Abousamra found justification for his position in the religious writings of Muslim extremists. Abousamra justified attacks on civilians, such as the September 11, 2001 attacks. Abousamra stated that civilians were not innocent because they paid taxes to support the government and because they were Kufar (non-believers).... Abousamra always justified their extremist views by citing Islamic teachings."

—from the 2009 criminal complaint against Ahmad Abousamra[130]

The Muslim American Society is the principal name under which the Muslim Brotherhood operates in the United States.[132] According to a captured internal Muslim Brotherhood document, the Brotherhood's "work in America is a kind of grand Jihad in eliminating and destroying the Western civilization from within and 'sabotaging' its miserable house by their hands and the hands of the believers so that it is eliminated and Allah's religion is made victorious over all other religions."[133]

What's more, on top of his father's dubious ties, Abousamra himself was a member of the Islamic Society of Boston, which was also attended over the years by jihadis such as Aafia Siddiqui, who was convicted of trying to murder American soldiers and may also have been plotting a jihad attack against an American city, and Abousamra's friend Mehanna, who is now in prison for aiding al-Qaeda. The Islamic Society of Boston was founded by al-Qaeda financier Abdurrahman Alamoudi.

The JTTF's Williams said confidently that Abousamra and Mehanna were "self-radicalized," but she actually had no way of knowing whether or not they (and others) were "radicalized" at the Islamic Society of Boston. In the wake of the Boston Marathon jihad bombing on April 15, 2013, FBI director Robert Mueller admitted that the only time FBI agents had visited the Islamic Society of Boston was "as part of our outreach efforts"—not to investigate what was taught there.[134]

However Abousamra came to believe that he should put his considerable talents at the service of violent jihad, the Islamic State had the full benefit of his expensive American education in computer technology—until the spring of 2015, when the computer whiz was reported to have been killed in an airstrike.[135]

The Girls of the Islamic State: The Jihadi Brides

The Islamic State has not only attracted young Muslim men but also hundreds of Muslim women from all over the world, and for the same reason that the men go: the lure of the caliphate. British authorities have estimated that ten percent of the Muslims from Britain who have traveled to the Islamic State are women, and the same proportion of women go to the Islamic State from continental Europe, Australia, and the United States.[136] These girls are overwhelmingly joining ISIS to become the wives of jihad warriors. A small number of women have also taken up arms themselves.[137]

Some have made the trip while as young as thirteen, and many girls in their mid-teens have gone, including two Muslim teens from Vienna, Sabina Selimovic, fifteen, and Samra Kesinovic, sixteen. Before they left, Samra had become notorious around her school for speaking out for jihad and leaving graffiti around the building reading, "I love al-Qaeda." The girls left a note for their parents, saying, "Don't look for us. We will serve Allah—and we will die for him."[138]

These girls are ready not just to die, but to kill for Allah as well. Before she left her home in Avignon, France, for the Islamic State, Nora el-Bathy, fifteen, posted on Facebook a photo of a veiled woman holding a rifle, with the caption, "Yes, kill! In the name of Allah."[139]

Others betray just how young they really are. The twins Zahra and Salma Halane, sixteen, left England for the Islamic State, where Zahra posed for a photo in which she is fully veiled and holding a rifle in front of the Islamic State's black flag of jihad. But soon after that she was back on social media lamenting the loss of her beloved kitten, who never returned home after her jihadist husband angrily threw it outside one night.[140]

Another reminder of these girls' extreme youth came in February 2015, when three Muslim schoolgirls from Britain, Amira Abase, fifteen, Shamima Begum, fifteen, and Khadiza Sultana, sixteen, sneaked away from their homes and families to join the Islamic State. Abase Hussen, Amira's father, appeared before the cameras clutching the girl's teddy bear and affecting shock, sorrow, and outrage that his daughter would do such a thing. He excoriated British authorities for failing to prevent the girls from leaving Britain. However, it later came to light that young Amira may have been acting on what she learned at home when she decided to make her trip to the caliphate: in his pre–teddy bear–clutching days, back in 2012, Abase Hussen had attended a rally led by firebrand British jihad cheerleader Anjem Choudary, at which rally-goers chanted "Allahu akbar" and "The followers of Mohammed will conquer America."[141]

One eighteen-year-old Muslim woman from Britain, Umm Khattab, said that she would like to see "David Cameron's head on a spike" and fled the Sceptered Isle. Once safely in the caliphate, she took to Twitter to exhort other Muslim girls from Britain to join her. In Britain, she claimed fancifully, it was almost impossible to live in an Islamically correct manner: Muslims, she said, had been forced to sign a petition to head off the prohibition of halal meat (that is, meat slaughtered according to the specifications of Islamic law).[142]

The Enforcers and Recruiters

A six-foot-tall woman named Umm Hamza, also known as "The Slaughterer," who is said to pack not only a gun, but several daggers and a cattle prod, is believed to be heading up the armed al-Khansa brigade of women patrolling Raqqa to ensure that women are obeying the strictures of Islamic law—and that enemy fighters aren't hiding behind niqabs to infiltrate the Islamic State. ISIS pays them a salary of about $150 a month, and they make their rounds covered in black from head to toe, including veils that completely obscure their faces.[143]

Aqsa Mahmood, one of Umm Hamza's colleagues among these female Sharia enforcers, is a native of Glasgow, Scotland, who has captured attention for her open praise of the murder of British soldier Lee Rigby on a London street in 2013 and also of the Boston Marathon and Fort Hood jihad massacres. In her view, these jihad attacks in the West are just as valuable as making the trip to the Islamic State: "If you cannot make it to the battlefield, then bring the battlefield to yourself."[144]

Aqsa is the daughter of an immigrant from Pakistan who starred for Scotland's cricket team. She attended Craigholme, an upscale private school. Her parents noted that when the uprising against Assad began in Syria, Aqsa, who had been quite secular, became interested in her religion and began reading the Qur'an avidly. Ultimately, she fled from her home in Scotland to the Islamic State in November 2013, when she was nineteen.

Since arriving there, Aqsa has taken to social media to exhort other young Muslim girls to follow in her footsteps. She has also pooh-poohed the idea that Muslims were drawn to jihad by poverty and social alienation.

Aqsa is the recruiter for the Islamic State who promised "a house with free electricity and water provided to you due to the Khilafah and no rent

NOT BUYING THE POVERTY-IS-THE-ROOT-CAUSE-OF-JIHAD THEORY

"The media at first used to claim that the ones running away to join the Jihad as being unsuccessful, didn't have a future and from broke down families etc. But that is far from the truth. Most sisters I have come across have been in university studying courses with many promising paths, with big, happy families and friends and everything in the *Dunyah* [material world] to persuade one to stay behind and enjoy the luxury. If we had stayed behind, we could have been blessed with it all from a relaxing and comfortable life and lots of money."

—Aqsa Mahmood on the Muslims from happy, prosperous families
who have left ample opportunities behind to join ISIS[145]

included." But her main selling point is that volunteers for ISIS will receive "an even BIGGER reward in the Aakhirah (afterlife)." She has told potential journeyers to the Islamic State that certainly they will miss their families, but "the family you get in exchange for leaving the ones behind are like the pearl in comparison to the Shell you threw away into the foam of the sea."[146]

To potential recruits, she emphasizes their duty as Muslims: "To those who are able and can still make your way, hasten hasten to our lands…This is a war against Islam and it is known that either 'you're with them or with us'. So pick a side."[147] Aqsa warns, however, that girls who follow in her footsteps will baffle and grieve their more secular-minded parents: "How does a parent who has little Islamic knowledge and understanding comprehend why their son or daughter has left their well-off life, education and a bright future behind to go live in a war-torn country. Most likely they will blame themselves, they will think they have done something. But until they truly understand from the bottom of their heart that you have done this action sincerely for Allah's sake they will live in hope that you will return."[148] Aqsa emphasized that although she missed her own mother, she would not go home.

The Sex Slaves

Nor will most of the non-Muslim women that the Islamic State has taken captive.

In line with the Qur'anic permission to Muslim men to enjoy the sexual favors of the "captives of the right hand," the Islamic State captured three thousand non-Muslim Iraqi women—Yazidis and Christians—in the summer of 2014, and forced them into sex slavery.

These unfortunate women and girls were looked after by the all-female al-Khansa Brigade. Female Muslims from Britain who were part of the Islamic State's police apparatus were given the responsibility of supervising the de facto brothels where the captives were forced to live and work.[149]

In April 2015, the Islamic State sold 216 Yazidi captives, including fifty-five boys and girls, back to non-Muslim humanitarian aid workers. Once freed, many began to give the details of what they had been through. Ziyad Shammo Aladany, an aid worker for an organization devoted to assisting Yazidis, explained that the boys as well as the girls had been "distributed among houses" in two cities that the Islamic State controlled, Mosul and Tal Afar. "They were treated very badly," said Shammo. "The girls were dragged away from their mothers. If the mothers pleaded them not to give away their daughters, they were beaten and tortured."

Then they were "forced to convert to Islam and pray, and say the Shahada [the Islamic profession of faith]. They also gave them lectures about Islam." After that, some of the girls were given to Islamic State jihadis, sometimes after ISIS victories, as the spoils of war.

"A lot of them," said Shammo, "have been sold to ISIS fighters, they have been raped in…public, and by more than two or three people at a time. They were tortured, beaten and subject to any type of violence."[150]

One nineteen-year-old Yazidi woman who escaped after being a captive of the Islamic State for four months told a horrific story. She was captured when the Islamic State invaded the Kurdish city of Sinjar. When the Islamic State jihadis entered her house, she recalled, "My mother started screaming and begging for mercy as the Daesh

NOT THAT THIS HAS ANYTHING TO DO WITH ISLAM

A twelve-year-old Yazidi girl recalled that when the Islamic State entered her village, "we were surrounded. They told us to convert (to Islam), but we wouldn't. They took us to the school in the village and separated the men. Then they took us away." She was sold to a fifty-year-old jihadist who raped her repeatedly.[151]

(Isis) fighters told my sister and me to join the group of younger women specially selected. But they tore us from her grasp. I saw other women in the building being dragged out to waiting lorries by their hair."

The men were separated from the woman, and the married women from the unmarried. "The Daesh took our names and ages and noted everything down. It was organised and they took us away like cattle." Among the Islamic State jihadis were some men she recognized from her town: "A local mechanic was among them. The Sunni men in our area became Daesh as soon as they got a smell of them approaching. No one even had to ask them to join."

She was then given to an Islamic State member and raped repeatedly—and then sold to another. Amid physical and mental abuse, she was forced to convert to Islam.[152]

The father of one girl who escaped said, "We had no hope. We knew thousands of women had been sold."[153] Slave auctions went on for days, as girls were sold for as little as $15, and some of those who were being offered for sale attempted suicide; several were successful. One girl who was sold to an Islamic State jihadi was taken by him to a home where his other sex slaves were waiting. When the new girl told him she had a husband, he beat her.[154] According to Islamic law, when an infidel woman is taken captive, her previous marriage is immediately annulled.

Another escapee recalled that at an auction of sex slaves, the girls all wept, and the men "were very happy." She was sold in Raqqa, and then also repeatedly raped and beaten.[155] Seeing no other way out of her situation, she tried suicide several times—to the disgust of her captors, who then promptly sold her to other jihadis. The girls' captors emphasized that the slavery was all about religion: "We said we are human beings. They said, 'You are our property.' They said, 'You are infidels. We will do what we want with you.'"

The Islamic State jihadis preferred younger girls—the younger, the better: "They raped girls who were nine or ten or even eight. They said they preferred the young ones. They would say the older ones know a few things, the young ones know nothing."[156]

One Yazidi woman described the house of horrors in a building in Syria where approximately sixty women were held as slaves: "From 9:30 in the morning, men would come to buy girls to rape them. I saw in front of my eyes ISIS soldiers pulling hair, beating girls, and slamming the heads of anyone who resisted. They were like animals.... Once they took the girls out, they would rape them and bring them back to exchange for new girls. The girls' ages ranged from 8 to 30 years ... only 20 girls remained in the end."[157]

The Deserters

It is not surprising, given how enamored the Islamic State is with blood, death, and destruction, that some of those who make their way to it with high ideals of living in the caliphate quickly become disillusioned.

In December 2014, ISIS jihadis in their Raqqa capital executed a hundred men for desertion. A local opponent of the group claimed that inside the Islamic State, "Morale isn't falling—it's hit the ground." He said that the disillusionment was besetting both the native jihadis and the foreigners: "Local fighters are frustrated—they feel they're doing most of the work and the dying...foreign fighters who thought they were on an adventure are now exhausted."[158]

The situation had so deteriorated in Raqqa that the Islamic State had given some military policemen the sole task of punishing jihadis who failed to perform their assigned duties. According to opponents of ISIS in Raqqa, four hundred jihadis had been arrested by November 2014.[159] It is not known what happened to them after that, but given the nature of the regime, it is unlikely that they are still alive.

A rare former Islamic State fighter who successfully escaped was Abu Almouthanna, a twenty-seven-year-old from Syria. He said he had been tortured by the Assad regime, which had also killed his family, and "when your family has been killed, you will want to kill, too." He first joined the Free Syrian Army (FSA), the group that both the Obama administration and Republican leaders such as John McCain had touted as the "moderates" who were going to save Syria from both Assad and the Islamic State. Then he joined Jabhat al-Nusra Front, the al-Qaeda affiliate that al-Qaeda leader Zawahiri had demanded that the Islamic State yield to in Syria.

After the Islamic State soundly defeated Jabhat al-Nusra in battle, Almouthanna and two thousand of his comrades joined the winning side. "I was happy to move to ISIS. They had the most money and the best weapons," he explained. "Other than that they were just the same."

He was sent to an Islamic State boot camp, where foreign jihadis trained him. He bunked with two Muslims from France and one from Britain who

WE HAD 'EM

A significant portion of the Islamic State's senior leadership served time in U.S. detention centers, including:

- Abu Bakr al-Baghdadi: caliph[160]
- Adnan Ismail Najem al-Bilawi (a.k.a. Abu Abed Abdul Rahman al-Bilawi): the Islamic State military chief who planned the conquest of Mosul[161]
- Haji Bakr (Samir Abd Muhammed al-Klifawi): assistant to the caliph, overseer of Syrian operations[162]
- Abu Louay (Abu Ali): Minister of General Security[163]
- Abu Kassem: Minister for Foreign Fighters and Suicide Bombers[164]
- Abu Suja: Coordinator for the Affairs of Martyrs and Women[165]
- Abu Abdul Salem (a.k.a. Abu Mohammed al-Sweidawi): Governor of Anbar and head of the military council[166]
- Abu Sima: Minister for Weapons[167]
- Abu Muhammad al-Adnani (Taha Sobhi Falaha): Chief Spokesman[168]

did little outside of training but study the Qur'an and boast of their coming exploits for Allah: "From Day One, they joked about cutting heads and making the enemy pay."

Almouthanna fought for the Islamic State for a little over a year. He had no trouble killing civilians, he said: "They were all enemies." He participated in public beheadings in town squares, with the townsfolk watching agog as the jihadis fought over who would have the privilege of actually performing the beheading. They vied for this privilege, Almouthanna said, because cutting off an infidel's head "brings them closer to Allah." After the fighting and beheading, slave women would cook dinner for the jihadis, and the camaraderie was close.

The brutality was not what led to Almouthanna's ultimate disenchantment; what led him to flee the group was a bloody battle with Jabhat al-Nusra that made Almouthanna realize that he was no longer fighting Assad, but instead spending all his time fighting against his fellow jihadis. He made it out of the Islamic State's domains successfully, but the stakes should he be recognized and captured are high: "The punishment for leaving is death."[169]

The Would-Be Rescuer

For some, the risk is worth taking. A Muslim first-year medical student from Britain, Ahmad Rashidi, ventured into the Islamic State to try to find a friend's daughters who had gone there to become jihadi brides. He succeeded in entering ISIS territory and finding one of the girls—whereupon her husband accused Rashidi of being "a spy and a journalist."[170] But then Rashidi struck on a stratagem that saved his life: he claimed that he was a doctor who had come to join the caliphate.

The jihadis were convinced. An Islamic State court freed Rashidi on the condition that he stay within the caliphate and practice medicine. Eventually he was accorded so much trust that he was allowed to pass freely in and out of Islamic State government offices. At one point he was even given access to one of the Islamic State's computers. On it he saw material that convinced him that "they want to be more better than al-Qaida. They want to do something more better than the World Trade Center."

Rashidi was eventually able to escape across the border into Turkey; he recalls his experience within the Islamic State as harrowing: "They are full of hate. You can see fire in their eye. If you smell like European, they are going to kill you."[171]

The same thing holds true of everyone who does not conform to their vision of Islam and the Islamic State, if they get the chance.

The Secret of Their Success: Former Saddam Men

The Islamic State is not just the gang of ruffians it is made out to be by the international media and Western leaders. Much of its senior leadership

Name	Islamic State	Saddam Hussein's Iraq
Adnan Ismail Najem al-Bilawi (a.k.a. Abu Abed Abdul Rahman al-Bilawi) (killed June 5, 2014)[172]	Islamic State military chief	Captain under Saddam Hussein
Haji Bakr (Samir Abd Muhammed al-Klifawi) (killed in 2014)[173]	Assistant to the caliph, overseer of Syrian operations for the Islamic State	Colonel in Saddam's Army
Abu Muslim al-Turkmani (killed in December 2014)[174]	Deputy to the caliph, overseer of the Iraqi provinces of the Islamic State	Lieutenant colonel in Saddam Hussein's special forces[175]
Abu Ali al-Anbari	Deputy to the caliph, overseer of the Syrian provinces of the caliphate	Major general under Saddam[176]
Abu Abdul Salem (a.k.a. Abu Mohammed al-Sweidawi)	Governor of Anbar and head of the ISIS military council	Lieutenant colonel under Saddam[177]
Abu Ahmed al-Alwani	Senior military official	Officer in Saddam's Army[178]

is made up of former military officers in Saddam Hussein's army. A selection of the men who we know have made this transition is listed below, with the role of each in the Islamic State's leadership followed by his former position in Saddam Hussein's Iraq.

The Islamic State even won over one of Saddam's principal deputies, Izzat Ibrahim al-Douri—the King of Clubs in the U.S. military's card deck of wanted Saddam officials. The Americans never captured al-Douri; he became the leader of the Sufi Naqshbandi Army (that's right, the "peaceful" Sufis), which allied with the Islamic State, and he was killed in April 2015 in fighting against the Baghdad government.[179]

Much of the military success of the Islamic State is owed to the planning of former Saddam military and intelligence officials.[180]

Coinage for the Caliphate

In November 2014, the Islamic State announced plans to mint its own currency.[181] The purpose of this currency would be to separate Muslims from "the tyrannical monetary system that was imposed on the Muslims and was a reason for their enslavement and impoverishment, and the wasting the fortunes [sic] of the Ummah (nation), making it easy prey in the hands of the Jews and Crusaders." The currency, said the Islamic State in its announcement, "will be minted from gold, silver and copper, and further instruction will be provided by the Treasury Department"—which was an early indication that the Islamic State had a Treasury Department at all.

Islamic State agents began buying up gold, silver, and copper in large quantities. One precious metals trader remarked, "They said it was for gifts for their wives, but now I know why, and all the traders say the same thing. We've been making trips to Baghdad to get more, and they buy all of it." Another said, "We don't ask why they're buying so much. But even silver in small shops outside the city is sold out."[182]

END THE FED!

The statement announcing the new ISIS currency said, "We ask Allah to strengthen the [Islamic] nation with this step and releasing it from the Satanic and 'interest-based' international economic system."[183] Charging interest is prohibited under Islamic law.

Images for the proposed coins include a map of the world, in line with the Islamic State's global pretensions, as well as the Al-Aqsa Mosque, the Minaret of Jesus in the Umayyad Mosque in Damascus, and other images designed to remind the bearer of Qur'anic passages and Islam's glory days.

Since none of the nations of the world recognize the Islamic State, this currency, if it is indeed ever minted, will for the foreseeable future be for internal use only.[184]

It is unclear what they plan to do with passports, since no border police in any country would accept a passport from the Islamic State, but ISIS has issued them anyway. Emblazoned with "State of the Islamic Caliphate" on the cover, each Islamic State passport also says: "The holder of the passport if harmed we will deploy armies for his service."[185] Given the trajectory of its history, that is a promise on which the Islamic State means to make good. And given the long journey of groups such as the Palestine Liberation Organization and even the Taliban to respectability, and the ongoing weakness and vacillation of the West, perhaps it is not unreasonable for the caliph and his minions to envision a day when these passports will be accepted everywhere.

Not Exactly the AP Stylebook: Islamic State Rules for Journalists

It is often difficult to get solid information out of the Islamic State, especially after the beheading of journalist James Foley. It became even tougher when the Islamic State issued rules for journalists in October 2014. Journalists must:

- Declare their allegiance and loyalty to the caliph.
- Submit all stories and photos to Islamic State media supervisors before sending them in to their employers.
- Not work for any local or international satellite TV network or offer any exclusives.
- Not work for Al Arabiya, Al Jazeera, or other networks based in Muslim countries that have joined air or ground missions against the Islamic State.
- Submit no anonymous pieces.
- Publish nothing without the permission of the Islamic State media office.
- Provide the Islamic State media offices with the names, addresses, and online handles of all those writing on blogs or social media about the Islamic State.
- Abide by local regulations when taking photos.
- Accept the supervision of Islamic State media offices, knowing that violation of these rules could lead to suspension and punishment.
- Accept any new rules or changes in rules for journalists.
- Submit a license request to the Islamic State media office and operate only with this license.[186]

THE CALIPHATE: WHAT IT MEANS AND WHY IT MATTERS

The Islamic State's June 29, 2014, proclamation of itself as the caliphate is the key to its appeal to so many Muslims worldwide.

The caliphate in Islamic theology is *the* Islamic nation, embodying the supranational unity of the Muslim community worldwide under a single leader, the caliph, or "successor"—that is, the successor of Muhammad as the spiritual, political, and military leader of the Muslims.

The claim couldn't have possibly been more momentous. The concept of the caliphate is extraordinarily important for Muslims, deriving its power from the fact that the Qur'an repeatedly exhorts Muslims to obey not only Allah, but Muhammad as well (3:32; 3:132; 4:13; 4:59; 4:69; 4:80; 5:92; 8:1; 8:20; 8:46; 9:71; 24:47; 24:51; 24:52; 24:54; 24:56; 33:33; 47:33; 49:14; 58:13; 64:12).

Muslims can read about Muhammad's deeds and sayings in the hadith, obey his words, and emulate him, in accord with the Qur'an's designation of Muhammad as the "excellent example" (33:21)—that is, the perfect model for Muslim behavior. But this obedience to Muhammad is also expressed in obedience to his successor. As the successor of Muhammad, the caliph does not hold the Prophet's status as an exemplar, but he does command the obedience of all Muslims, and loyalty to him transcends all ethnic and national loyalties.

The Significance of the Caliphate

The caliph is the symbol and center of the unity of the Muslims worldwide. In traditional Islamic theology, Muslims worldwide constitute a single community (*umma*), and are rightfully citizens only of the Islamic caliphate. The caliph, as the successor of Muhammad, is the only earthly authority to whom Muslims owe obedience.

Reliance of the Traveller, a manual of Islamic law that Cairo's prestigious and influential Islamic Al-Azhar University (where Barack Obama delivered his outreach speech to the Islamic world in June 2009) certifies as conforming "to the practice and faith of the orthodox Sunni community," explains more of why the caliphate is so pivotal for Muslims worldwide[1] (or at least for Sunnis, who are 85 to 90 percent of the world's Muslims; the Shi'ites have a very different idea of the authority within the Muslim community).

The caliphate, this Sharia manual says, is "both obligatory in itself and the necessary precondition for hundreds of rulings...established by Allah Most High to govern and guide Islamic community life." It quotes the Islamic scholar Abul Hasan Mawardi explaining that the caliph's role is "preserving the religion and managing this-worldly affairs."

The caliphate is a "communal obligation," according to *Reliance of the Traveller*, "because the Islamic community needs a ruler to uphold the religion, defend the sunna, succor the oppressed from oppressors, fulfill rights, and restore them to whom they belong." The "sunna" is what is acceptable practice for Muslims, established by the Qur'an and Muhammad's example.

And only the caliph is authorized to declare "offensive" jihad. That's the kind of jihad that *Reliance of the Traveller* is describing when it declares that the caliph "makes war upon Jews, Christians, and Zoroastrians…until they become Muslim or else pay the non-Muslim poll tax."[2] "Offensive" jihad is an obligation upon the Muslim community as a whole—so that individual Muslims are excused from fighting if other Muslims are doing it.

"Defensive" jihad, on the other hand, is an obligation for every Muslim and requires no caliph. In other words, when a Muslim land is attacked, it becomes the duty of every Muslim to defend it, even in the absence of a caliph to declare the jihad and lead the fight. Thus all jihads since 1924— including even the 9/11 attack—have been classified as "defensive," by their perpetrators and defenders, who justify them with reference to a long list of grievances. But once a caliph is in power, no such justification is needed.

The Ideal Caliph

One might have thought it an obvious point, but *Reliance of the Traveller* specifies that the caliph must be Muslim, as it is "invalid to appoint a non-Muslim (kafir) to authority, even to rule non-Muslim." And actually this point has important implications for those who have put their hopes upon the prospects of reform in Islam. For "if the caliph becomes a non-Muslim" or "alters the Sacred Law … or imposes reprehensible innovations while in office, then he

CAUTION: MORE JIHAD AHEAD

Since the caliph is obligated to wage offensive jihad, we can expect that with the coming of the Islamic State caliphate there will be even more jihad in the world than there has been recently.

loses his authority and need no longer be obeyed, and it is obligatory for Muslims to rise against him if possible, remove him from office, and install an upright leader in his place."

No wonder Egyptian President Abdelfattah el-Sisi, who called for real Islamic reform in his New Year's Day 2015 speech to the scholars of Cairo's Al-Azhar University, has since dialed back his position. On January 1, 2015, he called for a "religious revolution" pointing out that the "corpus of texts and ideas that we have sacralized over the centuries, to the point that departing from them has become almost impossible, is antagonizing the entire world." It seemed that he might even be appealing over the head of the sacred texts of Islam to some more enlightened idea of Allah's judgment of right and wrong:

> I am saying these words here at Al Azhar, before this assembly of scholars and ulema—Allah Almighty be witness to your truth on Judgment Day concerning that which I'm talking about now.
>
> All this that I am telling you, you cannot feel it if you remain trapped within this mindset. You need to step outside of yourselves to be able to observe it and reflect on it from a more enlightened perspective.
>
> I say and repeat again that we are in need of a religious revolution. You, imams, are responsible before Allah. The entire world, I say it again, the entire world is waiting for your next move...because this umma is being torn, it is being destroyed, it is being lost—and it is being lost by our own hands.[3]

But just a few weeks later, at the World Economic Forum in Davos, Switzerland, Sisi backed away from this criticism, retreating to the same tired themes of Islamic terrorists as a "minority" who have "distorted" their religion.[4] Obviously, even that less courageous language is not likely to pass muster with ISIS or the Muslim Brotherhood. But the original call for a real "religious revolution" in Islamic thought apparently risked turning even the more moderate Muslims against the Egyptian president. As even minor curriculum changes were introduced into Al Azhar, more traditional-minded students were incensed. One complained, "They want to change the curriculum.... They've turned it into 'fiqh-lite.'"[5] *Fiqh* is Islamic jurisprudence.

Besides being a Muslim, the caliph must also be free, male, and, if possible, a member of Muhammad's tribe, the Quraysh of Mecca. (The new caliph, Abu Bakr al-Baghdadi, claims to be a descendant of Muhammad.) He must also be "capable of expert legal reasoning (ijtihad)"; "courageous"; "possessed of discernment"; and "upright," although "if there are no upright leaders or rulers available, then the least corrupt is given precedence."

Reliance of the Traveller quotes scholar Mawardi stating that once the caliph is chosen, "the entire Islamic Community (Umma)" is "compelled to acknowledge fealty to him and submit in obedience to him." Contrary to the Muslim spokesmen who aver that the Islamic State's claim to the caliphate is not valid because al-Baghdadi was not chosen by the consent of the entire Muslim community worldwide, the manual asserts that "the caliphate of someone who seizes power is considered valid, even though his act of usurpation is disobedience, in view of the danger from the anarchy and strife that would otherwise ensue."[6]

And throughout Islamic history, there have been many who seized power—notably, the first caliphs of the great dynastic caliphates: Abu'l Abbas As-Saffah, the first Abbasid caliph, who supplanted the Umayyad caliph Marwan II ibn Muhammad in 750; the Ottoman sultan Murad I, who declared himself caliph in 1362 in defiance of the Abbasid caliph Al-Mustakfi I in Cairo; and others. The Islamic State is far from the first "self-appointed" caliphate. It is also far from the first whose claim has been disputed by other Muslims.

Declaring the Caliphate

As far as the Islamic State was concerned, restoring the caliphate was a divine imperative. ISIS made the case for it in a document entitled "This Is the Promise of Allah."

With nary a trace of irony, the Islamic State declaration asserts that without obedience to divine commands, "authority becomes nothing more than kingship, dominance and rule, accompanied with destruction, corruption, oppression, subjugation, fear, and the decadence of the human being and his descent to the level of animals." By contrast, the caliphate frees human beings from this oppression and subjugation: it is meant "for the purpose of compelling the people to do what the Sharia (Allah's law) requires of them concerning their interests in the hereafter and worldly life, which can only be achieved by carrying out the command of Allah, establishing His religion, and referring to His law for judgment."[7]

To us, the contrast between "oppression, subjugation, fear" and "compelling the people to do what the Sharia requires of them" may seem to be a distinction without a difference—especially considering that Sharia prescribes stoning, amputation, beheading, and even crucifixion for those who fail to do what Allah requires of them.

But as far as the Islamic State is concerned, "oppression, subjugation, and fear" (not to mention widespread decadence and men's "descent to the level of animals") come from mankind's obedience to manmade laws instead of the divinely ordained Sharia. How could what is mandated by the Supreme Being be oppressive? When the Islamic State carries out its beheadings and crucifixions, its jihadis do not consider themselves to be oppressing people, or ruling by fear. Where we see a reign of terror, they see the justice of Allah. And they are his instruments, the executors of his wrath, and the fulfillment of his promise to fight those who disbelieve by means of human beings who obey him: "Fight them; Allah will punish them by your hands and will disgrace them and give you victory over them and satisfy the breasts of a believing people and remove the fury in the believers' hearts" (9:14–15).

In "This Is the Promise of Allah," ISIS says that to establish this caliphate and thereby compel people to obey the Sharia, was "the purpose for which Allah sent His messengers and revealed His scriptures, and for which the swords of jihad were unsheathed."[8] On that point all other jihad groups would agree with the Islamic State, even if they reject its claim to constitute the caliphate. All of them share the common goal of restoring the caliphate, and the ultimate purpose of their waging jihad is to establish the hegemony of Islamic law throughout the world.

Justifying the Declaration

Before Islam, according to "This Is the Promise of Allah," the Arabs were weak and disunited; once they accepted Islam, Allah granted them unity and power. Then followed success unprecedented in world history.

THEY DID IT BEFORE, THEY CAN DO IT AGAIN

"Our dear ummah—the best of peoples—Allah (the Exalted) decrees numerous victories for this ummah to occur in a single year, which He does not grant others in many years or even centuries. This ummah succeeded in ending two of the largest empires known to history in just 25 years, and then spent the treasures of those empires on jihad in the path of Allah.[9] They put out the fire of the Magians (fire-worshippers) forever, and they forced the noses of the cross-worshippers onto the ground with the most miserable of weapons and weakest of numbers.... Yes, my ummah, those barefoot, naked, shepherds who did not know good from evil, nor truth from falsehood, filled the earth with justice after it had been filled with oppression and tyranny, and ruled the world for centuries."

—from "This Is the Promise of Allah," released June 19, 2014, by the Islamic State[10]

As far as the Islamic State was concerned, nothing had changed—or at least nothing should have changed—since the conquests of Islam's early days: "The God of this ummah yesterday is the same God of the ummah today, and the One who gave it victory yesterday is the One who will give

A PLACE FOR EVERYONE, AND EVERYONE IN HIS PLACE

"Here the flag of the Islamic State, the flag of tawhid (monotheism), rises and flutters. Its shade covers land from Aleppo to Diyala. Beneath it, the walls of the tawaghit (rulers claiming the rights of Allah) have been demolished, their flags have fallen, and their borders have been destroyed. Their soldiers are either killed, imprisoned, or defeated. The Muslims are honored. The kuffar (infidels) are disgraced. Ahlus-Sunnah (the Sunnis) are masters and are esteemed. The people of bid'ah (heresy) are humiliated. The hudud (Sharia penalties) are implemented—the hudud of Allah—all of them. The frontlines are defended. Crosses and graves are demolished. Prisoners are released by the edge of the sword. The people in the lands of the State move about for their livelihood and journeys, feeling safe regarding their lives and wealth. Wulat (plural of wali or 'governors') and judges have been appointed. Jizyah (a tax imposed on kuffar) has been enforced. Fay' (money taken from the kuffar without battle) and zakat (obligatory alms) have been collected. Courts have been established to resolve disputes and complaints. Evil has been removed. Lessons and classes have been held in the masajid (plural of masjid) and, by the grace of Allah, the religion has become completely for Allah. There only remained one matter, a wajib kifa'i (collective obligation) that the ummah sins by abandoning. It is a forgotten obligation. The ummah has not tasted honor since they lost it. It is a dream that lives in the depths of every Muslim believer. It is a hope that flutters in the heart of every mujahid muwahhid (monotheist). It is the khilafah (caliphate). It is the khilafah—the abandoned obligation of the era."

—the description in "This Is the Promise of Allah" of how life in the Islamic State fulfills the conditions for restoring the caliphate it victory today."[11] Accordingly, "The time has come for those generations that were drowning in oceans of disgrace, being nursed on the milk of humiliation, and being ruled by the vilest of all people, after their long slumber in the darkness of neglect—the time has come for them to rise."[12] The "vilest of all people" is a Qur'anic epithet for the "unbelievers among the People of the Book"—that is, Jews, Christians, and Zoroastrians who do not become Muslims (Qur'an 98:6).

And so the Islamic State announced, "The sun of jihad has risen. The glad tidings of good are shining. Triumph looms on the horizon. The signs of victory have appeared." It made its case that ISIS could rightfully embody the caliphate because in its domains the Muslims were exalted and the infidels were humiliated, paying the Qur'anic tax (jizya) and submitting in humiliation to the Muslims, as specified in the Qur'an (9:29)—in the process sketching out a chilling picture of non-Muslims subjugated under the supremacy of Islam.

So ISIS would turn what they claimed was every Muslim's dream into a reality and restore the caliphate. And "the khalifah [caliph] Ibrahim (may Allah preserve him) has fulfilled all the conditions for khilafah [caliphate] mentioned by the scholars." And from that point on, all Muslims would owe allegiance to the Islamic State's caliph: "We clarify to the Muslims that with this declaration of khilafah, it is incumbent upon all Muslims to pledge allegiance to the khalifah Ibrahim and support him (may Allah preserve him). The legality of all emirates, groups, states, and organizations, becomes null by the expansion of the khilafah's authority and arrival of its troops to their areas."

Thus the Islamic State exhorted:

> So rush O Muslims and gather around your khalifah, so that you
> may return as you once were for ages, kings of the earth and knights
> of war....By Allah, if you disbelieve in democracy, secularism,

nationalism, as well as all the other garbage and ideas from the west, and rush to your religion and creed, then by Allah, you will own the earth, and the east and west will submit to you. This is the promise of Allah to you. This is the promise of Allah to you.

Answering the Critics

What of those Muslims who doubted that the Islamic State's claim to have restored the caliphate was really legitimate?

We—by Allah—do not find any shar'i (legal) excuse for you justifying your holding back from supporting this state. Take a stance on account of which Allah (the Exalted) will be pleased with you. The veil has been lifted and the truth has become clear. Indeed, it is the State. It is the state for the Muslims—the oppressed of them, the orphans, the widows, and the impoverished. If you support it, then you do so for your own good.... It is time for you to end this abhorrent partisanship, dispersion, and division, for this condition is not from the religion of Allah at all. And if you forsake the State or wage war against it, you will not harm it. You will only harm yourselves.

ISIS warned Muslims that "they will look for something to criticize and will attempt to raise misconceptions. So if they ask you, 'How can you announce the khilafah when the ummah has not rallied behind you? For your authority is not accepted by the groups, factions, detachments, brigades, corps, banners, sects, parties, assemblies, councils, institutions, coordination teams, leagues, coalitions, armies, fronts, movements, and organizations.'"

The answer to all this dissension is a Qur'an verse: "But they will not cease to differ except whom your Lord has given mercy" (11:118–119). The document added: "They have never united on a single issue, nor will they ever unite on any issue except for those whom Allah has mercy upon. Furthermore, the Islamic State will bring together those who want unity."

The Islamic State anticipated a further question from skeptics: "If they tell you, 'You have stepped over them and acted on your own judgment. Why did you not consult the other groups, pardon them, and tolerate them?'" Again ISIS supplied the answer: "Then say to them, 'The issue is too urgent.'"

This argument was buttressed with another Qur'an quote: "And I hastened to You, my Lord, that You be pleased" (20:84), and then followed with criticism of other Muslim groups: "And say to them,

NOT THAT THIS HAS ANYTHING TO DO WITH ISLAM

In its declaration of the caliphate, the Islamic State asserted that when Muslims are obedient to Allah, they will be granted a successor of Muhammad to lead and unify them—and lose that successor when they are disobedient. This is a standard jihadist understanding of the disunity and weakness that they regard as besetting the Islamic world after the abolition of the caliphate in 1924.

Succession, establishment, and safety—a promise from Allah reserved for the Muslims, but with a condition. {They worship me [Allah] and do not associate anything with me} [An-Nur: 55 (*that is, Qur'an 24:55*—ed.)]. Having faith in Allah, keeping far from the gateways to shirk (polytheism) and its various shades, along with submitting to Allah's command in everything big and small, and giving Him the level of obedience that makes your lusts, inclinations, and desires to be in compliance with what the Prophet (peace be upon him) came with—only after this condition is met will the promise be fulfilled. For by fulfilling this condition comes the ability to build, reform, remove oppression, spread justice, and bring about safety and tranquility. Only by meeting this condition, will there be the succession, which Allah informed the angels about.[13]

The implication is that without total submission to the will of Allah, there can be no ability to build, or reform, or removal of oppression, or justice, safety, and tranquility. This makes the restoration of the caliphate all the more imperative.

'Whom would we consult? They never recognized the Islamic State to begin with, although America, Britain and France acknowledge its existence. Whom would we consult? Should we consult those who have abandoned us? Those who have betrayed us? Those who have disowned us and incited against us? Those who have become hostile towards us? Those who wage war against us? Whom would we consult, and whom did we step over?'"

And yet another objection was anticipated and dismissed: "And if they tell you, 'We do not accept your authority'. Then say to them, 'We had the ability to establish the khilafah, by the grace of Allah, so it became an obligation for us to do so. Therefore, we hastened in adherence to the command of Allah (the Exalted): 'It is not for a believing man or a believing woman, when Allah and His Messenger have decided a matter, that they should [thereafter] have any choice about their affair' [Al-Ahzab: 36 [*Qur'an 33:36*]]." In other words, they were able to restore the caliphate, and so they considered it their obligation to do so: if they hadn't, they would have been shirking their responsibility before Allah.

Meet the New Caliph

Less than a week after declaring itself the caliphate, the Islamic State gave the world a look at the new caliphate, releasing a video on July 5, 2014, of Abu Bakr al-Baghdadi speaking in the twelfth-century Great Mosque of al-Nuri in Mosul.[14] Around the same time, the Islamic State published "A Message to the Mujahedin and the Muslim Ummah in the Month of Ramadan," a statement from al-Baghdadi that appears to be the text of his inaugural speech as caliph.

Al-Baghdadi began with a pious effusion:

> Truly all praise belongs to Allah. We praise Him, and seek His help and His forgiveness. We seek refuge with Allah from the evils of our souls and from the consequences of our deeds.

Whomever Allah guides can never be led astray, and whomever Allah leads astray can never be guided. I testify that there is no god except Allah—alone without any partners—and I testify that Muhammad (peace and blessings be upon him) is His slave and Messenger.[15]

The new caliph followed that up with several quotations from the Qur'an, exhorting the believers to fear Allah (3:102; 4:1; 33:70–71; 2:183; 2:185). He then embarked upon an extended disquisition on the blessings of the month of Ramadan, which in 2014 began on June 28, the day before the declaration of the caliphate. The caliph's point was to exhort the faithful to jihad:

And there is no deed in this virtuous month or in any other month better than jihad in the path of Allah, so take advantage of this opportunity and walk the path of your righteous predecessors. Support the religion of Allah through jihad in the path of Allah. Go forth, O mujahidin in the path of Allah. Terrify the enemies of Allah and seek death in the places where you expect to find it, for the dunya (worldly life) will come to an end, and the hereafter will last forever.[16]

This, too, was buttressed with Qur'an quotes exhorting Muslims to wage war and not to prefer this life to the next, including: "So do not weaken and call for peace while you are superior; and Allah is with you and will never deprive you of [the reward of] your deeds. This worldly life is only amusement and diversion" (47:35–36).

Al-Baghdadi exhorted jihadis to "be monks during the night and be knights during the day"—that is, to devote their nights to prayer and their days to warfare. For "by Allah, we will never be mujahidin as long as we are stingy with our lives and our wealth. By Allah, we will never be truthful as long as we do not sacrifice our lives and wealth in order to raise high the word of Allah and bring victory to the religion of Allah." He then quoted another Qur'an verse—the one that promises Paradise to those who "fight in the cause of Allah, so they kill and are killed" (9:111).[17] "So take up arms, take up arms, O soldiers of the Islamic State! And fight, fight!"[18]

According to the new caliph, this warfare was necessary because Muslims are everywhere oppressed, being afflicted with "the worst kinds of torture. Their honor is being violated. Their blood is being spilled. Prisoners are moaning and crying for help. Orphans and widows are complaining of their plight. Women who have lost their children are weeping." He added that mosques were being "desecrated and sanctities are violated."[19]

All this was happening worldwide: "Muslims' rights are forcibly seized in China, India, Palestine, Somalia, the Arabian Peninsula, the Caucasus, Sham (the Levant), Egypt, Iraq, Indonesia, Afghanistan, the Philippines, Ahvaz, Iran [by the rafidah (shia)], Pakistan, Tunisia, Libya, Algeria and Morocco, in the East and in the West."[20]

What to do in response? Fight: "So raise your ambitions, O soldiers of the Islamic State! For your brothers all over the world are waiting for your rescue, and are anticipating your brigades."[21]

Al-Baghdadi predicted that the oppression would soon be over, and Muslims would rule everywhere:

Soon, by Allah's permission, a day will come when the Muslim will walk everywhere as a master, having honor, being revered, with his head raised high and his dignity preserved. Anyone who dares to offend him will be disciplined, and any hand that reaches out to harm him will be cut off.[23]

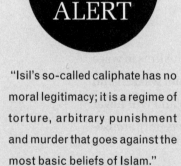

OSTRICH ALERT

"Isil's so-called caliphate has no moral legitimacy; it is a regime of torture, arbitrary punishment and murder that goes against the most basic beliefs of Islam."
—British Foreign Secretary Philip Hammond[22]

That great day was now dawning:

> So let the world know that we are living today in a new era.
> Whoever was heedless must now be alert. Whoever was sleeping
> must now awaken. Whoever was shocked and amazed must
> comprehend. The Muslims today have a loud, thundering state-
> ment, and possess heavy boots. They have a statement that will
> cause the world to hear and understand the meaning of terrorism,
> and boots that will trample the idol of nationalism, destroy the
> idol of democracy and uncover its deviant nature.[24]

(Apparently the caliph is not a big fan of democracy.)

It was therefore time for the Muslim community worldwide to "free
yourself from the shackles of weakness, and stand in the face of tyranny,
against the treacherous rulers—the agents of the crusaders and the atheists,
and the guards of the jews [sic]."[25]

After the fall of the last caliphate, al-Baghdadi said, "the disbelievers
were able to weaken and humiliate the Muslims, dominate them in every
region, plunder their wealth and resources, and rob them of their rights"—
by "attacking and occupying their lands, placing their treacherous agents
in power to rule the Muslims with an iron fist, and spreading dazzling and
deceptive slogans such as: civilization, peace, co-existence, freedom,
democracy, secularism, baathism, nationalism, and patriotism, among other
false slogans. Those rulers continue striving to enslave the Muslims, pulling them away from their religion with those slogans."[26]

(Peace and Coexistence don't seem to appeal to him either.)

Justifying Terrorism

Al-Baghdadi said this state of affairs presented Muslims with an unhappy
choice:

So either the Muslim pulls away from his religion, disbelieves in Allah, and disgracefully submits to the manmade shirk (polytheistic) laws of the east and west, living despicably and disgracefully as a follower, by repeating those slogans without will and honor, or he lives persecuted, targeted, and expelled, to end up being killed, imprisoned, or terribly tortured, on the accusation of terrorism.[27]

According to the caliph, it's not such a bad thing to be labeled a terrorist:

Because terrorism is to disbelieve in those slogans and to believe in Allah. Terrorism is to refer to Allah's law for judgment. Terrorism is to worship Allah as He ordered you. Terrorism is to refuse humiliation, subjugation, and subordination [to the kuffar—infidels]. Terrorism is for the Muslim to live as a Muslim, honorably with might and freedom. Terrorism is to insist upon your rights and not give them up.[28]

He then retailed a list of supposed infidel atrocities, concluding bitterly:

Terrorism does not include the insulting of the Lord of Mightiness, the cursing of the religion, and the mockery of our Prophet (peace be upon him). Terrorism does not include the slaughtering of Muslims in Central Africa like sheep, while no one weeps for them and denounces their slaughter.

All this is not terrorism. Rather it is freedom, democracy, peace, security, and tolerance! Sufficient for us is Allah, and He is the best Disposer of affairs.[29]

But now Muslims could be proud again:

Raise your head high, for today—by Allah's grace—you have a state and khilafah, which will return your dignity, might, rights, and leadership. It is a state where the Arab and non-Arab, the white man and black man, the easterner and westerner are all brothers. It is a khilafah that gathered the Caucasian, Indian, Chinese, Shami, Iraqi, Yemeni, Egyptian, Maghribi (North African), American, French, German, and Australian. Allah brought their hearts together, and thus, they became brothers by His grace, loving each other for the sake of Allah, standing in a single trench, defending and guarding each other, and sacrificing themselves for one another. Their blood mixed and became one, under a single flag and goal, in one pavilion, enjoying this blessing, the blessing of faithful brotherhood. If kings were to taste this blessing, they would abandon their kingdoms and fight over this grace. So all praise and thanks are due to Allah.[30]

Al-Baghdadi then called on Muslims to "rush" to the Islamic State, because "it is your state. Rush, because Syria is not for the Syrians, and Iraq is not for the Iraqis. The earth is Allah's. 'Indeed, the earth belongs to Allah. He causes to inherit it whom He wills of His servants. And the [best] outcome is for the righteous' [Al-A'raf: 128]. The State is a state for all Muslims. The land is for the Muslims, all the Muslims. O Muslims everywhere, whoever is capable of performing hijrah (emigration) to the Islamic State, then let him do so, because hijrah to the land of Islam is obligatory."[31]

The caliph especially urged professionals to heed this call:

We make a special call to the scholars, fuqaha' (experts in Islamic jurisprudence), and callers, especially the judges, as well as people with military, administrative, and service expertise, and

medical doctors and engineers of all different specializations
and fields.[32]

The warriors of jihad should not worry about the formidable military
might of the infidels, for success would come through obedience to Allah,
not by means of weapons:

> O soldiers of the Islamic State, do not be awestruck by the great
> numbers of your enemy, for Allah is with you. I do not fear for
> you the numbers of your opponents, nor do I fear your neediness
> and poverty, for Allah (the Exalted) has promised your Prophet
> (peace be upon him) that you will not be wiped out by famine,
> and your enemy will not himself conquer you and violate your
> land. Allah placed your provision under the shades of your
> spears. Rather, I fear for you your own sins. Accept each other
> and do not dispute. Come together and do not argue. Fear Allah
> in private and public, openly and secretly. Stay away from sins.
> Expel from your ranks those who openly commit sin. Be wary
> of pride, haughtiness, and arrogance. Do not become proud on
> account of gaining some victories. Humble yourselves before
> Allah. Do not be arrogant towards Allah's slaves. Do not under-
> estimate your enemy regardless of how much strength you gain
> and how much your numbers grow.[33]

He called upon them also to "persevere in reciting the Quran with com-
prehension of its meanings and practice of its teachings. This is my advice
to you. If you hold to it, you will conquer Rome and own the world, if Allah
wills."[34]

It would be an understatement to say that the new caliph's inaugural
speech was an essentially Islamic call. It was nothing else *but* Islamic—as

was the Islamic State's statement declaring the caliphate. The fact that both statements contained threats of the imminent conquest of non-Muslim lands only pointed up the dangers of the willful ignorance of Western authorities in insisting that the Islamic State was not Islamic: they were depriving themselves of the only means by which the outlook, motives, and goals of the Islamic State could be properly understood.

The Caliph's Wristwatch—and the West's Myopia

Instead of paying attention to what the caliph said and its implications, the Western media opted to focus on his wristwatch. Oliver Duggan wrote in the *Telegraph*, "His choice of accessory, which is believed to be either a Rolex, Sekonda or £3,500 Omega seamaster, has been highlighted as jarring with the content of his controversial speech."[35] The *New York Post* quoted a Muslim calling the caliph a hypocrite: "Why does the 'Caliph' wear a fancy watch if the possessions of this life ultimately mean nothing?"[36] The UK's *Daily Mail* chortled: "Terror warlord al-Baghdadi denounces the West—but is spotted wearing '£3,500 James Bond wristwatch."[37] "'Follow my every word and you too will have a Rolex'; Islamic State leader wears luxury watch to first-ever public address," laughed Twitchy.[38] "ISIS Leader Mocked for Wearing Expensive Wristwatch in First Public Appearance," said Daniel Politi in Slate.[39]

Apparently journalists didn't know about Islam's doctrines regarding plunder and the spoils of war. By wearing his expensive watch, the caliph was likely signaling to Muslims worldwide that if they joined his caliphate, they, too, would share in the spoils of war and be able to plunder the infidels of their expensive goods. In this, they would be following in Muhammad's example. But Western reporters and pundits persist in their ignorant assumption that Islam and its Prophet must somehow have the exact same attitude towards wealth as Christians and their Savior—after all, Islam and Christianity are both "religion."

ACTUALLY, MUHAMMAD IS NOT MUCH LIKE JESUS

The New Testament Gospel according to Mark, considered by most scholars the first Gospel to be written, quotes Jesus as saying: "One thing thou lackest: go thy way, sell whatsoever thou hast, and give to the poor, and thou shalt have treasure in heaven: and come, take up the cross, and follow me.... How hardly shall they that have riches enter into the kingdom of God!... It is easier for a camel to go through the eye of a needle, than for a rich man to enter into the kingdom of God."

Ibn Ishaq, the first biographer of Muhammad, quotes the prophet of Islam as saying: "Allah made booty lawful and good. He used it to incite the Muslims to unity of purpose. So enjoy what you have captured."[40] Ibn Ishaq recounts of the early Muslims: "Allah saw what was in their hearts [what they coveted] so he rewarded them with victory and with as much spoil as they could take. Allah promised that they would soon capture a great deal of booty."[41] And: "Allah taught them how to divide the spoil. He made it lawful and said, 'A fifth of the booty belongs to the Apostle (Mohammed),'" which is a reference to the Qur'anic stipulation that Muhammad gets a fifth of what is captured.[42]

The Caliphates That Nobody Noticed

Lending weight to the Islamic State's case to be the true caliphate that can rightfully demand the allegiance of the entire Muslim community worldwide was the fact that other Muslim groups in the modern world have tried and failed to do what the Islamic State has done.

There have been other attempts to restore the caliphate.

The Taliban

On April 4, 1996, members of the Taliban and al-Qaeda in the Afghan city of Kandahar proclaimed Taliban leader Mullah Omar the *Emir ul-Momineen* (Commander of the Believers)—one of the earliest titles of the caliph. Repairing to the Shrine of the Cloak, which houses what is said to be a cloak that Muhammad himself wore, Omar asked the keeper of the shrine to allow him to borrow the relic. Then he went to a mosque in the city, climbed onto its roof, and wrapped himself repeatedly in Muhammad's cloak while the ecstatic crowd repeatedly acclaimed him as the *Emir ul-Momineen*—the leader of Afghanistan, but not just of Afghanistan—of all the Muslims worldwide, the caliph.[43]

In May 2002, a U.S. official explained that al-Qaeda and the Taliban planned first to "take over the whole country" of Afghanistan, and then "expand the caliphate."[44] The American invasion of Afghanistan and toppling of the Taliban from power, however, quashed any hope that Omar and his followers might have had to get Muslims outside Afghanistan to accept his claim to be the caliph. Only one group did: the Salafist Group for Preaching and Combat in Algeria. It wrote to Abu Musab al-Zarqawi in Iraq in May 2006, praising his jihad against the foes of Islam, seeking his help in Algeria, and declaring that Mullah Omar was the "caliph of the Muslims."[45]

This pledge was likely motivated by the Algerian jihadis' need for help, and it represented the high-water mark of Mullah Omar's pretensions to be the caliph—aside from the heady moments in Kandahar when he had wrapped himself in the alleged cloak of his beloved prophet.

The Muslim Brotherhood

When the Islamic State declared its caliphate, it is likely that no one was more shocked, dismayed, and outraged than the members and supporters of the Muslim Brotherhood. That Egypt-based international Islamic organization had been founded in 1928 with the primary goal of restoring the caliphate, and it had had its best-ever chance to do so in 2012, when its Freedom and Justice Party came to power in Egypt. But only a year later, the Egyptian military removed the Freedom and Justice Party from power after a popular uprising and then moved swiftly to cripple the Brotherhood and prevent it from coming to power in Egypt again for the foreseeable future.

And then—only a few months after the Brotherhood had been driven from power—the upstart jihadis of ISIS came out of nowhere and declared their caliphate in Iraq and Syria, stealing not only al-Qaeda's thunder but the Brotherhood's as well.

When the imam and teacher Hasan al-Banna founded the Muslim Brotherhood in 1928, he was trying to reverse what he termed "a wave of dissolution which undermined all firm beliefs," a wave that he claimed was "engulfing Egypt in the name of intellectual emancipation. This trend attacked the morals, deeds and virtues under the pretext of personal freedom. Nothing could stand against this powerful and tyrannical stream of disbelief and permissiveness that was sweeping our country."

Al-Banna was particularly incensed by the abolition of the caliphate four years earlier; he denounced the new secular Turkish government for separating "the state from religion in a country which was until recently the site of the Commander of the Faithful." According to the Brotherhood's founder, the abolition of the caliphate and the establishment of secular Turkey were manifestations of a "Western invasion which was armed and equipped with all [the] destructive influences of money, wealth, prestige, ostentation, power and means of propaganda."[46]

To combat this attack, Muslims worldwide needed an organization of their own:

> Islam does not recognize geographical boundaries, nor does it acknowledge racial and blood differences, considering all Muslims as one Umma. The Muslim Brethren consider this unity as holy and believe in this union, striving for the joint action of all

Muslims and the strengthening of the brotherhood of Islam, declaring that every inch of land inhabited by Muslims is their fatherland...The Muslim Brethren do not oppose every one's working for one's own fatherland. They believe that the caliphate is a symbol of Islamic Union and an indication of the bonds between the nations of Islam. They see the caliphate and its re-establishment as a top priority, subsequently; an association of Muslims people should be set up, which would elect the imam.[47]

In other words, the association that would elect the imam (that is, the caliph) was supposed to be the Muslim Brotherhood.

According to Brynjar Lia, a historian of the Brotherhood: "Quoting the Qur'anic verse 'And fight them till sedition is no more, and the faith is God's' [Sura 2:193], the Muslim Brothers urged their fellow Muslims to restore the bygone greatness of Islam and to re-establish an Islamic empire. Sometimes they even called for the restoration of 'former Islamic colonies' in Andalus (Spain), southern Italy, Sicily, the Balkans and the Mediterranean islands."[48]

Al-Banna declared, "Islam is faith and worship, a country and a citizenship, a religion and a state. It is spirituality and hard work. It is a Qur'an and a sword."[49] In 1947, he wrote to King Faruq of Egypt and to "the kings, princes, and rulers of the various countries of the Islamic world," demanding, among other things, "a strengthening of the bonds between all Islamic countries, especially the Arab countries, to pave the way for practical and serious consideration of the matter of the departed Caliphate."[50]

Al-Banna proclaimed the Brotherhood's goal to recapture, under the banner of the caliph, all the lands that had once belonged to Islam, and in the traditional Muslim view, thus belonged by right to the Muslims forever:

We want the Islamic flag to be hoisted once again on high, fluttering in the wind, in all those lands that have had the good fortune to harbor Islam for a certain period of time and where the muzzein's call sounded in the takbirs and the tahlis. Then fate decreed that the light of Islam be extinguished in these lands that returned to unbelief. Thus Andalusia, Sicily, the Balkans, the Italian coast, as well as the islands of the Mediterranean, are all of them Muslim Mediterranean colonies and they must return to the Islamic fold. The Mediterranean Sea and the Red Sea must once again become Muslim seas, as they once were, even if Mussolini has usurped the right to rebuild the Roman Empire. This so-called empire of ancient times was founded on cupidity and lust. It is thus our duty to rebuild the Islamic Empire, that was founded on justice and equality and that spread the light of the true way among the people.[51]

The caliphate wouldn't content itself with just recapturing those lands, either. Historian Charles Wendell, who translated some of al-Banna's pivotal works into English, noted that "it seems beyond dispute" that al-Banna "envisioned as his final goal a return to the world-state of the Four Orthodox Caliphs . . . and, this once accomplished, an aggressive march forward to conquer the rest of the earth for God and His Sacred Law."[52]

The hope in 2012 was clear: had the Muslim Brotherhood retained and consolidated its power in Egypt, and (with American help) toppled Assad in Syria and Gaddafi in Libya, it could have established a caliphate stretching from Tunisia across North Africa and into Syria, which once declared would have attracted other Sunni Muslims, and become a significant power. Instead, the Brotherhood was toppled and shattered—and the upstarts in Mosul and Raqqa seized their own opportunity instead.

Jihadis Worldwide Pledge Allegiance to the New Caliphate

The names "ISIS" and "ISIL," while favored of the Western media and the Obama administration, are really misnomers—not just because the Islamic State has dropped the "in Iraq and the Levant" part of its name, but also because the Islamic State is no longer just in Iraq and Syria. It now commands the allegiance of jihad groups the world over. Here again we see the appeal of the concept of the caliphate; while al-Qaeda had (and has) numerous affiliates and allied groups around the world, these affiliations were often merely a matter of two groups making a common cause. But with the Islamic State it is a different story: the caliph Ibrahim, Abu Bakr al-Baghdadi, claims to be the earthly leader of all Muslims, and many jihad groups have accepted this claim, pledging their allegiance—making "bayat"—to him or declaring their support for the Islamic State's jihad.

Note that, as we have already seen, while al-Qaeda in the Arabian Peninsula proclaimed its "solidarity" with the Islamic State in August 2014, in November and December, however, several leaders of al-Qaeda in the Arabian Peninsula denounced the Islamic State's beheading videos—and the tensions between the two groups have increased since then. Terror analyst Saeed Al-Jamhi has explained: "There are disagreements within AQAP, as one group believes that ISIL is not affiliated with the global leadership of Al-Qaeda, while the other one, which is led by Jalal Baleedi, supports what ISIL is doing. This divides Al-Qaeda in Yemen and probably its role will fade while ISIL's role will increase."[53] But also note that this rift did not keep AQAP-trained Chérif and Saïd Kouachi and ISIS-pledged Amedy Coulibaly from carrying out coordinated terror attacks at the offices of *Charlie Hebdo* and a kosher grocery in France in January 2015.

Groups in the Western Sahara, Sudan, Tunisia and even farther afield offered help to the Islamic State.[54] Especially noteworthy was the "bayat" of Boko Haram, a notoriously bloodthirsty jihad group that had aroused

Jihad groups that have declared their support for the Islamic State	Country
AnsarTawhid (Supporters of Islamic Monotheism) in the Land of Hind	Afghanistan
Al-Tawhid (Islamic Monotheism) Battalion	Afghanistan
Khorasan Province	Afghanistan and Pakistan
Jund al-Khilafah (Soldiers of the Caliphate) in the Land of Algeria	Algeria
Junda al-Khilafah in the Land of Kinana	Egypt
Ansar al-Tawhid in the Land of Hind	India
Mujahideen (Warriors of Jihad) Indonesia Timor (Mujahideen East Indonesia)	Indonesia
Ansar al-Islam	Iraq
Al-Jazeera Province	Iraq
Ahrar al-Sunna (Free Sunnis) in Baalbek Brigade	Lebanon
Ansar al-Sharia	Libya
Shura Council of the Youth of Islam	Libya
Tripoli Province	Libya
Fezzan Province	Libya
Barqa Province	Libya

Jihad groups that have declared their support for the Islamic State	Country
Boko Haram	Nigeria
Caliphate and Jihad Movement	Pakistan
Abtalul Islam Media	Pakistan
Tehrik-e-Taliban Pakistan (the Pakistani Taliban)	Pakistan
Islamic Movement of Uzbekistan	Afghanistan and Pakistan
Supporters of the Islamic State in Beit al-Maqdis	Palestinian territories
Mujahedeen Shura Council in the Environs of Jerusalem	Palestinian territories
Islamic State in Gaza	Palestinian territories
Abu Sayyaf	The Philippines
Bangasamoro Islamic Freedom Fighters	The Philippines
Ansar al-Khilafah	The Philippines
Mujahideen of the Arabian Peninsula	Saudi Arabia
Army of the Companions (and many others)	Syria
al-Qaeda in the Arabian Peninsula	Yemen
Dhamar governorate	Yemen
Sana'a governorate	Yemen
Supporters of the Islamic State in Yemen	Yemen[55]

international disgust with its brutality, particularly toward Nigerian Christians, and its kidnapping and enslavement of schoolgirls in an operation that foreshadowed the Islamic State's foray into the kidnapping and sexual enslavement of non-Muslim women. Boko Haram was an established group with shadowy sources of wealth and no tangible earthly benefit to be gained by allying itself with the Islamic State and pledging its allegiance to the caliph Ibrahim. Nevertheless in April 2015, it renamed itself the Islamic State in West Africa.[56]

Its only possible motive was a theological imperative. The same could be said of Abu Sayyaf, a jihad group that had won renown and inspired fear in the Philippines for years before it pledged its fealty to the Islamic State in September 2014, and of the bloodthirsty Pakistani Taliban, Tehrik-e-Taliban Pakistan.[57]

The Pakistani Taliban, the Shura Council of the Youth of Islam in Libya, the Mujahedeen Shura Council in the Environs of Jerusalem, and others among these groups had previously been aligned with al-Qaeda, but when the Islamic State declared its caliphate, they backed the strong horse, and shifted their allegiance.

Chapter Seven

THE CALIPHATE'S BLOODY HISTORY

The caliphate, for all its importance in Islam, was not constructed by Muhammad, or (by most accounts) attributed to Allah in the Qur'an—at least in any clear or explicit way. Rather it was born out of necessity.

According to Islamic tradition, Muhammad had just completed unifying Arabia and was beginning to move against the Byzantine Empire in Syria and Palestine when his final illness struck. Such severe pain came upon him that he feared he had been poisoned, as he had been several years earlier after his massacre of the Jews at the oasis of Khaybar in Arabia. He called out to his youngest and favorite wife: "O Aisha! I still feel the pain caused by the food I ate at Khaibar, and at this time, I feel as if my aorta is being cut from that poison."[1]

On his deathbed, Muhammad is said to have uttered the incandescent phrase: "I have been made victorious with terror."[2] He also gave the order to "turn *Al-Mushrikun* (polytheists, pagans, idolaters, and disbelievers in the Oneness of Allah and in His Messenger Muhammad) out of the Arabian Peninsula."[3]

He is not recorded as saying anything, however, about who should succeed him as the political, spiritual, and military leader of the Muslims. He had no sons who had survived to adulthood; Aisha said that if he had chosen a successor, it would have been Abu Bakr, one of his most devoted followers.[4] However, other Muslims insisted that Muhammad had actually chosen one of his earliest followers, his son-in-law Ali ibn Abi Talib, to succeed him.

Even traditions revered by Sunnis (as distinguished from Shi'ites, the party of Ali—*shiat Ali*, whence the word Shia) contain evidence for Muhammad's choice of Ali. One hadith has Muhammad asking Ali, "Aren't you satisfied with being unto me what Aaron was unto Moses?"[5] This could signify that Ali was to be Muhammad's successor (*khalifa*, caliph), for the Qur'an depicts Moses saying to Aaron, "Take my place among my people" (7:142).

Aisha, however, haughtily dismissed Ali's claim (for a variety of reasons the two of them had been at odds for years): "When did he appoint him by will? Verily, when he died he was resting against my chest (or said: in my lap) and he asked for a washbasin and then collapsed while in that state, and I could not even perceive that he had died, so when did he

IF YOU BELIEVE THAT, I HAVE SOME SWAMPLAND IN FLORIDA...

Abu Bakr had expressed the unshakeable fervor of his devotion to Muhammad when a skeptic doubted Muhammad's story about traveling to Jerusalem and then to Paradise on a winged white horse with a human head: "If he says so then it is true. And what is so surprising in that? He tells me that communications from God from heaven to earth come to him in an hour of a day or night and I believe him, and that is more extraordinary than that at which you boggle!"[6]

appoint him by will?"[7] She quoted Muhammad as saying, "It is not befitting that a group, among whom is Abu Bakr, be led by other than him."[8] Ali was duly passed over for Abu Bakr, one of Muhammad's most fanatical followers.

The controversy over Ali continued. He was passed over for caliph twice more, when Muhammad's companions Umar and then Uthman were chosen to succeed Abu Bakr. Finally, according to Islamic tradition, Ali got his chance in 656. Abu Bakr, Umar, Uthman, and Ali are considered the four "Khulafa Rashidun" or "Rightly Guided Caliphs," and the period of their reigns (632–661) is known as the first and greatest golden age of Islam.

It was a golden age awash with blood.

Abu Bakr, the First Rightly Guided Caliph: The Wars of Apostasy

Islamic tradition records that Abu Bakr's reign as caliph was brief (only two years) but eventful. The first crisis he faced was the one of legitimacy: he wasn't the charismatic prophet who had unified Arabia, and with that prophet dead, the *umma* was in danger of breaking apart. Prophets started arising all over Arabia and rejecting Abu Bakr's authority: Aswad al-Ansi in Yemen; Talha ibn Khuwaylid of the Asad tribe; the prophetess Sajah of the Tamim tribe; and Musaylima of the Hanifa tribe.[9] Other Arabic tribes simply preferred to govern themselves rather than be ruled from Medina. All these rebels declared that while they had pledged allegiance to Muhammad, that allegiance ended with his death, and it wasn't transferable to any successor.

Abu Bakr and the Muslims maintained that the rebellious Arabs had not just pledged allegiance to Muhammad as a person; they had entered Islam, and the penalty for leaving Islam was death, as per Muhammad's dictum: "Whoever changed his Islamic religion, then kill him."[10] Abu Bakr sent his best warrior, Khalid ibn al-Walid, to crush the most virulent rebellions, and three other commanders (one of whom being his rival, Ali ibn Ali Talib) to defeat the rest in what became known as the Wars of Apostasy (the "Ridda" Wars). The prophets were defeated and their followers forced back into Islam, and the other rebellious Arab tribes were likewise brought back into the fold.[11]

Historians continue to argue, as they have for centuries, over whether the Wars of Apostasy were primarily religious or primarily political.[12] In Islam, however, this is a distinction without a difference. The apostate Arabs refused to pay the compulsory alms (*zakat*) into the treasury, which could arguably be seen as a rebellion against the caliph as a political leader (though the requirement to pay zakat is also a religious duty—one of the five Pillars of Islam). But they also refused to pray the mandatory Islamic prayers. "Islam," explains a modern-day proselytizing article, "is an all-embracing way of life. It extends over the entire spectrum of life, showing us how to conduct all human activities in a sound and wholesome manner."[13] As far as Abu Bakr and his supporters were concerned, to reject his authority was a political act, but it also amounted to the religious act of rejecting Islam—the two were not separable. Eulogizing Abu Bakr, Umar put it this way: "he successfully waged the apostasy wars, and thanks to him, Islam is now supreme in Arabia."[14]

In the same way, as we have seen, the Islamic State today has declared that to reject its authority is to place oneself outside the fold of the Muslims.

The Wars of Apostasy successfully concluded, Abu Bakr began to expand

NOT THAT THIS HAS ANYTHING TO DO WITH ISLAM

After Muhammad's death, Abu Bakr is said to have proclaimed, "Whoever worshipped Muhammad, then Muhammad is dead, but whoever worshipped Allah, then Allah is alive and shall never die."[15]

his domains, launching wars against both of the two great powers of the day, the Persian Empire and the Eastern Roman (Byzantine) Empire. During his caliphate, the Arabs invaded Iraq and began the process of wresting it from the Persians. As Abu Bakr was dying in August 634, Khalid ibn al-Walid won a decisive battle against the Byzantines at Ajnadain in Syria. The Byzantines' hold on their Syrian province was drastically weakened. Two years later, Khalid and his forces defeated the Byzantines at the Battle of Yarmouk in Syria, further weakening the Christian empire and paving the way for more conquests.[16]

Islamic tradition also credits Abu Bakr and his successor, Umar ibn al-Khattab, with beginning the process of collecting the various revelations of the Qur'an and establishing the definitive text for the Muslim holy book. During the Wars of Apostasy, according to Islamic tradition, many people who had memorized parts of the Qur'an were killed during a battle, and the Qur'an was in danger of being lost altogether.[17] Umar realized what was at stake and urged Abu Bakr to act; Abu Bakr chose a Muslim named Zaid bin Thabit, who was said to be a *hafiz*—one who had memorized the whole Qur'an—to consult the people who had memorized parts of the Qur'an, collect the Qur'an's revelations together, codify, and publish them (although if he had really been a hafiz, he wouldn't have needed to do anything but sit down and write it all out himself from memory). Islamic tradition ultimately credits Uthman, the third caliph, with completing this work.[18]

Umar ibn al-Khattab, the Second Rightly Guided Caliph: The Empire Expands

In his final illness Abu Bakr chose Umar to succeed him, and the transition went smoothly.[19] Umar's ten-year caliphate was a time of energetic expansion, as his men completed the conquests of Persia, Syria, Palestine, Egypt, Libya, and more.[20] He oversaw the conquest and Islamization of a significant portion of the Byzantine Empire.

Islamic tradition holds that the conquering Muslims offered the conquered people conversion to Islam, submission as inferiors under Islamic rule, or death—just as the Islamic State does today. In 636, when the Arabs took Basra in Iraq, Umar instructed his lieutenant Utbah bin Ghazwan to "summon the people to God; those who respond to your call, accept it from them, but those who refuse must pay the poll tax out of humiliation and lowliness. If they refuse this, it is the sword without leniency. Fear God with regard to what you have been entrusted."[21]

Umar emphasized that the Muslims must be sure to collect the jizya tax from the subjugated peoples, as it was nothing less than the Muslims' source of livelihood: "I advise you to fulfill Allah's *dhimma* (financial obligation made with the *dhimmi*) as it is the *dhimma* of your Prophet and the source of the livelihood of your dependents."[22]

It is a myth commonly believed nowadays that the conquered people welcomed Umar's armies as liberators, as their tax rates were lower than those of the Byzantines, and that the Muslims were generally less oppressive rulers. John Esposito, the Catholic apologist for Islam at Georgetown University, has said, "In many ways, local populations found Muslim rule more flexible and tolerant than that of Byzantium and Persia."[23] The online "MacroHistory and World Timeline" states flatly: "In Egypt, Constantinople's Catholic authorities had persecuted, flogged, tortured and executed Monophysite Christians, and the Monophysites saw the Arabs as liberators. So too did Egypt's peasants, who had felt oppressed by tyrannical, mostly Greek, landlords."[24]

This is, however, politically motivated modern-day mythmaking. The German professor Harald Suermann of the Institute of Oriental and Asian Studies at Bonn University notes that the evidence of *The Panegyric of the Three Holy Children of Babylon*, a Christian homily dating from soon after the Arab conquest, clearly refutes this idea. Suermann points out "[T]he *Panegyric* calls the Muslims 'oppressors'. This evidence suggests that the idea that the Copts received the Muslims as liberators is no longer tenable."[25] Parts of the seventh-century homily are, disturbingly, applicable to the conquests of the Islamic State more than thirteen hundred years after the sermon was written—where, for example, the text says that the conquerors "give themselves up to prostitution, massacre and lead into captivity the sons of men, saying: 'We both fast and pray.'"[26]

Other accounts from close to the time of these conquests cast the invaders in a decidedly negative light—perhaps understandably, since they were written by the defeated.

John of Nikiou, a seventh-century Coptic Christian bishop, wrote in the 690s about what happened when Umar's army had arrived in his native town some fifty years before:

> Then the Muslims arrived in Nikiou. There was not one single soldier to resist them. They seized the town and slaughtered everyone they met in the street and in the churches—men, women and children, sparing nobody. Then they went to other places, pillaged and killed all the inhabitants they found.... But let us now say no more, for it is impossible to describe the horrors the Muslims committed when they occupied the island of Nikiou ...

Umar's commander, Amr ibn al-As, was extremely brutal:

> Amr oppressed Egypt. He sent its inhabitants to fight the inhabitants of the Pentapolis [Tripolitania] and, after gaining a victory, he did not

LIBERATORS, OR OCCUPATION FORCE?

Umar himself is said to have asked rhetorically: "Do you think that these vast countries, Syria, Mesopotamia, Kufa, Basra, Misr [Egypt] do not have to be covered with troops who must be well paid?"[27] Yet if local populations welcomed Muslim rule as more flexible and tolerant than that of Byzantium and Persia, why was there any need for troops?

allow them to stay there. He took considerable booty from this country and a large number of prisoners.... The Muslims returned to their country with booty and captives. The patriarch Cyrus felt deep grief at the calamities in Egypt, because Amr, who was of barbarian origin, showed no mercy in his treatment of the Egyptians and did not fulfill the covenants which had been agreed with him.

Like the Islamic State jihadis when they entered Mosul in June of 2014, Amr's men began to demand payment of the jizya, the tax on non-Muslims prescribed in the Qur'an:

> Amr's position became stronger from day to day. He levied the tax that had been stipulated...But it is impossible to describe the lamentable position of the inhabitants of this town, who came to the point of offering their children in exchange for the enormous sums that they had to pay each month, finding no one to help them because God had abandoned them and had delivered the Christians into the hands of their enemies.[28]

When the Arabs conquered Armenia in 642—in scenes that may remind us of the Islamic State's genocidal rampage through the Yazidi population of Northern Iraq in August 2014—they killed untold numbers of people and took captive many more: "The enemy's army rushed in and butchered the inhabitants of the town by the sword.... After a few days' rest, the Ismaelites [Arabs] went back whence they had come, dragging after them a host of captives, numbering thirty-five thousand."[29]

According to legend, Sophronius, the patriarch of Jerusalem, turned the city over to a magnanimous and tolerant Umar after the Arab conquest in 637. Taking Umar around the city, Sophronius invited the caliph to pray inside the Church of the Holy Sepulchre, but Umar replied, "If I had prayed inside the Church, you would be losing it and it would have gone from your hands because after my death the Muslims would seize it saying, 'Umar has prayed here.'"[30] This is pious fiction. In reality, Sophronius lamented the advent of "the Saracens who, on account of our sins, have now risen up against us unexpectedly and ravage all with cruel and feral design, with impious and godless audacity."[31]

This is a far cry from the legend, often taken as historical fact, that Umar graciously turned down Sophronius's invitation to pray in the Church of the Holy Sepulchre, for fear that his followers would use his prayer as a pretext to turn the church into a mosque.[32] In his actual writings, Sophronius never mentions this incident, or Umar.

Nevertheless, in the popular legend, Umar and Sophronius conclude a pact in which the Christians are not allowed to build new churches, carry arms, or ride on horses, and must pay a poll tax, *jizya*, to the Muslims, but are generally allowed to practice their religion and live in relative peace.[33] In fact this "Pact of Umar" is not likely to be authentic, but it does reflect the core tenets of the Islamic legal system of the dhimma, or contract of protection, which denies equality of rights to non-Muslims in the Islamic state and is oppressive in numerous

NOT THAT THIS HAS ANYTHING TO DO WITH ISLAM

In a sermon from December 636 or 637, Sophronius laments "so much destruction and plunder" and the "incessant outpourings of human blood." He says that churches have been "pulled down" and "the cross mocked," and that the "vengeful and God-hating Saracens...plunder cities, devastate fields, burn down villages, set on fire the holy churches, overturn the sacred monasteries, oppose the Byzantine armies arrayed against them, and in fighting raise up the trophies [of war] and add victory to victory."[34]

SPEAKING IN GOBBLEDYGOOK

"Speaking in social-anthropological terms—and this provides an important corrective to the view that Islam is fundamentally oppressive, if not persecutory—the rules of the Pact of 'Umar and other restrictions served as a means to create and preserve a 'natural' hierarchy, in the sense that it characterizes most religious societies in premodern times."

—spectacularly ineffective myth-busting from Mark R. Cohen in *The "Golden Age" of Jewish-Muslim Relations: Myth and Reality* (p. 33) (one wonders why only Islam found a need to "create and preserve" this purportedly "natural" hierarchy—supposedly shared by "most" religions—by means of the elaborate rules of dhimmitude)

other ways. As we have already seen, the Islamic State has imposed the same system upon the Christians who remain in its domains—no building or repairing churches, no public Christian worship, no Christian aid and comfort to the Muslims' enemies, and so forth.

Umar lived by the sword, and he died by the sword. In 644, Fayruz al-Nihawandi (a.k.a. Abu Luluah), a slave who had been captured by the Muslims during the conquest of Persia, stabbed Umar multiple times while he was leading prayers in the mosque in Medina. He died three days later.[35]

The Third Rightly Guided Caliph, Uthman: Armed Revolt

The next "Rightly Guided Caliph" was Uthman ibn Affan, under whom the rapid expansion of the Arab empire continued. Ali ibn Abi Talib, Muhammad's son-in-law, was passed over again, and his partisans, the party of Ali (*shiat Ali*, whence the word Shia), never accepted Uthman as the legitimate caliph, just as many Muslims today do not accept the pretensions of the Islamic State's caliph Ibrahim today.

Ali's supporters mocked Uthman for having run away during some of the early battles of the Muslims, "like a donkey runs from the lion."[36] Uthman didn't deny this; he just said he had permission: a hadith depicts a Muslim asking the caliph Umar's son Abdullah, who was an old man by this time, if he was aware that Uthman fled from the Battle of Uhud, was absent also from the Battle of Badr, and didn't even attend when Muhammad's closest companions pledged their fealty to him. Abdullah explains that Allah "excused" Uthman from Uhud, that Uthman was absent from Badr because Muhammad asked him to stay behind and care for his ailing wife, who was Muhammad's daughter, and that Uthman was on another assignment from Muhammad when the prophet's companions gathered to pledge their loyalty.[37]

Uthman thus claimed the authority of both Allah and Muhammad to excuse his apparent cowardice. The fact that this defense wasn't universally dismissed as an unacceptable act of presumption demonstrates the stature that the caliph had in the eyes of at least some of the Muslims.

Uthman is also credited with compiling the Qur'an as it stands today (finishing the work begun by Umar) and distributing the copies of the correct version to the Muslim provinces, which now stretched across North Africa and the Middle East and into Persia. The story goes that in the early 650s, a Muslim named Hudhaifa bin al-Yaman warned Uthman that the Muslims were in danger of becoming like the Jews and Christians: "O chief of the Believers! Save this nation before they differ about the Book (Quran) as Jews and the Christians did before."[38] So the caliph appointed a commission to standardize and codify the Qur'anic text, and once this work was done in 653, Uthman is supposed to have distributed the final version and burned all the variants.[39] The Qur'an isn't mentioned anywhere in the historical record for several decades after Uthman's caliphate, so the historical value of this later story about the third caliph is very low, but it does illustrate the authority of the caliph: no one else would have had the stature to edit and standardize what were considered divine revelations—but Uthman is credited with the achievement despite the fact that his authority was so widely challenged.

Besides the opposition of Ali's supporters, Uthman also faced armed revolt from Egypt and elsewhere; the rebels offered the title of caliph to several prominent Muslims, including Ali, but could find no takers. Finally, Uthman was assassinated in 656 by some of those who had rebelled against his rule. The challenges to his caliphate by the party of Ali and the Egyptian insurrectionists exemplify what became a recurring feature of the history of the caliphate: despite his status as successor of Muhammad, there were always some Muslims who refused to accept the caliph's rule—and seldom a shortage of heavily armed men ready to supplant him by force.

The Fourth Rightly Guided Caliph: Ali Finally Gets His Chance

After the assassination of Uthman, Muhammad's son-in-law Ali, who had first sought to become caliph twenty-four years earlier upon the death of Muhammad, finally got his chance. However, as was perhaps inevitable, his authority was never fully accepted, and his rocky five years as caliph coincide with the period known as the First Fitna (Disturbance) or First Civil War.[40]

Some of the most prominent companions of Muhammad refused to accept Ali's authority, including Muhammad's last and favorite wife, Aisha. Upon learning that Uthman had been assassinated, Aisha organized an armed uprising against Ali, culminating in the Battle of the Camel, fought in Basra on November 7, 656—so named because Aisha, fully veiled as Muhammad had ordered for all his wives, directed her forces from the back of a camel, on which she was concealed inside a howdah.

Aisha's men lost and she was captured, but Ali magnanimously forgave her and spared her life.[41] Ali faced another rebellion, led by Muawiya, the governor of Syria, who claimed the caliphate for himself. Ali fought Muawiya in the Battle of Siffin in 657, near Raqqa, the present-day capital of the Islamic State. After a bloody battle, to avoid further bloodletting both claimants agreed to accept the decision of a panel of arbitrators.[42]

Their leader, Abu Musa al-Ashari, announced their decision: "We have devised a solution after a good deal of thought and it may put an end to all contention and separatist tendencies. It is this. Both of us remove Ali as well as Muawiya from the caliphate. The Muslims are given the right to elect a caliph as they think best."[43]

Ali was indignant and reneged on his pledge to accept the arbitrators' decision, thereby enraging a group of his supporters who then left his camp, earning forever the name Khawarij, or Kharijites, "those who left." The Kharijites—whom we have already met as the historical group to whom any new group of rigorist Muslims known for violence against fellow Muslims they regard as heretics is inevitably compared—rejected both Ali and Muawiya, declared that all who didn't reject them as well were unbelievers, and plotted to assassinate both of them, as well as other Muslim leaders—but the plot was foiled.[44]

Ali defeated many of the Khawarij at the Battle of Nahrawan near Baghdad in 658, and gradually the sect died out, but the Ibadi school of Islamic thought that is dominant in Oman today has historical links with the Kharijites. And more importantly, as we have seen, many modern Muslim and non-Muslim scholars castigate contemporary jihad groups, including the Islamic State, as neo-Kharijites.[45] There certainly are similarities between the Kharijites and the Islamic State: in their readiness to pronounce takfir—that is, declare to be unbelievers—Muslims who oppose them and to say they can lawfully be killed; in their extremely rigorous understanding of how Islamic law should be applied; and in their rejection of the authority of Muslim rulers they consider to have strayed from Islamic norms.

Islam has always been susceptible to these rigorist movements; they can easily find justification in the Qur'an and the teachings of Muhammad.

Given all this rebellion and civil strife, it came as no surprise to anyone when Ali was finally assassinated in January 661—by a Khawarij, Abdul Rahman ibn Muljam, who stabbed him with a sword coated with poison while he was praying in the Great Mosque of Kufa in Iraq, which he had made his capital.[46]

That ended the twenty-nine-year period of the Rightly Guided Caliphs, who are still considered by many Muslims today to be the representatives of a golden age that Muslims must strive to restore. And yet it was the period of the Wars of Apostasy; the brutal conquest of huge swaths of the Middle East, North Africa, and Central Asia; the systematic oppression of the non-Muslim populations in those lands; and bloody civil strife among Muslims that, as we shall see, ultimately led to the Sunni-Shi'ite schism that persists, and remains violent, to this day.

Contrary to assertions—which were heard after the Islamic State's declaration of the caliphate—that historically the caliph was always chosen by the peaceful and unanimous consent of the worldwide Muslim community, the caliphate was often rent by dissent, rival claimants, and bloodshed.[47] In late June 2014, the internationally renowned Muslim Brotherhood sheikh Yusuf al-Qaradawi denounced the Islamic State's proclamation of itself as the caliphate: "We look forward to the coming, as soon as possible, of the caliphate...but the declaration issued by the Islamic State is void under Sharia and has dangerous consequences for the Sunnis in Iraq and for the revolt in Syria." Qaradawi said that the Islamic State was "known for its atrocities and radical views," and that the title of caliph could "only be given by the entire Muslim nation."[48] Yet the history of the Rightly Guided Caliphs is full of "atrocities and radical views," and demonstrates that the title of caliph was most often not "given by the entire Muslim nation." During the "golden age" when they ruled, three of the four "Rightly

Guided Caliphs" were assassinated, and three of the four faced violent challenges to their authority.

The Umayyad Caliphate

Ali's rival Muawiya succeeded him, and the caliphate became a family dynasty; when Muawiya died in 680, he was followed as caliph by his son, Yazid I. This succession, however, touched off another period of civil war, the Second Fitna, as some of the Muslims refused to accept the hereditary accession to the caliphate.[49] Hussein, the son of Ali and grandson of Muhammad, refused to swear allegiance to Yazid. At the Battle of Karbala in Iraq in 680, Hussein and his six-month-old son were killed.[50] The split between the supporters of Yazid and those of Hussein solidified into a schism that persists to this day between the Sunnis and the *shiat Ali*, the party of Ali, the Shi'ites.

Yazid's party was by far the largest, and came to be known as the Umayyad caliphate, after the Meccan family to which Muawiya belonged. At their peak the Umayyads ruled a vast empire stretching from Spain to India, but they had to deal with internal strife and rebellion on a more or less perpetual basis. The caliph Abd al-Malik, who ruled from 685 to 705 and built the Dome of the Rock on the Temple Mount in Jerusalem, fought a protracted conflict with a rival caliph, Abdullah ibn al-Zubayr, who had never accepted the hereditary succession, and who at one point ruled much more of the Islamic world than did Abd al-Malik.[51]

The wars, both civil and foreign, continued. Several Muslim revolts against the caliphate were put down in Iraq in the early eighth century. The caliph Sulayman (715–717) tried and failed to conquer Constantinople, then the greatest city in the world.[52] Yazid II (720–724) ordered that all Christian images throughout the caliphate be destroyed, believing that Allah would let him reign for forty years if he did so.[53] So the Islamic State is hardly the first caliphate to destroy pre-Islamic artifacts.

LIVING ON THE WEALTH OF THE CONQUERED

The collection of the jizya remained of cardinal importance for the Umayyad caliphate's finances. In the early eighth century, al-Jarrah ibn Abdullah al-Hakami, the Muslim governor of Khurasan in Central Asia (modern Afghanistan) saw that the large number of people converting to Islam was eroding the tax base, as converts were exempt from the jizya. So he decreed that only those converts who demonstrated a comprehensive knowledge of the Qur'an and were circumcised would be exempt from paying the jizya. Not surprisingly, an anti-Umayyad movement soon grew up in that area.[54]

The Umayyads expanded into Spain and even into southern France before being stopped at the Battle of Tours by Charles Martel (Charles the Hammer) in 732. A few years later, Muslims in Spain revolted against Umayyad rule. Discontent was spreading: the caliph Al-Walid (743–744) was widely despised for his open drinking and debauchery, for which he tried to compensate by violently persecuting a sect called the Qadaris—Muslims who had the temerity to claim that human beings had free will and were not simply under Allah's absolute control.[55]

Then in 750, a rival clan, the Abbasids, overthrew the Umayyad caliphate altogether. The Abbasid caliphate was to prove more durable, lasting in various permutations nearly eight hundred years.

The Abbasid Caliphate

The Abbasid caliphate takes its name from Muhammad's uncle, Abbas ibn Abd al-Muttalib, from whom its caliphs were descended.[56] Although this caliphate lasted until the sixteenth century and at its height ruled over territory from Spain to India roughly corresponding to the expanse ruled by the Umayyads, from the beginning it was beset by challenges from within, losing control over Spain and North Africa, including Egypt, within its first five decades.

The Abbasids never regained complete control over those territories. In the tenth century, a Shi'ite movement originating in Syria gained control of North Africa and established the Shi'ite Fatimid caliphate, which lasted until the latter half of the twelfth century.[57] And in Islamic al-Andalus (Muslim Spain) in 929, Abdul Rahman III, the last living member of the Umayyad royal family, declared his own caliphate centered in Córdoba and challenging the Abbasids in North Africa.[58] There were now three competing caliphs: the Abbasid in Baghdad, the Umayyad in Córdoba, and the Fatimid in Tunisia and, after 969, in Cairo.

Also in the tenth century, the Abbasids lost much of Iraq, Iran, and the surrounding regions to the Shi'ite Buwayhid (or Buyid) dynasty.[59] The Buyids then gave way to the Seljuq Turks (who were Sunni), who also gained control of more Abbasid domains, reducing the caliph to a figurehead with little real political power outside of his base around Baghdad.[60] The Seljuqs also won a stunning victory over the Byzantines at the Battle of Manzikert in eastern Anatolia in the summer of 1071, ending forever the Byzantine hold on Anatolia, and paving the way for the advent of the Ottoman Empire and modern Turkey.[61]

In 1258 the Mongols sacked Baghdad, ending Abbasid rule there, but the Abbasids relocated to Cairo and continued their caliphate, drastically weakened and fragmented, until the Ottomans, the last Muslim group to lay effective claim to the caliphate before the Islamic State, removed them from power in Cairo in 1517.[62]

FOLLOWING IN MUHAMMAD'S FOOTSTEPS

The first Abbasid caliph, Abul Abbas, was known as al-Saffah— the Blood Shedder—a title that he richly deserved for the ways by which he persuaded his foes not to mount active resistance to his rule.[63]

The history of the Abbasid caliphate thus vividly illustrates the fact that the unity of the Muslims that is supposed to be guaranteed and enabled by the caliph is more of a theological fiction than a reality. Only rarely did the caliph actually unite all the Muslims, and even more rarely did he sleep easily in his bed without having to worry about rivals who were determined to unseat and supplant him, or diminish his domains to insignificance and his theological and juridical authority to that of a figurehead.

The Golden Age of Tolerance?

Despite the failure of any of its earthly manifestations to live up to its ideals, however, the caliphate remained a potent symbol for Muslims worldwide, and to this day many, both Muslims and non-Muslims, regard the early period of the Abbasid caliphate as the high-water mark for Muslim cultural and societal advancement. The Abbasid caliphate in Baghdad from the eighth century to 1258 is generally considered to be the great cultural and intellectual golden age of Islam, with Baghdad becoming an international center of culture and learning. This is the time of Muslim philosophers Ibn Rushd and Ibn Sina (known in the West as Averroes and Avicenna). Claims for the Golden Age under the Abassids are often inflated nowadays by people trying to show another face of Islam besides violence and terror, but in any case, this vaunted Golden Age of Islam did not generally extend to the caliphate's subject people.

Like any laws, Sharia laws are often honored in the breach, and at various periods many Jews and Christians did attain to positions of power and influence. But at other times the laws mandating their subjugation and humiliation were strictly reinforced. The Abbasid caliph al-Mutawakkil (847–861) was so intent on making sure that Jews and Christians were thoroughly humiliated and subjugated that he ordered them to wear yellow clothing so that they could always be recognized as non-Muslims and treated accordingly. He also demanded that they put images of devils on their homes, and not ride horses, but only mules or donkeys.[64]

And in the Umayyad domains of al-Andalus, so widely touted these days as a beacon of tolerance and proto-multiculturalism, things were little better. Historian María Rosa Menocal speaks of Andalusia as a fount of "our cultural memories and possibilities."[65] In his foreword to Menocal's book on Islamic al-Andalus, Harold Bloom laments that "there are no Muslim Andalusians visible anywhere in the world today."[66] However, historian Richard Fletcher has noted that "Moorish Spain was not a tolerant and enlightened society even in its most cultivated epoch."[67] On December 30, 1066, Muslim mobs rampaged through Jewish areas of Granada and murdered around four thousand Jews.[68] What had enflamed them was that the Berber King Badis had appointed a Jew, Samuel ibn Naghrila, to be vizier of Granada, and that Samuel had passed on the office to his son Joseph. The Muslims were outraged that these Jews had authority over Muslims, which they saw as a "breach of Shari'ah."[69]

The Muslim jurist Abu Ishaq composed a poem that incited the mobs: "I myself arrived in Granada and saw that these Jews were meddling in its affairs.... So hasten to slaughter them as a good work whereby you will earn God's favour, and offer them up in sacrifice, a well-fattened ram."[70] A Muslim chronicler (and later Sultan of Granada), Abd Allah, said that "both the common people and the nobles were disgusted by the cunning of the Jews, the notorious changes they had brought in the order of things, and the positions they occupied in violation of their pact [i.e., the dhimma]." He recounted that the mob "put every Jew in the city to the sword and took vast quantities of their property."[71]

Joseph ibn Naghrila was murdered, and his dead body crucified on Granada's city gates, in accord with the Qur'an's command to crucify those who "spread corruption in the land" (5:33).[72]

The Ottoman Caliphate

One of the principal challenges to the authority of the Abbasid caliphate came from the Ottoman Turks, who had migrated from Central Asia to Anatolia in the late thirteenth and early fourteenth centuries and gained power over other Turkish domains in Anatolia. In 1362, the Ottoman sultan Murad I proclaimed himself the caliph, rejecting the authority of the Abbasid caliph Al-Mustakfi I in Cairo, who by then was recognized by few Muslims outside his immediate domains in any case.

Ninety-one years later, the Ottoman claim to constitute the authentic caliphate was considerably strengthened by the Sultan Mehmet II's conquest of Constantinople (and the consequent destruction of the Christian Byzantine Empire) on May 29, 1453. Islamic tradition holds that Muhammad himself had prophesied the Muslim conquest of Constantinople.

ONE DOWN, ONE TO GO

The modern-day Sheikh Yusuf al-Qaradawi, writing about "signs of the victory of Islam," has referred to a hadith:

The Prophet Muhammad was asked: "What city will be conquered first, Constantinople or Romiyya [Rome]?" He answered: "The city of Hirqil [i.e. the Byzantine emperor Heraclius] will be conquered first"—that is, Constantinople—Romiyya is the city called today "Rome," the capital of Italy. The city of Hirqil [that is, Constantinople] was conquered by the young 23-year-old Ottoman Muhammad bin Morad, known in history as Muhammad the Conqueror, in 1453. The other city, Romiyya, remains, and we hope and believe (that it too will be conquered). This means that Islam will return to Europe as a conqueror and victor, after being expelled from it twice—once from the South, from Andalusia, and a second time from the East, when it knocked several times on the door of Athens.[73]

The Muslims had first tried to conquer Constantinople in 711 and had made numerous attempts after that; Mehmet's victory was the culmination of seven hundred years of efforts to destroy the great Christian empire. The caliphate, going back to the four Rightly Guided Caliphs, had always been a might-makes-right proposition, and Mehmet's resounding victory was taken as a clear sign of Allah's favor on the Ottomans. The Abbasid claim to the caliphate was weaker than ever, and the Ottoman stronger.

The Ottomans continued to pressure Christian Europe. On October 7, 1571, they were defeated by the Holy League, a group of Mediterranean Christian states, in the Battle of Lepanto, preventing further Ottoman expansion into Europe. Nonetheless, they kept coming, impelled by Muhammad's prophecy about the conquest of Rome following that of Constantinople, and by the jihad imperative. In the summer of 1683 the Ottomans besieged Vienna, as they had done unsuccessfully in 1529; the siege was broken on September 11—a date on which Muslim warriors of a later century would choose to embark on their own jihad.

Unable to conquer Christian Europe, the Ottomans contented themselves with making the lives of the Christians within their domains miserable, ensuring that they would "feel themselves subdued," as per the Qur'an's command (9:29). One specifically Ottoman feature of this persecution was the *devshirme*, the seizure, enslavement, forced conversion, and impressment into military service of Christian boys. The Sultan Orkhan began this practice in the fourteenth century, and his successors continued it until late in the seventeenth.

Taken from their homes at a young age, the boys were told to convert to Islam or they would be killed. Then they were given strict military training; once they successfully completed it, they would join the Janissaries, the caliph's special forces.[74] All in all, around two hundred thousand boys were enslaved and exploited in this way.[75] The reality of life as a dhimmi in the Ottoman caliphate being what it was, some families welcomed the seizure of their sons, as they saw it as a path to a better life than they could possibly provide.[76]

After failing to capture Vienna, the Ottoman caliphate went into a long, slow decline and by the middle of the nineteenth century was being referred to derisively as "The Sick Man of Europe." This decline led to some reforms that relaxed the Sharia's institutionalized oppression of Christians. Under Western pressure in the nineteenth century, the caliph agreed to significant departures from Islamic law regarding the subjugated dhimmis.

Stratford Canning, the British Ambassador to the Sublime Porte (the Ottoman government), in 1842 protested to the caliph Abdulmecid I after seeing two Christians who had converted to Islam and then returned to Christianity executed in accord with Islam's death penalty for apostasy. He urged the caliph to "give his royal word that henceforward neither should Christianity be insulted in his dominions, nor should Christians be in any way persecuted for their religion."[77]

Needing British support, Abdulmecid agreed, and Queen Victoria sent him congratulations. Then, with the British and French allied with the Ottomans against Russia in the Crimean War, Canning used the increasing Ottoman dependence on the Western powers to continue to press the Porte for further reform of the dhimmi laws. This pressure culminated in the Hatti-Humayun decree of 1856, which declared that all Ottoman subjects were equal before the law, regardless of religion.

The Europeans added this decree to the Treaty of Paris that ended the Crimean War, praising "the Sultan's generous intentions towards the Christian population of his Empire." But the British and French severely disappointed Canning by assuring the Ottomans and the world that they did not consider themselves to have any right "to interfere either collectively or individually in the relations of the Sultan with his subjects or in the internal administration of the Empire."

Canning knew this would doom the reform: without Western pressure, the Ottomans would continue to enforce Islamic law. The Porte, he said, would "give way to its natural indolence and leave the firman [decree] of reform...a lifeless paper, valuable only as a record of sound principles."[78]

And that's how it played out. The British consul James H. Skene wrote to another British official on March 31, 1859, that "the Christian subjects of the sultan at Aleppo still live in a state of terror." He attributed this fact to the trauma they had suffered nine years earlier, when

> houses were plundered, men of distinction among them were murdered, and women violated.... They were not allowed to ride in the town, not even to walk in the gardens. Rich merchants were fain to dress in the humblest garb to escape notice; when they failed in this they were often forced to sweep the streets or act as porters in order to give proofs of their patience and obedience; and they were never addressed by a Mussulman without expressions of contempt.[79]

This contempt was mandated by the Qur'anic command to Muslims to be "merciful to one another" but "harsh to unbelievers" (48:29)—prescripts whose effect we see today in the Islamic State's treatment of Christians and Yazidis.

Another British consul, James Brant, wrote in July 1860 about "the inability of the Sultans [sic] Government to protect its Christian subjects," referring to massacres of Christians by Muslim mobs in Ottoman domains.[80] Yet another British consul, James Finn, wrote at the same time that "oppression against Christians usually begins with the fanatic populace, but it is neither repressed nor punished by the Government."[81]

These reports and Stratford Canning's efforts to compel the Ottoman caliphate to ease the hardships mandated by Islamic law for religious minorities make for interesting reading from a contemporary vantage point. In sharp contrast to the British officials' forthright and unapologetic efforts to curb the enforcement of Islamic law in the Ottoman Empire, today the president of the United States and virtually every leader in what was once known as Christendom respond only with fulsome praise for the belief system that is motivating the Islamic State to persecute Christians with a ferocity not seen since Roman times.

In the latter half of the nineteenth century and the beginning of the twentieth, the Ottoman caliphate's gradual decline accelerated. The caliphate, the symbol and source of the unity of Muslims worldwide, was so diminished in influence by the time World War I broke out and the Ottomans joined the Central Powers against Britain, France, and its archenemy Russia, that the caliph Mehmet V declared a jihad and nobody came.

Mehmet issued a *fatwa* (religious ruling) answering yes to this question:

When it occurs that enemies attack the Islamic world, when it has been established that they seize and pillage Islamic countries and capture Moslem persons

NOT THAT THIS HAS ANYTHING TO DO WITH ISLAM

And when your Lord said to the angels, "Indeed, I will make upon the earth a caliph," they said, "Will You place upon it one who causes corruption therein and sheds blood, while we declare Your praise and sanctify You?" Allah said, "Indeed, I know that which you do not know."

—Qur'an 2:30

This verse doesn't necessarily refer to a defined office of successor of Muhammad—most Islamic scholars consider it a reference to Adam, the "caliph" of Allah on earth. But by the sheer use of the word itself, it does give the idea of the caliphate broad Qur'anic sanction.

and when His Majesty the Padishah of Islam thereupon orders the jihad in the form of a general mobilization, has jihad then, according to the illustrious Koran verse: March out light and heavy [hearted], and strive with goods and persons [in the way of Allah; that will be better for you' (K[oran] 9:41)], become incumbent upon all Moslems in all parts of the world, be they young or old, on foot or mounted, to hasten to partake in the jihad with their goods and money?[82]

The war lost, there was widespread discontent in the diminishing Ottoman domains against the sultanate/caliphate that had led the once-great Empire down the road to disaster. Amid the postwar atmosphere of imperial collapse, one Turkish woman reflected the sentiments of many when she asked, "Of what use was the Caliphate to us during the war? We proclaimed a holy war and what good did that do?"[83]

Kemal Atatürk, the founder of secular Turkey, agreed. The Turkish Grand National Assembly abolished the sultanate on November 1, 1922, but seventeen days later chose the Ottoman Crown Prince, Abdulmecid II, to be the caliph—the first and only Ottoman caliph not to be also the sultan of the Empire. Atatürk viewed Abdulmecid with contempt, remarking: "The Caliph has no power or position except as a nominal figurehead"—by that time, simply a statement of fact.

On March 3, 1924, Atatürk abolished the caliphate altogether and sent Abdulmecid into exile. The last caliph boarded the Orient Express, bound for Switzerland. As the grand train sped through Hungary, past the site where his predecessor Suleyman the

CAN'T GET NO RESPECT

· · ·

When the caliph asked for an increase in his pay, Atatürk thundered: "The Caliphate, your office, is no more than an historical relic. It has no justification for existence. It is a piece of impertinence that you should dare write to any of my secretaries."[84]

Magnificent's heart was said to have been buried after he died while on a jihad campaign, Abdulmecid murmured, "My ancestor came with a horse and flags. Now I come as an exile."[85]

"Islam," said Atatürk, "this theology of an immoral Arab, is a dead thing."[86]

The caliphate certainly was—until June 29, 2014.

Chapter Eight

IS THE ISLAMIC STATE ISLAMIC?
(IS THE POPE CATHOLIC?)

I t would be patently obvious to everyone that the Islamic State is Islamic—were it not for the fact that Barack Obama, Joe Biden, John Kerry, David Cameron, and virtually every other authority in the Western world insist that it's not.

This is the primary reason why Western authorities unanimously refuse to call the Islamic State by the name it calls itself: the Islamic State.

They *Think* They're Islamic

"ISIL does not operate in the name of any religion," said Deputy State Department spokesperson Marie Harf in August 2014. "The president has been very clear about that, and the more we can underscore that, the better."[1] Really? As far as the Islamic State itself is concerned, there is no question that it is Islamic—in fact, it holds that any Muslim who doesn't get on board

> ### Did you know?
> - Islamic State beheading victims appear calm in the videos because they are told they're just going through a rehearsal
> - Hostages are given Arabic names to reassure them
> - "Captives of the right hand"—that is, sex slaves—are allowed in addition to the four wives a Muslim man can have
> - Muslim intellectuals proposed reviving slavery before ISIS did it

with the State's claim to represent Islam is placing himself outside the fold of true Islam. In June 2014, a video circulated of a masked Islamic State commander telling a cheering crowd: "By Allah, we embarked on our Jihad only to support the religion of Allah.... Allah willing, we will establish a state ruled by the Quran and the Sunna.... All of you honorable Muslims are the soldiers of the Muslim State." He promised that the Islamic State would establish "the Sharia of Allah, the Quran, and the Sunna" as the crowed repeatedly responded with cries of "Allahu akbar."[2]

But for virtually every authority in the Western world and many Muslim leaders as well, the Islamic State is a vicious perversion of the Qur'an, the Sunnah, and the Sharia of Allah—thus they insist that whatever the group is called, it must not be called "Islamic" or identified in any way with the religion of Islam.

A Caliphate by Any Other Name Would Smell as Rancid

Considerable confusion has arisen over what exactly to call the Islamic State. It calls itself just that—the Islamic State—but with "Islamic" so prominent in that name, Western officials eager to reassure their people that they have nothing to fear or be concerned about in Islam would rather be waterboarded than call it that.

And so they take refuge in acronyms. The most commonly used name for the group is ISIS, which stands for the name the group discarded in June 2014: *ad-Dawlat al-Islamiyah fi al-Iraq wa sh-Shams*: the Islamic State of Iraq and *al-Shams*. Al-Shams is the Arabic term for the Levant, the Mediterranean region generally understood as

OSTRICH ALERT

"ISIL speaks for no religion. Their victims are overwhelmingly Muslim, and no faith teaches people to massacre innocents."
—Barack Obama[3]

comprising Syria, Lebanon, Israel, and Jordan. Many assume that ISIS stands for the Islamic State of Iraq and Syria, but al-Shams is a larger region than Syria alone.

In light of the meaning of *Shams*, some translators have rendered the group's former name in English as the Islamic State of Iraq and the Levant, or ISIL—the acronym that Barack Obama and his administration prefer, for reasons unknown.

In September 2014, French Foreign Minister Laurent Fabius announced that he would henceforth be using the Arabic acronym for *ad-Dawlat al-Islamiyah fi al-Iraq wa sh-Shams*: Daesh. "This is a terrorist group and not a state," he explained. "I do not recommend using the term Islamic State because it blurs the lines between Islam, Muslims and Islamists. The Arabs call it 'Daesh' and I will be calling them the 'Daesh cutthroats.'"[4]

Apparently Secretary of State John Kerry thought this was a great idea, as he began referring to the group as "Daesh" in December 2014.[5] This may have been calculated to raise the group's ire, since after dropping "in Iraq and al-Shams" from after "the Islamic State," the group threatened to cut out the tongues of anyone who referred to them as Daesh, the acronym for the longer name.[6] Now that they were claiming the world, to refer to them as pertaining only to Iraq and the Levant was an implicit denial of their claim to have restored the caliphate. Plus, as we have seen, "Daesh" sounds like the Arabic words for someone who "crushes something under foot" or "sows discord."

Fabius and Kerry may have been intending to signal to ISIS leaders a calculated disrespect. But it was also

OSTRICH ALERT

"Islam is about peace and brotherhood. There are 1.6 billion Muslims in this world, and the true Islamic faith has nothing to do with what ISIL represents. And so to start labeling them as Islam or as Islamic State in any respect, I think gives them far more dignity than they deserve." —Homeland Security Secretary Jeh Johnson, February 22, 2015[7]

THEY MEAN WHAT THEY SAY

In February 2015, the Islamic State showed that they meant business about being called the name they wanted; they gave a boy sixty lashes in public for referring to them as "Daesh."[8] He was lucky not to have his tongue amputated—the prescribed penalty for his crime.

handy that calling the Islamic State "Daesh" among English speakers obscured the "Islamic" aspect of its name even more than calling it "ISIS" or "ISIL."

It is increasingly common journalistic practice to refer to the Islamic State simply as "Islamic State," without the definite article, as if it were some Dantescan college sports team. This is not so much an attempt to demonstrate by shorthand that it is not Islamic as that it is not a state—and a group with illegitimate pretensions to both.

As if all these different names weren't confusing enough, Egypt's leading Islamic authority, Dar al-Ifta, announced that it would be calling the group "al-Qaeda Separatists in Iraq and Syria": QSIS.[9] A group of imams in Britain called on British Prime Minister David Cameron to call it "the un-Islamic State."[10]

The Islamic State Laughs

The Islamic State has professed contempt and amusement over all this confusion and denial. In his September 21, 2014, address calling for strikes in the U.S. and Europe, Islamic State spokesman Abu Muhammad Adnani ridiculed John Kerry ("that uncircumcised old geezer") and Barack Obama ("the mule of the jews", Adnani's capitalization) for declaring that the Islamic State was not Islamic—as if the American president and secretary of state were Islamic authorities:

The media portrayed the crusaders as good, merciful, noble, generous, honorable and passionate people who feared for Islam and the Muslims the "corruption and cruelty of the khawarij (a deviant, extremist sect) of the Islamic State" as they allege. To the extent that Kerry, the uncircumcised old geezer, suddenly became an Islamic jurist, issuing a verdict to the people that the Islamic State was distorting Islam, that what it was doing was against Islamic teachings, and that the Islamic State was an enemy of Islam. And to the extent that Obama, the mule of the jews [sic], suddenly became a sheikh, mufti (Islamic scholar that issues verdicts), and an Islamic preacher, warning the people and preaching in defense of Islam, claiming that the Islamic State has nothing to do with Islam. This occurred during six different addresses he made in the span of a single month, all of them about the threat of the Islamic State.[11]

The Western media has taken little notice of the Islamic State's self-description and contempt for those who deny its Islamic character. A steady stream of articles by Muslim and non-Muslim academics and commentators maintains that, despite appearances to the contrary, ISIS has nothing to do with Islam.

However, this avalanche of reassurances only leaves us with an inexplicable mystery: If the Islamic State so brazenly violates the Qur'an and outrages Muhammad's example, why is it so appealing to the most devout young Muslims that over twenty thousand Muslims from all over the world have now joined it in Iraq and Syria, with five thousand joining its Libyan wing?[12]

The answer is not complicated, despite intense and ongoing efforts to complicate it.

The Islamic State's theology is straightforward. While apologists for Islam in the West insist that the Qur'an's words must not be taken at face value

OSTRICH ALERT

"It makes no sense to turn the ISIS threat into a fight about Islam."

—*Forbes*, February 26, 2015[13]

and maintain that only a tiny minority of Muslims do take them literally, the Qur'anic justifications for the Islamic State's actions are based on the plain words of the text. And the Islamic State's appeal to tens of thousands of Muslims from all over the world testifies to the resonance of their literal reading of Islam's holy book.

What Is It about ISIS and Lopping Off Heads?

It has been a seemingly endless parade, beginning just weeks after ISIS declared its new caliphate: public beheadings, lovingly filmed and included in slick propaganda videos appealing to Muslims around the world to join the Islamic State.

These very public beheadings have horrified the world; in large part, they were responsible for the wave of public concern about ISIS in America that led to the U.S.-led airstrikes against the Islamic State. Many have taken them as a sign that for all its vaunted media savvy, the Islamic State will ultimately be undone by its own savagery, as the world will ultimately have had enough of this horror and will move to destroy ISIS once and for all.

Why, then, does the Islamic State behead anyone at all, much less film the beheadings and post them on social media? Because from their standpoint, beheadings are a recruitment tool—one that is rooted in the Qur'an. The Muslim holy book says straightforwardly, "When you meet the unbelievers, strike the necks" (47:4).

The Islamic State knows that young Muslims who are aware of that verse will not recoil in horror and disgust from their beheading videos, but rather realize that the Islamic State is acting in fidelity with the Qur'an. Thus the beheadings will bolster the Islamic State's claim to constitute the new caliphate.

The beheading videos also "strike terror into the hearts of the enemies of Allah"—another Qur'anic imperative (8:60). Thus, as far as the jihadis

Victims of Islamic State Beheadings: A Partial List

SYRIAN SOLDIERS: On July 25, 2014, Islamic State supporters posted to social media photos of soldiers of the Assad regime beheaded in Raqqa—one ISIS supporter said seventy-five soldiers had been beheaded.[14]

JAMES FOLEY: The Islamic State posted video of the beheading of American journalist Foley on August 20, 2014.[15]

ALI AL-SAYYED: Eight days later, on August 28, 2014, the Islamic State posted photos of the beheading of Lebanese Army Sergeant al-Sayyed on social media.[16]

STEVEN SOTLOFF: The beheading video of Israeli-American journalist Sotloff was published September 2, 2014.[17]

DAVID HAINES: British humanitarian aid worker Haines's beheading video was published on September 13, 2014.[18]

15 RELATIVES OF POLICE OFFICERS IN AFGHANISTAN: On September 20, 2014, masked men calling themselves soldiers of the Islamic State beheaded fifteen family members of Afghan police officers.[19]

HERVÉ GOURDEL: A French mountaineering guide, Gourdel was kidnapped in Algeria. The Algerian Islamic State affiliate Jund al-Khilafah (Soldiers of the Caliphate) released a video showing his beheading, "A Message of Blood for the French Government," on September 24, 2014.[20]

ALAN HENNING: The Islamic State released the beheading video of British humanitarian aid worker Henning on October 3, 2014.[21]

PETER KASSIG: American humanitarian aid worker Kassig converted to Islam while in captivity, taking the name Abdul-Rahman. His conversion did not save him, as he had served in the U.S. military in Iraq, and thus as far as the Islamic State was concerned had to be punished as a "Crusader."[22] A video showing his beheading—and also that of twenty-one Syrian soldiers—was published on November 16, 2014.[23]

HARUNA YUKAWA AND KENJI GOTO: The Islamic State released the beheading video of Yukawa in January 2015, after the Japanese government did not pay the demanded ransom of $200 million. Shortly thereafter, after Japanese Prime Minister Shinzo Abe made it clear that he was not going to accede to the Islamic State's demands, Goto's beheading video was released as well.[24]

21 EGYPTIAN CHRISTIANS: On February 15, 2015, the Islamic State posted a video entitled, "A Message Signed with Blood to the Nation of the Cross." It showed the Islamic State's Libya affiliate beheading twenty-one Coptic Christians from Egypt who had gone to Libya to find work.[25]

WHY ARE THE VICTIMS SO CALM?

One curious feature of the Islamic State's beheading videos is that they include propaganda statements from the hostages who are about to be executed. These hostages are invariably quite calm, reading the statements prepared for them clearly and without hesitation. This anomaly has let some to speculate that the hostages in ISIS beheading videos are drugged—and even that the videos are entirely fake. Fueling this speculation is the fact that we know that many of the Islamic State hostages were extensively tortured: James Foley, for instance, was beaten, waterboarded, and made to go through mock executions. Islamic State hostages have been kept in a general state of terror and deprivation, with no blankets or mattresses and very little food. They have often been confined in darkness for days on end. ISIS has shown gruesome footage—victims' heads are typically sawn off with relatively small knives, a process that takes some time—of the execution of hostages to the terrified survivors.[26] After all this, the moment of a hostage's own execution would be the crowning horror, and calm would be the last reaction we would expect from the hostages. A defector from the Islamic State has explained the mystery. It was his job, he says, to make sure that the hostages did not panic. For this reason, the beheadings are extensively rehearsed. According to the defector, the jihadist doing the beheading "would say to me, 'Say to them, no problem, only video, we don't kill you, we want from your government [to] stop attacking Syria. We don't have any problem with you; you are only our visitors.' So they don't worry. Always I say to them, 'Don't worry, doesn't matter, nothing dangerous for you.' But at the end I was sure [they would die]." In the same way, the Islamic State jihadi preparing to behead his victim would say to him, "It's a rehearsal, don't [be] afraid." He would instruct the hostages to say, "I'm living in ISIS and will stay and continue." The hostages were given Arabic names to reassure them further. Japanese hostage Kenji Goto was renamed "Abu Saad" and told: "You should be Muslim and come with us."[27] In the end, they killed him.

of the Islamic State are concerned, the world's revulsion and disgust at their beheading videos are only confirmation that they're on the right track.

And about Those Slave Girls

Similar calculations apply in regard to the Islamic State's practice of kidnapping Yazidi and Christian women and pressing them into sex slavery. The Qur'an says straightforwardly that in addition to wives ("two or three or four"), Muslim men may enjoy the "captives of the right hand" (4:3, 4:24). These are specified as being women who have been seized as the spoils of war" (33:50) and are to be used specifically for sexual purposes, as men are to "guard their private parts except from their wives or those their right hands possess" (23:5–6).

If these women are already married—no problem. Islamic law directs that "when a child or a woman is taken captive, they become slaves by the fact of capture, and the woman's previous marriage is immediately annulled."[28]

The Islamic State did not originate this belief in the right that Muslim warriors have to make sex slaves of captive women. Not only is this the traditional understanding of how things should work, firmly grounded in the obvious literal meaning of the passages of the Qur'an quoted above, but also in recent years, Muslim thinkers have been suggesting that it is time to revive the practice. The Egyptian Sheikh Abu-Ishaq al-Huwayni declared in May 2011 that "we are in the era of jihad," and that "if we could conduct one, two, or three jihadist operations every year, many people throughout the earth would become Muslims." Those who rejected the invitation to convert to Islam (da'wa) should be enslaved:

And whoever rejected this *da'wa*, or stood in our way, we would fight against him and take him prisoner, and confiscate his wealth, his children, and his women—all of this means money. Every *mujahid* who returned from jihad, his pockets would be full. He would return with three or four slaves, three or four women, and three or four children. Multiply each head by 300 *dirhams*, or 300 *dinar*, and you have a good amount of profit. If he were to go to the West and work on a commercial deal, he would not make that much money. Whenever things became difficult (financially), he could take the head (i.e. the prisoner) and sell it, and ease his (financial) crisis. He would sell it like groceries.[29]

This statement, understandably enough, touched off a firestorm, leading al-Huwayni to reassure everyone that he wasn't suggesting that *Muslims* could be enslaved in this way—only infidels:

OSTRICH ALERT

"[Islamic State] extremists are beheading people and parading their heads on spikes, subjugating women and girls, killing Muslims, Christians and anyone who gets in their way. This is no liberation movement—only a perverted, oppressive ideology that bears no relation to Islam."
—UK Shadow Home Secretary Yvette Cooper[30]

Jihad is only between Muslims and infidels.... Do you understand what I'm saying? Spoils, slaves, and prisoners are only to be taken in war between Muslims and infidels. Muslims in the past conquered, invaded, and took over countries. This is agreed to by all scholars—there is no disagreement on this from any of them, from the smallest to the largest, on the issue of taking spoils and prisoners. The prisoners and spoils are distributed among the fighters, which includes men, women, children, wealth, and so on.

When a slave market is erected, which is a market in which are sold slaves and sex-slaves, which are called in the Qur'an by the name *milk al-yamin*, "that which your right hands possess" [Qur'an 4:24]. This is a verse from the Qur'an which is still in force, and has not been abrogated. The *milk al-yamin* are the sex-slaves. You

go to the market, look at the sex-slave, and buy her. She becomes
like your wife, (but) she doesn't need a (marriage) contract or a
divorce like a free woman, nor does she need a *wali*. All scholars
agree on this point—there is no disagreement from any of them.
[...] When I want a sex slave, I just go to the market and choose
the woman I like and purchase her.[31]

Around the same time, a female Kuwaiti activist and politician, Salwa
al-Mutairi, also spoke out in favor of the Islamic practice of sexual slavery
of non-Muslim women, emphasizing that the practice accorded with Islamic
law and morality:

I received a message that was a little strange. A merchant told
me that he would like to have a sex slave. He said he would not
be negligent with her, and that Islam permitted this sort of thing.
He was speaking the truth. The topic that he brought up is an old
topic. I have been working on it for two years now.

I was working with this man, a young man, who (liked)
women a lot. I was sympathetic to his situation, and also dedicated to my work. I was given the opportunity to visit Mecca,
and when I did so, I brought up (this man's) situation to the
muftis in Mecca. I told them that I had a question, since they
were men who specialized in what was *halal*, and what was
good, and who loved women. I said, "What is the law of sex
slaves?"

The mufti said, "With the law of sex slaves, there must be a
Muslim nation at war with a Christian nation, or a nation which
is not of the religion, not of the religion of Islam. And there must
be prisoners of war."

"Is this forbidden by Islam?" I asked.

"Absolutely not. Sex slaves are not forbidden by Islam. On the contrary, sex slaves are under a different law than the free woman. The free woman must be completely covered except for her face and hands. But the sex slave can be naked from the waist up. She differs a lot from the free woman. While the free woman requires a marriage contract, the sex slave does not—she only needs to be purchased by her husband, and that's it. Therefore the sex slave is different than the free woman."

Of course, I also asked religious experts in Kuwait (about this issue), and they told me about the problem with the passionate man, or even the man who is committed to his religion. For every good man in our religion, the only solution for him—when forbidden women come around, if he's tempted to sin, then the solution to this issue is for him to purchase sex slaves. I hope that Kuwait will enact the law for this category, this category of people—the sex slaves....

I hope that a law will be enacted for this category, and they will open the door for this, just as they have opened the door for servants (to come into the country). They should open the door for sex slaves, by enacting a sound law, so that our children don't waste away in the abyss of adultery and moral depravity. Allah-willing, this will work out. I believe, look, the (sex slaves could come from) a country like Chechnya, where there is a war between an (Islamic) state and another state. Certainly there are prisoners. These prisoners could be purchased. They could be purchased and sold to the merchants in Kuwait. This is better than (the merchants) committing that which is forbidden. There is nothing wrong with this.

Harun al-Rashid [the Abbasid caliph from 786 to 809] had many more sex slaves than this. When he died he had 2,000 sex slaves. But he only had one wife. This was not forbidden. Our *shari'a* permits such a thing as this. Praise be to Allah, here in Kuwait there are many merchants who are committed (to Islam). I hope the best for Kuwait, Allah-willing.[32]

Unfortunately, this isn't the view of just a couple of nut cases. Boko Haram, the notorious jihad group in Nigeria that ultimately allied with the Islamic State, made international headlines and inspired Michelle Obama to join the #BringBackOurGirls protest on Twitter in April 2014 when it captured over two hundred non-Muslim girls and pressed them into sex slavery.

And for some Muslims living in the West, Islamic justifications for enslaving infidel women captured in war seem to have bled over into an attitude that the daughters of their non-Muslim neighbors are fair game. From Yorkshire to Minneapolis, groups of Muslim men have engaged in sex trafficking and the forced prostitution of non-Muslim women on an appalling scale. Britain has seen a horrifying number of cases of "Asian

GREAT WORLD RELIGION OR *PENTHOUSE*?

"A Muslim state must [first] attack a Christian state—sorry, I mean any non-Muslim state—and they [the women, the future sex-slaves] must be captives of the raid. Is this forbidden? Not at all; according to Islam, sex slaves are not at all forbidden. Quite the contrary, the rules regulating sex-slaves differ from those for free women [i.e., Muslim women]: the latter's body must be covered entirely, except for her face and hands, whereas the sex-slave is kept naked from the bellybutton on up—she is different from the free woman; the free woman has to be married properly to her husband, but the sex-slave—he just buys her and that's that."

—female Kuwaiti politician explains how sex slavery should work[33]

sex gangs" ("Asian" is a common euphemism for "Muslim" in the British media): groups of Muslim men who cajole or kidnap non-Muslim girls, often in their early teens, and force them into prostitution.[34] As many as fourteen hundred minors may have been abused in this way in Rotherham, South Yorkshire, alone—the British city where the phenomenon first came to light.[35] Meanwhile, Muslims from the Twin Cities area in Minnesota ran an interstate sex trafficking ring until they were caught and indicted in late 2010.[36]

But in the Islamic State, the trafficking in girls is not in any way surreptitious. Sex slavery is an institution recognized by law. And where the non-Muslim world sees barbarism and cruelty, devout and knowledgeable young Muslims see the Islamic State's enslavement of young non-Muslim girls and gain respect for a group that is willing to defy the world's opprobrium to practice what it regards as pure Islam. The Islamic State made this abundantly clear in the October 2014 issue of its *Dabiq* magazine, in which it said, "Enslaving the families of the kuffar [non-believers] and taking their women as concubines is a firmly established aspect of the Sharia."[37] In a November 2014 video of gleeful Islamic State jihadis laughing and bantering at a sex slave auction, one of the fighters declares, "Today is the slave market day. Today is the day where this verse applies, '[Guard your private parts] Except with their wives and the (captives) whom their right hands possess, for (then) they are not to be blamed.'"[38]

The Islamic State amplified this point in December 2014, when it issued a pamphlet explaining how sex slaves should be treated and why the practice was acceptable in Islam.

The pamphlet was entirely in line with classic Islamic theology regarding sex slaves. It explained that *al-Sabi*—the slave—was "a woman from among *ahl al-harb* (the people of war) who has been captured by Muslims"—that is, a non-Muslim woman taken as the spoils of war. It was permitted to use these women in this way because of their "unbelief":

"Unbelieving (women) who were captured and brought into the abode of Islam are permissible to us, after the imam distributes them (among us)."

The Islamic State asserted that "there is no dispute among the scholars that it is permissible to capture unbelieving women (who are characterized by) original unbelief (*kufr asli*), such as the *kitabiyat* (women from among the People of the Book, i.e. Jews and Christians) and polytheists. However, (the scholars) are disputed over (the issue of) capturing apostate women." In other words, there was some question over whether women who had left Islam could be used as sex slaves. But since "the consensus leans towards forbidding it," the Islamic State announced that it was inclined not to use ex-Muslim women in this way.

Other rules allow Muslims "to buy, sell, or give as a gift female captives and slaves, for they are merely property, which can be disposed of (as long as that doesn't cause the Muslim ummah) any harm or damage." An owner cannot sell his slave if she becomes pregnant by him. Upon his death, his slaves will be "distributed as part of his estate, just as all [other parts] of his estate [are distributed]."

The instructions are quite detailed. "A man may not have intercourse with the female slave of

NOT THAT THIS HAS ANYTHING TO DO WITH ISLAM

"Question 4: Is it permissible to have intercourse with a female captive?

"It is permissible to have sexual intercourse with the female captive. Allah the almighty said: '[Successful are the believers] who guard their chastity, except from their wives or (the captives and slaves) that their right hands possess, for then they are free from blame [Koran 23:5–6].'…"

—from a pamphlet on sex slaves issued by the Research and Fatwa Department of the Islamic State[39]

his wife, because [the slave] is owned by someone else.... A man may not kiss the female slave of another, for kissing [involves] pleasure, and pleasure is prohibited unless [the man] owns [the slave] exclusively."

And if a slave gets out of line, it is "permissible to beat the female slave." A runaway is to be "reprimanded (in such a way that) deters others like her from escaping." It is forbidden for a Muslim man to marry his slaves, except under certain strict circumstances.[40]

The Islamic State's guidelines on sex slavery are remarkably similar to what the other proponents of the practice had said several years before the Islamic State was established. And no wonder—they were all drawing their understanding from the same principles of Islamic law. Thus the October 2014 issue of the Islamic State magazine *Dabiq* explained that in practicing sex slavery, the group was simply reviving an institution justified under Sharia. The article noted that, scrupulously, "one fifth of the slaves were transferred to the Islamic State's authority to be divided as khums"—that is, the cut of the spoils of war due to Islamic leaders, in line with the Qur'an: "And know that anything you obtain of war booty—then indeed, for Allah is one fifth of it and for the Messenger..." (8:41).[41]

Qur'anic Punishments

On December 15, 2014, the Islamic State released a document entitled "Clarification [regarding] the Hudud"—that is, punishments Allah specifies in the Qur'an. This was essentially the Islamic State's penal code, and every aspect of it was drawn from Islamic teaching.

The "Clarification" mandates death for blasphemy against Allah or Muhammad. The document also specifies that murder with stealing will be punished by death and crucifixion (of the dead body). Murder alone will be punishable by just death. Stealing as part of banditry will be rewarded with the amputation of the right hand and the left leg, and terrorizing people will result in exile.[42]

All these penalties are derived from this Qur'anic verse: "Indeed, the penalty for those who wage war against Allah and His Messenger and strive upon earth corruption is none but that they be killed or crucified or that their hands and feet be cut off from opposite sides or that they be exiled from the land. That is for them a disgrace in this world; and for them in the Hereafter is a great punishment, except for those who return before you apprehend them. And know that Allah is Forgiving and Merciful" (5:33–34).

Blasphemy against Islam is likewise punishable by death, also as per the Qur'an: "If they violate their oaths after pledging to keep their covenants, and attack your religion, you may fight the leaders of paganism—you are no longer bound by your covenant with them—that they may refrain" (Qur'an 9:12).

In fact all of the Islamic State's penalties line up with the Qur'an and Muhammad's words in the hadith. Adulterers, for example, are to be stoned to death; fornicators will be given a hundred lashes and exile.

Stoning for adultery is in the hadith—a hadith which the caliph Umar claimed had once been in the Qur'an:

> 'Umar said, "I am afraid that after a long time has passed, people may say, 'We do not find the Verses of the Rajam (stoning to death) in the Holy Book,' and consequently they may go astray by leaving an obligation that Allah has revealed. Lo! I confirm that the penalty of Rajam be inflicted on him who commits illegal sexual intercourse, if he is already married and the crime is proved by witnesses or pregnancy or confession." Sufyan added, "I have memorized this narration in this way." 'Umar added,

"Surely Allah's Apostle carried out the penalty of Rajam, and so did we after him."[43]

Sodomy (homosexuality) is also to be punished by death, as per Muhammad's reported words: "If you find anyone doing as Lot's people did, kill the one who does it, and the one to whom it is done" (Sunan Abu Dawood 38:4447).

The hand of the thief will be amputated: "The thief, the male and the female, amputate their hands in recompense for what they committed as a deterrent from Allah. And Allah is Exalted in Might and Wise" (Qur'an 5:38).

Those who drink alcohol will be lashed eighty times, also as per a hadith:

Abu Huraira said, "A man who drank wine was brought to the Prophet. The Prophet said, 'Beat him!'" Abu Huraira added, "So some of us beat him with our hands, and some with their shoes, and some with their garments (by twisting it) like a lash, and then when we finished, someone said to him, 'May Allah disgrace you!' On that the Prophet said, 'Do not say so, for you are helping Satan to overpower him."[44]

Slanderers will likewise get eighty lashes: "And those who accuse chaste women and then do not produce four witnesses—lash them with eighty lashes and do not accept from them testimony ever after. And those are the defiantly disobedient" (Qur'an 24:4).

Those caught spying for the unbelievers will be put to death: "Let not believers take disbelievers as allies rather than believers. And whoever does that has nothing with Allah, except when taking precaution against them in prudence. And Allah warns you of Himself, and to Allah is the destination" (Qur'an 3:28).

Apostates will also be put to death: "They wish you would disbelieve as they disbelieved so you would be alike. So do not take from among them allies until they emigrate for the cause of Allah. But if they turn away, then seize them and kill them wherever you find them and take not from among them any ally or helper" (Qur'an 4:89).[45]

Punishment by Fire

On February 3, 2015, the Islamic State released a video showing the burning alive of the Jordanian pilot Muath al-Kaseasbeh—and brought upon itself a new chorus of condemnation. The Saudi Muslim cleric Salman Al-Odah wrote: "Burning is an abominable crime rejected by Islamic law regardless of its causes. It is rejected whether it falls on an individual or a group or a people. Only God tortures by fire."[46]

Indeed, there is a hadith to this effect:

> Narrated 'Ikrima: Some Zanadiqa (atheists) were brought to 'Ali and he burnt them. The news of this event, reached Ibn 'Abbas who said, "If I had been in his place, I would not have burnt them, as Allah's Apostle forbade it, saying, 'Do not punish anybody with Allah's punishment (fire).' I would have killed them according to the statement of Allah's Apostle, 'Whoever changed his Islamic religion, then kill him.'"[47]

But as is so often the case with hadith, there is also a contradictory one (likely because these sayings were fabricated by competing factions among Muslims and have little historical value). In the contradictory hadith, Muhammad is depicted as saying that those who don't answer the call to prayer should be set on fire, along with their houses: "Certainly I decided to order the Mu'adh-dhin (call-maker) to pronounce Iqama (the second call to Islamic prayer) and order a man to lead the prayer and then take a fire flame to burn all those who had not left their houses so far for the prayer along with their houses."[48]

The clerics who condemned the burning alive of al-Kaseasbeh also did not mention this story from Muhammad's conquest of Khaybar:

> Kinana b. al-Rabi', who had the custody of the treasure of B. al-Nadir, was brought to the apostle who asked him about it. He denied that he knew where it was. A Jew came…to the apostle and said that he had seen Kinana going round a certain ruin every morning early. When the apostle said to Kinana, "Do you know that if we find you have it I shall kill you?" he said Yes. The apostle gave orders that the ruin was to be excavated and some of the treasure was found. When he asked him about the rest he refused to produce it, so the apostle gave orders to al-Zubayr b. al-Awwam, "Torture him until you extract what he has," so he kindled a fire with flint and steel on his chest until he was nearly dead. Then the apostle delivered him to Muhammad b. Maslama and he struck off his head, in revenge for his brother Mahmud.[49]

And ISIS had a Qur'anic justification for the immolation of the Jordanian pilot, as well: "AND IF YOU PUNISH (AN ENEMY), PUNISH WITH AN EQUIVALENT OF THAT WITH WHICH YOU WERE HARMED." That verse is a call out in the feature on the burning of the pilot in the March 2015 issue of the Islamic State's slick online English-language propaganda magazine *Dabiq*. As the article explained,

> In burning the crusader pilot alive and burying him under a pile of debris, the Islamic State carried out a just form of retaliation for his involvement in the crusader bombing campaign which

continues to result in the killing of countless Muslims who, as a result of these airstrikes, are burned alive and buried under mountains of debris.... This āyāh [the verse of the Qur'an in the call out, quoted above] sufficiently demonstrates the shar'ī validity [the rightness in Islamic law] of burning someone alive in a case of qisās (retribution).... in addition to the aforementioned āyah from Sūrat An-Nahl [the book of the Qur'an titled "The Bee,"] the fuqahā' used as evidence for these exceptions the following āyah [verse of the Qur'an] from Sūrat Al-Baqarah [another book of the Qur'an, titled "The Cow"]. {So whoever has assaulted you, then assault him in the same way that he has assaulted you} [Al-Baqarah: 194].

The article in *Dabiq* also pointed to a hadith about "the 'Uranī men whose eyes were gouged out by the Prophet (sallallāhu 'alayhi wa sallam) with heated iron" and to several historical examples of burning alive used as a punishment in the era of the Rightly Guided Caliphs.[50]

Besides Islamic punishments, the Islamic State authorities are also reviving the jizya tax on the "People of the Book"—demanding that the Christians of Mosul "pay the *jizya* with willing submission, and feel themselves subdued" as Muslims are commanded in the Qur'an to force Christians to do (9:29) and, also in line with the Qur'an, killing those who "turn away" from Islam (4:89), among whom they count all the Muslims fighting on the side of the "Crusaders," that is, the Western powers. Thus the headline of the *Dabiq* article justifying the burning alive of the Jordanian pilot calls him "murtadd"—the word for apostate, derived from the verb for "turn away."[51]

Brutal—like Muhammad

The Islamic State regularly justifies its own brutality by invoking Muhammad's example. The September 2014 issue of *Dabiq* includes copious citations of the Qur'an and hadith, along with invocations of incidents from Muhammad's life in which he was just as brutal and bloodthirsty as the Islamic State has ever been.

One *Dabiq* article justifies the shooting of Muslims in Syria who had been accused of rebelling against the authority of the caliphate by recalling a particularly spine-chilling incident from the early Muslim accounts of Muhammad's life—one that we have already seen referred to in passing to justify the pilot's burning alive:

> Narrated Abu Qilaba: Anas said, "Some people of 'Ukl or 'Uraina tribe came to Medina and its climate did not suit them. So the Prophet ordered them to go to the herd of (Milch) camels and to drink their milk and urine (as a medicine). So they went as directed and after they became healthy, they killed the shepherd of the Prophet and drove away all the camels. The news reached the Prophet early in the morning and he sent (men) in their pursuit and they were captured and brought at noon. He then ordered to cut their hands and feet (and it was done), and their eyes were branded with heated pieces of iron, They were put in 'Al-Harra' and when they asked for water, no water was given to them." Abu Qilaba said, "Those people committed theft and murder, became infidels after embracing Islam and fought against Allah and His Apostle."[52]

"This hadith," the *Dabiq* article explains, "shows the severity of the prophetic punishment against the treacherous, false claimants of Islam." The executed

OSTRICH ALERT

"If you want to know why ISIS exists, don't bother searching Islamic texts, or examining Islamic traditions."

—*Salon* magazine, February 19, 2015[53]

Syrians, it asserts, were guilty of a "wicked deed" that called for a punishment similar to that which Muhammad had meted out.[54]

There is, of course, no end to the articles assuring Americans that the Islamic State is misunderstanding and misinterpreting Islamic texts, but this message has not gotten through to the thousands of Muslims from the West who have already joined the Islamic State, and the others who attempt to do so every day.

Those who glibly dismiss the numbers of these Muslims as only a minuscule percentage of the billion-plus Muslims worldwide are missing the point. If twenty-five thousand young Christians had flocked from all over the world to join a terror group, no one would wave the phenomenon away by pointing out that there are over a billion Christians in the world.

If the Islamic State is not Islamic, its success represents a massive failure on the part of Muslim authorities. They have failed, and failed spectacularly, to communicate the true, peaceful tenets of their religion—teachings that are so obvious to non-Muslims such as John Kerry and Joe Biden—to tens of thousands of their young people. They are presiding over a catechetical disaster of proportions unknown in the history of the world: never before has such global havoc been wrought by people acting upon a massive misunderstanding of the core beliefs of their own religion.

The thing is, those young people can read the Qur'an. They can see what it says, and see that the Islamic State is acting in accord with the plain words of a book that repeatedly tells its readers that it is clear (6:114, 11:1, 16:89, 41:3)—and also with the example of Muhammad and the rulings of traditional Islamic jurisprudence. Articles explaining how the Qur'an really means

OSTRICH ALERT

"The extremism that we see, the radical exploitation of religion which is translated into violence, has no basis in any of the real religions. There's nothing Islamic about what ISIL/Daesh stands for, or is doing to people."

—Secretary of State John Kerry[55]

UNFORTUNATELY, THERE'S A LOT IN THERE FOR MASS-MURDERING SOCIOPATHS TO LIKE

Professor Caner K. Dagli of the College of the Holy Cross in Worcester, Massachusetts, explains away ISIS's reading of the Qur'an: "Its members search for text snippets that support their argument, claim that these fragments are reliable even if they are not, and disregard all contrary evidence—not to mention Islam's vast and varied intellectual and legal tradition. Their so-called 'prophetic methodology' is nothing more than cherry-picking what they like and ignoring what they do not."[56]

something quite different from what it seems to say keep appearing, but they have not managed to staunch the flow of foreign jihadis into the Islamic State.

It would be refreshing if their authors, instead of devoting their efforts to calming jittery infidels and convincing us that there is no problem within Islam that anyone, Muslim or non-Muslim, need address, would formulate programs designed to convince young Muslims that the Islamic State's understanding of Islam is wrong. But no such programs exist in mosques in the U.S. or anywhere else at this time. Programs of that kind would require Muslim leaders to confront what no one anywhere on the political spectrum seems willing to examine: the Qur'anic roots of the Islamic State's "extremism."

Nothing is gained, however, by ignoring and avoiding uncomfortable questions—and meanwhile, the only beneficiary of all this denial is the Islamic State.

But Muslims Have Condemned the Islamic State!

In September 2014, the Hamas-linked Council on American-Islamic Relations (CAIR) and the Fiqh Council of North America held a press conference in Washington at which they announced with great fanfare that they had refuted the religious ideology of the Islamic State.

They issued a lengthy "open letter" (not, interestingly enough, a fatwa, which would be an actual religious ruling) addressed to the Islamic State's Caliph Ibrahim, Abu Bakr al-Baghdadi, explaining how he was misunderstanding Islam. The international media was, predictably, thrilled.[57] But unfortunately, and not surprisingly, there is less to this repudiation of the Islamic State than meets the eye.[58] Even the "moderates" who signed on to this open letter endorsed elements of Islam that most non-Muslim Westerners consider to be "extremist."

And it will not change the mind of a single jihadi. This letter is not an Islamic case against the Islamic State's jihad terror that will move Islamic State fighters to lay down their arms, but rather a deceptive piece of propaganda designed to fool gullible non-Muslim Westerners into thinking that the case for "moderate Islam" has been made.

The disingenuous nature of the open letter should have been clear from the outset—from the involvement not only of Hamas-linked CAIR, but also of some of the 126 signers.

These included Professor Mustafa Abu Sway, who holds the Integral Chair for the Study of Imam Ghazali's Work at al Quds University in Jerusalem—and is a Hamas activist; Dr. Jamal Badawi, an unindicted co-conspirator in the Holy Land Foundation Hamas terror funding case; Mustafa Ceric, former grand mufti of Bosnia and Herzegovina, who has called for Sharia in Bosnia; Professor Caner Dagli, a venomously hateful Islamic apologist at Holy Cross College in Worcester, Massachusetts, who traffics in Nazi imagery about "unclean" unbelievers; Ali Gomaa, former grand mufti of Egypt, who endorses wife-beating, Hizballah, and the punishment of apostates from Islam; Hamza Yusuf Hanson, founder and director of Zaytuna College, USA, who blamed the West for Muslim riots over a teddy bear named Muhammad; Ed Husain, senior fellow in Middle Eastern Studies for the Council on Foreign Relations, who claimed in

September 2014 that seizing British jihadis' passports so that they couldn't return to the UK from the Islamic State would only create more jihadis; Muhammad Tahir Al-Qadri, founder of Minhaj-ul-Qur'an International, Pakistan, who drafted Pakistan's notorious blasphemy law and had already issued a disingenuous and hypocritical Fatwa Against Terrorism; and Muzammil Siddiqi, chairman of the Fiqh Council and former head of the Hamas-linked Islamic Society of North America (ISNA).[59]

Hardly names to inspire confidence in the group's "moderation."

And sure enough, in the course of their very lengthy open letter, the signatories endorse these six elements of what is usually considered to be "extremist" Islam:

NOT THAT THIS HAS ANYTHING TO DO WITH ISLAM

"Fight them until there is no more rebellion and religion is all for Allah."

—Qur'an 8:39

"Against them make ready your strength to the utmost of your power, including steeds of war, to strike terror into the enemies of Allah and your enemies...."

—Qur'an 8:60

"We will cast terror into the hearts of those who disbelieve for what they have associated with Allah of which He had not sent down authority. And their refuge will be the Fire, and wretched is the residence of the wrongdoers."

—Qur'an 3:151

1. Jihad

Recently "jihad" has been the subject of a massive rebranding campaign—undertaken by none other than the very same Council on American-Islamic Relations that promoted this disingenuous letter. In 2013 CAIR began running bus ads featuring cheerful-looking Muslims with slogans such as "My Jihad is to stay fit despite my busy schedule. What's yours?,"

"My Jihad is to not judge people by their cover. What's yours?," and "My Jihad is to build friendships across the aisle. What's yours?"[60]

The 2014 open letter continued the campaign to whitewash the concept of jihad. "All Muslims see the great virtue in jihad," it says, repeatedly claiming that jihad warfare is strictly defensive. "There is no such thing," the scholars assert, "as offensive, aggressive jihad just because people have different religions or opinions. This is the position of Abu Hanifa, the Imams Malik and Ahmad and all other scholars including Ibn Taymiyyah, with the exception of some scholars of the Shafi'i school."

On its surface, it sounds moderate to renounce "offensive" jihad to convert or subjugate non-Muslims and claim the right only to defend fellow Muslims when they're attacked. But remember that in Sunni Islamic law, only the caliph has the authority to declare offensive jihad, while defensive jihad is obligatory upon all Muslims when a Muslim land is attacked, and need not be declared by anyone. Thus since 1924 (when the caliphate was abolished by Atatürk) to this day (except for those who accept the Islamic State's claim to have revived it), all jihad attacks, even 9/11, have been cast by their perpetrators as defensive.

So endorsing only "defensive" jihad is not as moderate as it sounds.

In any case, the Shafi'i school, which even the open letter's signatories have to admit does endorse "offensive" jihad, is one of the four great schools of Sunni jurisprudence. If some Shafi'i scholars allow for "offensive, aggressive jihad just because people have different religions or opinions," can it really be said to be un-Islamic? Are the scholars pronouncing takfir on the Shafi'i school (declaring them heretics)? Or just deceiving gullible non-Muslims?

2. Dhimmitude

"Regarding Arab Christians," the scholars remind the Islamic State caliph, "you gave them three choices: jizyah (poll tax), the sword, or conversion to Islam." Jizya, as we have seen, is the tax specified in the Qur'an (9:29) to be levied on "the People of the Book" as a sign of their dhimmitude, their subjugation and submission to Muslim hegemony. This, the scholars say, was wrong, because "these Christians are not combatants against Islam or transgressors against it, indeed they are friends, neighbours and co-citizens. From the legal perspective of Shari'ah they all fall under ancient agreements that are around 1400 years old, and the rulings of jihad do not apply to them."

The letter's explanation of jizya, however, is hopelessly self-contradictory.

The scholars tell the caliph that the Arab Christians are friends of the Muslims, who "did not wage war against you" and thus should not have been subjugated as dhimmis. But then in the very next paragraph they mention a "second type of jizyah," which "is levied on those who do not wage war against Islam." So if, as the signatories to the letter aver, "there are two types of jizyah in Shariah," and only the first "applies to those who fought Islam," then how is the Islamic State transgressing against Islam by levying the jizya on those who did not wage war against Islam?

These "moderate" scholars are apparently fine with a religion-based poll tax, a sign of the subjugation of the religious minority, in an Islamic state. In this the authors also contradict their earlier claim that jihad is only defensive; now "those who do not wage war against Islam" are to be made to pay the jizya, which in the Qur'an is the end goal of Muslims' fighting the People of the Book: "Fight those who believe not in Allah nor the Last Day, nor hold that forbidden which hath been forbidden by Allah and His Messenger, nor acknowledge the religion of Truth, (even if they are) of the People of the Book, until they pay the Jizya with willing submission, and feel themselves subdued" (Qur'an 9:29).

3–5. Stoning for Adultery, Amputation for Theft, Execution of Apostates

In Islamic law *Hudud* refers to the punishments fixed by Allah himself for serious crimes, including the stoning of adulterers, the amputation of thieves' hands, and the execution of apostates from Islam. While Islamic apologists in the U.S. routinely claim that these punishments are not really part of Sharia or Islam at all, these "moderate" scholars say: "Hudud punishments are fixed in the Qur'an and Hadith and are unquestionably obligatory in Islamic Law."[61] Their quibble with the Islamic State is that it has been cruel and merciless in applying these punishments.

This is telling. In its campaigns against laws that would block the imposition of Islamic Sharia law in the United States, CAIR has claimed that these punishments are not an integral or essential part of Sharia.[63] Now, CAIR has admitted otherwise.

TAQIYYA WATCH

"The Islamic State has nothing to do with Islam. Everything Mohammed stood for is the opposite of what they do—he condemned violence."
—Amjad Mahmood Khan, Ahmadiyya Muslim Youth Association[62]

6. The Caliphate

"There is agreement (ittifaq) among scholars," say the scholars, "that a caliphate is an obligation upon the Ummah."

A caliphate is an obligation. That is, Muslims should strive to establish a single multinational, multiethnic empire, to which alone they owe political loyalty. In other words, they owe no loyalty to the nations in which they currently reside.

This is a notable and extremely important admission. The Islamic State is appealing to so many young Muslims in the West because it claims to be the caliphate. Caliphates are established and sustained on the principle of Might Makes Right. If the Islamic State sustains itself and survives, more and more Muslims will pledge allegiance to it.

To be sure, Hamas-linked CAIR, the Fiqh Council, and all the signers of this open letter really do oppose the Islamic State. But they don't oppose it because it is transgressing against the commands of what they believe to be a religion of peace. They oppose it because they want to establish a caliphate led by the Muslim Brotherhood, and the Islamic State constitutes competition. This is clear from their sly endorsements of jihad, the Sharia, and the concept of the caliphate in this letter. But with so many infidels so eager to be fooled, their work is easy.

Chapter Nine

ON THE ISLAMIC STATE'S TO-DO LIST
(ROME, NON-MUSLIMS, AND THE FINAL SHOWDOWN)

I n his inaugural address as caliph of the Islamic State, Abu Bakr al-Baghdadi, the caliph Ibrahim, asserted that "the Muslims were defeated after the fall of their khilafah [caliphate]. Then their state ceased to exist, so the disbelievers were able to weaken and humiliate the Muslims, dominate them in every region, plunder their wealth and resources, and rob them of their rights."[1]

This was not a new idea; in fact, it was the foundation of the global Muslim effort to restore the caliphate. On June 21, 2013, Mohammed Malkawi, founder of the Chicago-based pro-Sharia, pro-caliphate organization known as Hizb ut-Tahrir (Party of Liberation) America, sounded the very same theme when he complained that "ever since the Caliphate was destroyed, the world has lost an exemplar of justice, a model for humanity in its entirety. Since then, the world has been held hostage by wolves, who do not respect the honor of a man or a believer. Two world wars cost the lives of over 70 million people, yet they accuse us of terrorism. They killed over 70 million people, and dropped atomic bombs on Japan, yet they level accusations against us."[2]

Malkawi admitted that the caliphate would be bad for infidels: "They say that the caliphate makes the infidels angry. Don't we want to make the infidels angry? Isn't this Islam?" He added: "Let America and Britain hate the caliphate. Let Britain, America, and the entire West go to hell, because the caliphate is coming, Allah willing."[3]

The record of the new caliphate shows that the West and the free world in general have abundant reason to hate it.

The Islamic State's To-Do List: Conquering Rome and Europe

Early in 2015, the Islamic State released an e-book entitled *Black Flags from Rome*, as part of its series detailing its plans for world conquest. Other titles in the series included *Black Flags from the East*, *Black Flags from Syria*, *Black Flags from Arabia*, and *Black Flags from Persia*.

All of these e-books detail why and how the various areas specified in their titles can and must be conquered by ISIS. *Black Flags from the East*, *Black Flags from Syria*, *Black Flags from Arabia*, and *Black Flags from Persia* detail the Islamic State's plans for the conquest of the Muslim areas outside its domains, with particular emphasis on two of its most formidable foes, Saudi Arabia and Iran. *Black Flags from Rome* explains how the ISIS jihad will also be extended into non-Muslim domains—and details how it will succeed in Europe.

Black Flags from Rome begins with a quotation from the Qur'an that sets the tone for the whole thing (punctuation, including parentheses and brackets, are as in the original in all the quotations that follow): "And I (Allah [God]) wanted to do a favour to those who were weak and oppressed in the land, and to make them rulers…(Quran 28:5)."[4]

Borrowing Leftist Fantasies: The Rise of "Far-Right Racist Groups"…

The theme of the whole piece is that the Muslims in Europe are "weak and oppressed," and that they can and will rise up against non-Muslim Europeans and conquer Rome and Europe for Islam.

To portray Muslims in Europe as oppressed, *Black Flags from Rome* paints a paranoid and contrary-to-reality picture of a European continent full of "armed gangs" that are "forming into militias for racist politicians," and "far-right racist groups" being "funded by racist rich people."[5]

These violent gangs of racists are—for reasons that are unclear—focused in particular upon Islam. The right wing groups started off "as people who were against immigration," but soon "their leaders were paid to oppose Islam especially."[6]

> Europe is returning to the Dark Ages [due to the financial reces-
> sion]. Armed gangs are forming into militias for racist politicians,
> and a young Muslim minority is their enemy. All this while a
> Caliphate is growing across the Mediterranean sea next door.[7]

NOT THAT THIS HAS ANYTHING TO DO WITH ISLAM

"We want, Allah willing, Paris before Rome and before Al-Andalus, [and] after that we will blacken your life and blow up your White House, Big Ben, and the Eiffel Tower, Allah willing…. We want Kabul, Karachi, the Caucasus, Qom, Riyadh, and Tehran. We want Baghdad, Damascus, Jerusalem, Cairo, Sana', Doha, Abu Dhabi, and Amman. And Muslims shall return to ruling and leadership everywhere."

—Islamic State spokesman Abu Muhammad Al-Adnani, March 12, 2015, in an audio message entitled, "So They Kill and Are Killed"

ISIS suggests that European governments are behind these anti-Muslim racists—whereas the reality is that the European political establishment viciously hounds even peaceful groups that attempt to combat Islamization using only free speech.

As far as the Islamic State is concerned, the strife between Muslims and these European racist gangs is coming to a head—and it will culminate in the Islamic conquest of Rome.

Increasingly Assertive and Aggressive Muslim Populations

The document offers a history of Muslim immigration into Europe, identifying three waves. The first immigrant generation "was satisfied with a basic living" and "did not want to offend their European rulers and felt grateful to them for giving them a job, a home to live in and a mosque to pray at in their European land." They were grateful for these things because they hadn't had them back home, and that, too, was the Europeans' fault: "They had been prevented from these basic human rights in their homelands by the puppet rulers (which the colonisers had put on thrones before they left.) So these immigrants were grateful for even a little."

The second generation, which the Islamic State places between 1960 and 1980, was focused on ensuring that "their families were rich and had high ranking jobs so they support the poorer family members 'back home.'"[8] The third generation, thriving now, is different: "Unlike their parents version of Islam, which was more cultural and subservient, this new generation, would start studying the life of Allah (God's) Messenger, Muhammad (peace be on him) and comparing it to their situation in Europe."

As a result of these studies, this generation "had given up the victim subservient slave mentality the previous generations had. This generation would be emboldened and more confident in their newly (re)discovered beliefs. They would see the world from a new perspective, and unlike the previous generations who only dedicated on earning money for supporting the family 'back home', this new generation would see the world through the eyes of a global Ummah (Muslim nation) which transcended all national boundaries."[9]

The Islamic State's e-book doesn't say it, but aiding and abetting this generational shift was the European embrace of multiculturalism, which led to the rejection—as "racist" and "ethnocentric"—of the earlier idea that immigrants must be assimilated. Immigrants into Europe (and the United States as well) were encouraged to keep and celebrate their own cultures and traditions rather than embrace those of their new home—an idea that played right into the hands of those who believed that all earthly loyalties must take a second place to the believers' adherence to the "global Ummah" that "transcended all national boundaries."

Smuggling Lessons

Meanwhile, according to the ISIS e-book, "Many Jihad preachers and supporters who left Afghanistan came to Europe as refugees in the early 90s, and later married convert Muslim women and got permanent stay where they lived. Countries with the biggest Jihadi populations in Europe were; Belgium, France, and later the UK."[10] These preachers took advantage of lax and conflicting laws in European countries:

> The Jihad preachers and supporters in the West took advantage
> of the different laws within each country. In the early 90s, many
> went to Belgium (located: North of France) due to its relaxed laws
> against supporting armed groups. However, once the Belgium
> government found out there were many Jihadis' there, it made
> stricter laws against them so many fled to the UK where the laws
> were also soft (this would change in the 2000s). France has a
> huge Muslim Arab population, and they knew that many Arab

Jihadis' from the GIA were in their country. They would try to arrest them but many of the leaders who inspired the youth were in the UK. But the UK would not hand the preachers over to France because the preachers had not broken any laws in the UK. This caused the European intelligence agencies to be bitter against each other in the early to mid-90s.[11]

The GIA was the Armed Islamic Group, a jihad group in Algeria. *Black Flags from Rome* offers a fascinating glimpse into how such groups operated in Europe, with jihadis smuggling weapons from there into Algeria:

They would receive donations from supporters in Europe and with them donations buy weapons for the GIA. From where? From Europe, and transport them into the Islamic Maghrib. They would buy the weapons and then take them to a car mechanic who worked for them, who would dismantle the car and place the cash and weapons inside the cars (deep in the interior framework) and fix the car back together again. These cars would then be driven by GIA members pretending to be natives going on a holiday from France to Spain, and from Spain by Ferry (ship) to Morocco, and from Morocco into Algeria. A middle-person would then collect the car in Morocco and take it to the location of the fighters who would receive the car, dismantle it and extract what was inside. This is how they smuggled weapons from France to Algeria.[12]

This isn't just anecdotal history, it's strategizing for the next jihad: "No doubt, if a war in Europe is to spark in the future, this whole process will be reversed and weapons will be smuggled in a similar way from the Islamic Maghrib into the heart of Europe...."[13]

"Extremists" and "Moderates"

The other side, according to *Black Flags from Rome*, was mobilizing as well: "In 1998, the New World Order was beginning to take place, and European countries began to work together in fighting against Islam."[14] And after 9/11, "the Western intelligence agencies began to change their laws and co-operate together to capture and lock up the preachers who were the most outspoken within the 90s. Groups and organisations made by the preachers were closed down and banned. Spies and listening devices were installed in the Muslim mosques and community centres everywhere."[15] But the Western officials' task was difficult, as "many AQ [al-Qaeda] members captured in Muslim lands had shaven their beards for deception and hiding their devout Muslim identity."[16]

Black Flags from Rome remarks upon the absurdity of Western authorities' inability or unwillingness to deal with the ideological roots of the challenge they were facing:

> The Western policy makers had to play a powerful balancing act. They would fight the Muslim world while trying to stop Muslims from becoming 'radicalised' and reactionary violent. This was almost impossible, so they came up with a clever plan. They would begin to divide Muslims in the media as 'extremists' (who supported Jihad) and 'moderates.' (those who didn't).[17]

The Islamic State rejects the distinction, preferring instead to distinguish between real Muslims, whom they consider to be following Islam, and those who, in their opinion, are not. As far as ISIS is concerned, the "moderates" are on the wrong side—and they continue to appeal to Muslims in the West on the basis of their claim that only the "extremists" are properly following the Qur'an and the example of Muhammad.

Meanwhile, those classified as "extremists," such as the famed jihad preacher in Britain, Anjem Choudary, skillfully exploit the weaknesses of the tolerant West:

> People like Anjem Choudhary were lawyers before they were practising Muslims, so they knew how the law works. Everyday they would study the latest version of the Anti-Terrorism Act [Law], and then call for Islamic law while staying within the guidelines of the British and Western law. This way, they could never be doing anything illegal while fulfilling the obligation of calling for Islam to be the highest.
>
> They would use the 'freedom of expression' given to them to spread their beliefs. This put the European governments in a big dilemma....[18]

Where Have You Gone, Samuel Huntington? (The Clash of Civilizations Is On)

The European governments, the Islamic State claims, solved this dilemma in an ingenious way:

> So they plotted a new plot. If the Muslims were going to make 'Shariah groups' which stay within the law, then they too will make 'Anti-Shariah groups' which stay within the law. So rich anti-Islam people began funding far-right groups in different parts of the world whose only main focus is to fight Islam while staying within the guidelines of the law of the land.[19]

In a passage that is ironic in light of the Islamic State's sexual enslavement of hundreds of infidel women, *Black Flags from Rome* dismisses as "right-wing" "propaganda" the huge scandal of Muslim gangs sexually exploiting young non-Muslim girls in Britain:

> These charismatic leaders of right-wing groups would start to recruit more people to their causes, and protests, and would therefore receive even more funding. People who were normally neutral would start to receive their propaganda and start accepting it. The news media outlets would spread news that Muslim males were making 'grooming gangs' which abuse 'white girls', which would make even more people join the right-wing groups.[20]

The rising tensions set the stage for what was to come:

> In simple words, a clash of civilizations was occurring. A neo-Nazi order was forming in Europe as a reaction to real political Shari'ah-Islam. The future of Europe would be a violent one, until—'you will raid/attack Rome, and Allah will enable you to conquer it.'[21]

Bringing It All Back Home

The Syrian jihad enabled thousands of Muslims from Europe to become trained and battle-hardened: "Here they could learn basic armed/shooting combat, assassination techniques, how to make explosives from homemade materials etc."[22]

They would bring this training back to their home countries: "There were small armies of the Islamic State within every country of Europe by late 2014, and the intelligence agencies didn't even know about it! January 2015 was when these shocking secrets would be discovered, and all the world would see the depth of the Islamic State and Al Qa'idah infiltration in Europe."[23] (Note the casual linking of the Islamic State and al-Qaeda, with no hint of antagonism

ON THE ISLAMIC STATE TO-DO LIST: MURDER MORE "BLASPHEMERS"

In line with the brothers' murder of the Muhammad cartoonists, *Black Flags from Rome* endorses al-Qaeda's hit list of eleven people "wanted dead or alive for crimes against Islam." Most were Muhammad cartoonists or transgressors of Sharia blasphemy laws in some way. In *Black Flags from Rome*, the murdered *Charlie Hebdo* editor Stephane Charbonnier's face is circled; the others listed are all still alive as of this writing:

- Carsten Juste, the former editor of *Jyllands-Posten*, the Danish newspaper that in 2007 published cartoons of Muhammad that touched off worldwide Muslim riots;

- Terry Jones, the Florida pastor who widely publicized his intention to burn the Qur'an;

- Kurt Westergaard, the artist who drew the most famous of the *Jyllands-Posten* Muhammad cartoons;

- Geert Wilders, the Dutch politician who is a vocal opponent of the Islamization of Europe;

- Lars Vilks, another Muhammad cartoonist;

- Flemming Rose, culture editor of *Jyllands-Posten* when the Muhammad cartoons were published, and the man primarily responsible for their publication;

- Morris Saadiq, a Coptic Christian activist who promoted the film about Muhammad, *The Innocence of Muslims*, that the Obama administration blamed for the September 11, 2012, jihad massacre in Benghazi;

- Salman Rushdie, author of *The Satanic Verses*, which got him a death fatwa from the Ayatollah Khomeini for blasphemy against Muhammad;

- Molly Norris, the *Seattle Weekly* cartoonist who created Everybody Draw Muhammad Day and then went into hiding after receiving death threats;

- Ayaan Hirsi Ali, the Somali ex-Muslim who collaborated with murdered filmmaker Theo van Gogh on *Submission*, a film about the oppression of women in Islam that featured Qur'an verses written on the bodies of nude women.[24]

These were all featured in a graphic depicting pastor Terry Jones being shot in the head, with the legend:

YES WE CAN

A BULLET A DAY KEEPS THE INFIDEL AWAY

Defend Prophet Muhammad peace be upon him

All the men were pictured, but in keeping with Islam's rules of modesty, Norris and Hirsi Ali were fastidiously listed by name only.[25] Apparently it is possible to lust after even apostates and blasphemers.

between the two.) The way the world discovered the "shocking secrets" was by the Kouachi brothers' massacre at the *Charlie Hebdo* offices in Paris.

Surprise! The Left Will Help

These will not be the only targets, of course. After describing the *Charlie Hebdo* and Hyper Cacher attacks in detail, the Islamic State explains how intelligence agencies collect huge amounts of data, "but they will not study it unless you are caught under the radar."[26] As attacks such as the ones in Paris become more common, law enforcement authorities will not be able to keep up:

> As the Western nations get poorer, their intelligence collection
> agencies will continue to exist, but they simply won't have
> enough manpower (less jobs) to analyse it all. With less attacks
> in the West being group (networked) attacks and an increasing
> amount of lone-wolf attacks, it will be more difficult for intelli-
> gence agencies to stop an increasing amount of violence and
> chaos from spreading in the West.[27]

As this violence and chaos spreads, Leftist non-Muslim Europeans will help pave the way for the Islamic conquest of Europe, for

> a growing population of left-winged activists (people who are against; human/animal abuses, Zionism, and Austerity measures etc) look up to the Muslims as a force who are strong enough to fight against the injustices of the world.... Many of these people (who are sometimes part of Anonymous and Anarchy movements) will ally with the Muslims to fight against the neo-Nazis' and rich politicians. They will give intelligence, share weapons and do undercover work for the Muslims to pave the way for the conquest of Rome.

When will this alliance be cemented? When, sooner or later, Leftist protesters realize that taking up arms alongside Muslims is the only viable way of achieving their goals:

> If you have ever been at a pro-Palestine / anti-Israel protest, you will see many activists who are not even Muslims who are supportive of what Muslims are calling for (the fall of Zionism). It is most likely here that connections between Muslims and Leftwing activists will be made, and a portion from them will realise that protests are not effective, and that armed combat is the alternative. So they will start to work together in small cells of groups to fight and sabotage against the 'financial elite'.[28]

There Are Lots of Guides to Seeing Europe. This One Is Different

Black Flags from Rome also explains "How to take, hold and expand territory," saying that "there are already 'Muslim No Go Zones' and even

'White only zones' existing within European countries," and explaining how Muslims can steadily expand their zones of control, until ultimately there is a "big national armed force of Muslim fighters. Muslim fighters from all European countries will continue the fight, breaking borders until they can reach; Northern Rome."[29]

The e-book details how to make Molotov cocktails and the kinds of bombs that the Tsarnaev brothers used in their jihad attack at the Boston Marathon. It also expresses confidence in the rather unlikely idea that Russia will aid the Muslims in conquering Europe. This wishful thinking exposes the entire plan as rather fanciful, but one aspect of it is quite realistic: at least some Muslims in Europe will be committing murder in the name of Islam, jihad, and the Islamic State in the near future.

There is nothing fanciful about that at all.

Black Flags from Rome ends with a series of photographs of the Colosseum and other Roman landmarks. At this point, the e-book starts to resemble a twisted tourist manual. But when the jihadis go sightseeing in Rome, they won't be armed with cameras and maps. The photographs are included so that, once the jihadis do arrive, they will know where to go with their sledgehammers and drills.

Indeed, they are already there. Late in April 2015, Islamic State supporters in Rome and Milan tweeted photos of landmarks in each city, including the Colosseum in Rome, with signs held in front of them reading, "We are on your streets, we are locating targets."[30]

End Times Timetable

There is a timetable to all this. *Black Flags from Rome* begins with an epigraph from a hadith in which Muhammad is depicted as saying that after the Muslims conquer Rome, the End Times will begin, with Muslims warring against the Antichrist:

'You will raid/attack Arabia and Allah will give you victory over it, then you will raid/attack Persia (Iran) and Allah will give you victory over it, then you will raid Rome (Italy) and Allah will give you victory over it, then you will raid/attack al-Dajjal (the AntiChrist) and Allah will give you victory over him.' [Saheeh Muslim [54/50].[31]

As far as the Islamic State is concerned, that is prophecy that is certain to come true: first the jihadis will conquer Saudi Arabia, then Shi'ite Iran, and then Rome and Europe—at which point their battles will become eschatological, as they will fight and defeat the Dajjal, the Islamic version of the Antichrist, who will make war against the Muslim faithful before the second coming of Jesus Christ the Muslim Prophet and the consummation of all things.

In line with this scenario, the Islamic State sees itself first defeating Russia and Iran, whereupon the Romans—that is, the Europeans—will gather at Dabiq, a northern Syrian town. Why there? Because Muhammad is depicted in the same hadith as also predicting that Dabiq will be the site of the final battle between the believers and the unbelievers:

The Last Hour would not come until the Romans would land at al-A'maq or in Dabiq. An army consisting of the best (soldiers) of the people of the earth at that time will come from Medina (to counteract them). When they will arrange themselves in ranks, the Romans would say: Do not stand between us and those (Muslims) who took prisoners from amongst us. Let us fight with them; and the Muslims would say: Nay, by Allah, we would never get aside from you and from our brethren that you may fight them. They will then fight and a third (part) of the army would run away, whom Allah will never forgive. A third (part of the army) which would be constituted of excellent martyrs in Allah's eye, would be killed and the third who would never be put to trial would win and they would be conquerors of Constantinople.

Then, apparently the end will come, as Jesus the Muslim Prophet (not to be confused with Jesus the Savior of Christianity) will then return to the earth and defeat the enemies of Allah:

> And as they would be busy in distributing the spoils of war (amongst themselves) after hanging their swords by the olive trees, the Satan would cry: The Dajjal [the Antichrist] has taken your place among your family. They would then come out, but it would be of no avail. And when they would come to Syria, he would come out while they would be still preparing themselves for battle drawing up the ranks. Certainly, the time of prayer shall come and then Jesus (peace be upon him) son of Mary would descend and would lead them in prayer. When the enemy of Allah would see him, it would (disappear) just as the salt dissolves itself in water and if he (Jesus) were not to confront them at all, even then it would dissolve completely, but Allah would kill them by his hand and he would show them their blood on his lance (the lance of Jesus Christ).[32]

The Islamic State, taking all this as a literal foretelling of the future, says that the Europeans will "go on the offensive and arrive with 80 flags to Dabiq (near the Turkish/Syrian border), with more than 100,000 soldiers. This is when the great Malhama (Armageddon begins). It is such a big event that it is even mentioned in Christian Biblical scripture and refers to the time near Judgment Day."[33]

Whatever one believes of Christian or Muslim eschatology, that Judgment Day is coming—because the Islamic State is working toward it, and will continue to do so. And because the United States and the European Union, meanwhile, prefer to continue to reassure themselves that this is not a religious war, or even a proper war at all, and that the whole thing will blow over fairly soon, once jihadis have jobs and social standing. But the Islamic State is confident that it will come down to a military showdown. *Black Flags from Rome* says that the European Union and the United States will fight the Islamic State at Dabiq, while "those who cannot reach Syria go on the offensive elsewhere depending on where they are located."

Around this time the "puppet rulers in Muslim lands"—that is, rulers of Muslim countries who do not rule by Islamic law and pledge their allegiance to the new caliphate—"may be defeated." This could be, says *Black Flags from Rome*, by the year 2020—"equivalent to 100 years since the fall of the Ottoman Caliphate." If this happens, it will give "Islamic armed groups alot of freedom to travel in Muslim lands, and on the Mediterranean sea, and also to use the airspace to target Europe with missiles they will have now captured from the Arab puppet regimes."[34]

But despite their faith in this eschatology, there is work for the jihadis to do. The Islamic State envisions itself one day encompassing the entire world, but there are two primary infidel polities that it wants to conquer first and foremost. Besides Rome, there is Israel.

WISHFUL THINKING FROM ONE OF THE "PUPPET RULERS IN MUSLIM LANDS"?

"This cowardly Islamic State group...does not resemble our religion in any way."
—King Abdullah II of Jordan[35]

The Apple of Every Jihadi's Eye

The Islamic State followed *Black Flags from Rome (Europe)* in April 2015 with another e-book, *Black Flags from Palestine (Magic, Deception & War)*. It envisions the fall of Rome to the Islamic State in 2020 being followed in 2022 by "the beginning of the end of Israel."[36]

Israel, we're told, will soon "expand out to pick up the broken pieces of the war torn countries neighbouring it, so they can make their 'Greater Israel' which spans from the Nile (Egypt) to the Euphrates (Iraq)."[37] Aware that this claim will be skeptically received, *Black Flags from Palestine* adds, "Prophet Muhammad (peace be upon him) informed us: 'War is deception.' Mossad's motto is: 'by way of deception, you shall do war.'"[38]

Black Flags from Palestine traffics in a considerable amount of deception of its own, retailing centuries-old blood libels against the Jews as if they were fact, emphasizing the Jews' use of "black magic" throughout their history, and even providing a summary of nineteenth-century czarist forgery *The Protocols of the Elders of Zion* as if it were a factual account of Jews' goals for the world.[39]

After a concise and highly anti-Jewish history of the Jews, the Islamic State author gets to the heart of the present conflict:

> Then World War 2 would begin, some Jews would be put in concentration camps by Germany, only for the survivors to be rewarded with Palestine (why not Germany?) as compensation. No questions were asked. The Palestinians objected to their houses being taken bulldozed, but the world looked away, and continues to look away...
>
> Allah had taken away Palestine from the Muslims and given it to their enemy.[40]

This too, he says, was prophesied by Muhammad:

> It's reported the Messenger of Allah, Muhammad (saws) warned the believers that: "The (people) do not break the covenant with

Allah and His Messenger, but Allah will enable their enemies to overpower them and take some of what is in their hands." (source: Ibn Majah)[41]

The Muslims' attempt to counter the establishment of Israel foundered because Egypt's irreligious leader Gamal Abdul Nassir betrayed the Muslim Brotherhood and prevented it from restoring the caliphate:

> It is within this era that the Muslim Brotherhood rose in Egypt under the guidance of Hassan al-Banna. His goals were to revive the global Caliphate by a careful plan of winning the Muslim population to an Islamic revivalist message through Islamic Da'wah (invitation and teaching), while a secret military arm of the Muslim Brotherhood would infiltrate the Egyptian army and do a coup to remove the king and take hold of power in Egypt. A man called Gamal Abdul Nassir was within this Muslim Brotherhood military wing, but he was not too religious, he craved power a lot.
>
> As soon as the Muslim Brotherhood did the coup, the Egyptian King Farouk was toppled and the Muslim Brotherhood was about to take hold of the reins of power in Egypt. However, Gamal Abdul Nassir suddenly got his own men who rounded up the Muslim Brotherhood members—he knew their names because he had worked with them—and locked them up in prison and put them through Hell-like torture. The Islamic Caliphate-revival cause had been delayed and betrayed by 50 years due to the cursed Arab dictator Gamal Abdul Nassir....[42]

Without Islam, Arab nations were corrupt, and Arab soldiers were consequently poorly trained:

In the Arab-Israel [conflict], the Egyptian troops had not even received proper training prior to battle. The foot soldiers role in an Arab army before battle was to simply be a servant to the commander, to polish his shoes and to be subservient to his daily chores. The commander could not train him out of fear that he may learn too much armed skills and snatch power behind his back.

Could an army who doesn't trust its own soldiers really win a battle? This is the state of the Arab world without Islam.[43]

It was imperative for the Muslims to recover their full obedience to Islam, so that they could cleanse the holy land:

It is the land which Allah has blessed, the land which He has sent thousands of Messengers' to, and a land which has had many devout worshippers (Arabic: Abdaal) throughout history. The name of this land doesn't matter; Jerusalem was called Eelya by the Romans and Arabs in the past during the time of Prophet Muhammad (saws). What matters is the moral nature of the people ruling such a blessed place. If they are righteous believers, then they make the people living under them good and righteous in this holy land, but if they are not righteous and cause corruption in this holy land—then that makes them Allah (God)'s enemy. Allah will purify this land from corrupt people, even if they were *God's chosen people*.[44]

The Palestine Liberation Organization was not suited to perform that work of purification, as it was "a Communist movement who didn't really care about Islamic teachings. They considered religion backwards and did not take the guidance of Allah seriously."[45] Yet this purification much needs to be done, as

Israel is like Florida in America. It is packed with sunshine, shopping malls, clubs and beaches. The people of modern Israel are like America in their materialism and many do not have much care for religion (only a minority are religious). It also has its fair share of criminal gangs who are a nuisance for the Israeli government. You would imagine the modern Israel is like GTA [the video game *Grand Theft Auto*] Vice city more than the chosen land for God's chosen people.[46]

.... Israel is the country most similar to America in the Middle Eastern world. It is filled with crimes; murder, drugs, corruption, and even adultery and homosexuality is widespread within this holy land. People within Israel live a life of hedonism and materialism, and the whole system from the top to bottom is run on bribery, blackmail and favours.[47]

It is not surprising that this corrupt and criminal nation would have the United States intelligence apparatus wrapped around its finger: "Many people are aware of Edward Snowden's leaks on the NSA (America's 'National Security Agency'), but what many people don't know is that any intelligence which the NSA collects is directly forwarded to Israel."[48]

Israel doesn't just rely on the U.S., however; it has dark, fearsome capacities:

Finding the location of the Mujahideen and preventing their weapons from working are just some of the low-level examples I have read of the dark arts (black magic) being used against the Jihad. I am not alone in this view, many Christians are even aware that the Intelligence Agencies have a strong connection with black magic and other beings (spirits, jinn etc) to help them expand their outreach in Intelligence activities, to help them in their blackmail and torture methods, and even to help them control the people! Drugs and herbs are part of the black magic because they can alter peoples senses.

All these 'Magic tools' are used by Israel to portray itself to look like an invincible force which is undefeatable.[49]

Yet it too has formidable enemies, including Hamas, "an organisation whose goal is to liberate Palestine entirely and to leave no trace of Israel on the map. It is not allowed for a Muslim to believe Israel is a legitimate state, because they have stolen land which belongs to the Muslims (any land which has been a Muslim land in the past belongs to the Muslims until the Day of Judgment)."[50]

Hamas's mistake, however, is "using the elections through democracy to gain a major vote and then rule over the Muslim people through a slow and gradual implementation of Islamic Laws. The Islamic State and Al Qa'idah disagree with this method totally and say that democracy is shirk (polytheism), because people cannot vote whether Allah (God)'s law should be highest or not, rather Allah's Law should always be highest whether people vote for it or not. These differences in politics are what cause the

HARRY POTTER, PAVING THE WAY FOR THE ANTICHRIST

According to the Islamic State, the Antichrist will soon come to the earth, and is already busy corrupting the youth: "The scar on Harry Potter's forehead (& in other popular culture) is a sign of sorcery and is preparing children to accept the mark of the beast on their foreheads as something 'kool.'"[51]

Muslim Brotherhood and Al Qa'idah + the Islamic State to differ and even fight sometimes."[52]

But the Islamic State is on the rise:

> In late 2014, the Islamic State was expanding its influence into al-Sham (Greater Syria) extremely quickly. It wasn't just spreading through war, but also through ideology. Many groups in Greater Syria; Jordan, Lebanon, and even Palestine began to pledge allegiance to the Caliph Abu Bakr al- Baghdadi. This startled Israel because they themselves had only imagined the Islamic State would have a presence within Iraq and Syria only. If the Islamic State had a presence in Palestine, it meant they could attack Israel at anytime, even without the permission of Hamas.[53]

As the jihad against Israel and the rest of the free world ramps up, the Islamic State author betrays a youth spent reading science fiction, watching *Star Wars* movies, and playing video games:

> In the near future, soldiers will fight in Urban cities against rebels who are against the New World Order. Soldiers will mainly consist of mercenaries working for PMCs (Private Military Companies) who are sold to the highest bidder.
>
> As soon as a soldier is recruited, he is injected with nano-machines which will stimulate the soldiers' pituitary glands' to release specific hormones suited to the context of a battle. These nano-machines will be controlled by the army HeadQuarters, so for example: if the soldiers are in an intense fight, the nano-machines will be adjusted by commanders in the HeadQuarters to raise the 'Rage/Anger' hormones level high, and to restrict/cut down

the Fear emotion within their bodies. All the troops within the unit will have the same 'level of emotion' and will therefore work more effectively together as a united force against a common enemy.[54]

Israel will employ these Private Military Companies because "it is better for them that a non Jew dies than a Jew."[55]

Why will Israel's fall begin in 2022? Because, says *Black Flags from Palestine*, the former Israeli Prime Minister Menachem Begin said so in 1982: "Israel will enjoy the 40 years of peace, mentioned in Torah."[56]

Year 2022 may well be when Israel's years of peace and safety end, and the major wars will begin against it. We already mentioned in the ebook: Black Flags from Rome—that the conquest of Rome may happen by 2020, but Allah only knows best.

As a result of this, Israel is working hard day and night before 2022 to make the a perfect war machine. It is 'racing against time' to make a sophisticated combo of war machines on the ground, above the ground, and underground which will give defence and victory to Israel from all sides.

But will it win?[57]

Free people the world over can only hope so. But ISIS has other plans, as the author of *Black Flags from Palestine* explains in a passage that reveals a great deal about the Islamic State's overall agenda:

The Islamic State is breaking the borders and throwing the puppet Arab kings off their thrones, and merging the different provinces and countries under the Islamic State Caliphate. They are breaking the borders because these are the two things which are weakening the Muslim Ummah:

i -Nationalism psychologically divides the Muslims, and

ii - the puppet Kings Physically enforce the separation of Muslims so Palestine cannot be liberated.

The Islamic State aims to smash these borders so Muslim Mujahideen (fighters) can call each other for backup from anywhere in the world, and there is no border or king to stop them. Just like the Caliphate in the early times of Islamic history which spanned across the known world[.] This is why you will practically see Mujahideen of the Islamic State travelling from Syria to Iraq and back without the need of any passport except the statement of belief: Laa ilaaha illAllah Muhammadur-Rasool Allah (there is no god but Allah, Muhammad is the Messenger of Allah) as their passport. The Islamic State is trying to break all borders till it can make a corridor pathway into Palestine towards Israel.[58]

Hamas "is surrounded by enemies and cannot expand out deeper into Israel and consolidate more territory. So it remains ineffective in the overall picture of liberating the entire Muslim world from Zionist subjugation." But the Islamic State will step into the breach, and "if Israel destroys this batch of fighters, it doesn't matter; the corridor allows even more reinforcements of Mujahideen from different parts of the Muslim world to continue the fight."[59]

Ultimately this onslaught will exhaust the Jewish state:

Israel will face many different types of threats. If it is attacked by rockets, it requires the Iron Dome, if it is attacked on the ground, it needs tanks, soldiers and ground vehicles, if it is attacked from tunnels underground, it needs to spend funds on finding the tunnels and destroying them. These variety of attack types makes the Israeli state exhausted, uncertain as to where it should spend the majority of its defence money on before a war, causing it to make many errors. Even if Israel has an 'unlimited' amount of money, the mere fact that it has an enemy who is coming on the attack from all sides, all the time will itself exhaust it and keep it in a state of constant fear.[60]

After Rome and Europe are conquered, the jihad against Israel will receive needed reinforcements from European converts to Islam—but will have to hurry to gather and instruct these converts before the Antichrist arrives:

> After the Armageddon/Malhamah, and the conquest of Rome—
> Muslims will start collecting the spoils of war. They know they
> have a tough fight ahead. Now that the leadership of Europe will
> have been killed or fled, the Muslims will be able to inform non
> Muslims living in Europe the message of Islam, the mercy and
> brotherhood, and they will be able to clear the misunderstandings
> many Europeans may have about Islam and the Muslims. But they
> will not have much time, because within 7 months the AntiChrist
> will arrive. And so the truth seekers and freedom fighters from
> Europe will join the believers, whereas the rest will stay away—
> they will be the ones who will be misled by al-Dajjal.[61]

The first converts will come from the jihadis' allies on the Left: "Good, honest people (like Edward Snowden) who are willing to sacrifice the comforts of life for something greater will most likely be the type of converts who will join the guided Islamic cause."[62] However,

> The freedom fighters and truth seekers in Europe will range from
> left wingers, to even right wingers and those in between. They
> will be able to see the open mindedness and mercy of Islam and
> the Mujahideen after many years of deception on the media.

They will be like the early converts after the Conquest of Makkah, meaning—they will join the Jihad straightaway after accepting Islam. They will be a good replenishment for the losses Muslims have faced in the Armageddon (Malhamah). It's important to note that during this time period, Christianity and the Pope in the Vatican will be fully engulfed by the Zionist system, and many truth-seekers from the Christians will look into Islam.[63]

Then there will be the battle with the Antichrist. The final showdown between good and evil will now be on the horizon, and will take place at—you guessed it—Ben Gurion International Airport:

According to Islamic Prophecy, the leader of the believers (Ameer al-Mu'mineen) during this time period will be the Imam al-Mahdi (the Guided one). He will be like Prophet Muhammad (peace be on him) in excellent character but not in looks.

According to the prophecy, a pathway will have been made by the army of black flags from the East (Khorasan / Afghanistan) all the way towards Jerusalem, in their midst will be the Mahdi (guided one).

The goal of the Mujahideen will be to pave a pathway towards the core centre of Israel, most specifically towards the Gate of Lud (Arabic) [Lod: Hebrew].

Today we see the Gate of Lod is actually Israel's main international airport—Ben Gurion International Airport (previously called Lydda Airport, RAF Lydda, and Lod Airport). And as we all know, the international airport of a country is one of its most secure and protected areas.

However, once the Mujahideen approach the Gate of Lod, they will be sieged in a building. This will be the biggest test of faith for both the Muslims and the Jews because al-Dajjal (the AntiChrist) will have landed in that area when the Muslims have been sieged. No-one can defeat and kill the AntiChrist except the true Christ (Jesus) himself. Not even the Mahdi can kill the AntiChrist, so the believers will remain sieged in this building, praying to Allah (God) for the true Messiah to arrive.

It will be during this time that Jesus, the son of Mary (peace be on them) will descend down from the sky in Damascus, he will travel towards Jerusalem and see that the Dajjal has landed and has surrounded the building containing the Mahdi and the believers.

This is not the second coming of the Jesus of Christianity. This is Jesus the Muslim prophet of the Qur'an, who will, according to a hadith, make war upon Christianity and destroy it:

> The Prophet said: There is no prophet between me and him, that is, Jesus. He will descent (to the earth). When you see him, recognise him: a man of medium height, reddish fair, wearing two light yellow garments, looking as if drops were falling down from his head though it will not be wet. He will fight the people for the cause of Islam. He will break the cross, kill swine, and abolish jizyah. Allah will perish all religions except Islam. He will destroy the Antichrist and will live on the earth for forty years and then he will die. The Muslims will pray over him.[64]

He will abolish jizya, the special tax that the subjugated Christians are to pay in the Islamic State, because there will be no more Christians: "Allah will perish all religions except Islam."

This Islamic "purification" and eschatological scenario is bathed in blood, not just of the Christians but of the Jews also. *Black Flags from*

Palestine quotes the notorious hadith in which Muhammad is shown prophesying the wholesale murder of Jews by Muslims:

> The last hour would not come unless the Muslims will fight against the Jews and the Muslims would kill them until the Jews would hide themselves behind a stone or a tree and a stone or a tree would say: Muslim, or the servant of Allah, there is a Jew behind me; come and kill him; but the tree Gharqad (boxthorn) would not say, for it is the tree of the Jews.[65]

All of this is Islamic fable seen through twenty-first century video-game sensibilities, but the people who believe in it are well-financed, well-armed, and fanatically determined. They are already in control of half the territory of Syria[66] and a sizeable chunk of Iraq, they rule over eight million people,[67] and jihadis under their influence are able to carry out terror attacks in virtually any part of the world, from Saudi Arabia to France to Texas to Australia. They will keep advancing, and keep advancing, and keep advancing—until they are stopped.

Warfare in the Streets in the U.S.

Another Islamic State publication, *How to Survive in the West*, is a detailed manual for subterfuge and subversion in the United States and Europe. The ominous epigraph:

> Indeed, Allah has purchased from the believers their lives and their properties [in exchange] for that they will have Paradise. They fight in the cause of Allah (God), so they kill and are killed. [It is] a true promise [binding] upon Him in the Torah and the Gospel and the Qur'an. And who is truer to his covenant than Allah?

So rejoice in your transaction which you have contracted.
And it is that which is the great success.
        (Quran 9: 111)[68]

Like *Black Flags from Rome*, *How to Survive in the West* begins on a note of self-pity, claiming that Muslims were being unfairly targeted in the West:

> A real war is heating up in the heart of Europe. Many Muslims are putting a lot of effort into showing the world that we are peaceful citizens, we're spending thousands of Euros to do Da'wah (invitation to Islam) campaigns to show how good we are in society, but we're miserably failing. The leaders of disbelief repeatedly lie in the media and say that we Muslims are all terrorists, while we denied it and wanted to be peaceful citizens. But they have cornered us and forced us into becoming radicalised, and that will be the cause of their defeat and be the cause for the conquest of Rome.[69]

Islam and Muhammad are being insulted, and it's time for Muslims to fight back:

> As Muslims, we need to be prepared for what is coming our way. Media propaganda is the first step to justify what will happen later. So if Muslims are portrayed as evil terrorists, then the mass killing which happens to us afterwards will not be a big deal, infact it will be a sigh of relief for the fooled masses of people.
>
> So what are Muslims supposed to do? Are we supposed to petition to a deaf 'free press' because our Prophet is being insulted day and night? Are we supposed to sit back until the

police raids our homes for having the Quran and surah al-Tawbah on our shelves?[70]

We as free Muslims cannot sit back and get locked up for something which is not a crime in the sight of Allah. In the Ummah (Nation) of Prophet Muhammad (saws), we have been taught to physically fight to defend ourselves and our religion, no matter where we are in the world.[71]

So *How to Survive in the West* teaches Muslims "how to live a double-life, how to keep your Secret life private, how to survive in a threatening land, how you can Arm and strengthen the Muslims when the time for Jihad comes to your country, and neighborhood."[72]

A great deal of subterfuge will be needed: "If you are a convert to Islam, you should try to hide your Islam as much as possible.... If you are a born Muslim: then don't make it too obvious you have become a practicing Muslim.... if you are a practising Muslim, and you have a beard already, then don't remove it if it will bring unwanted attention to yourself. I.e. your family, friends and colleagues will get more suspicious why you removed it, forcing them to spy on you more."[73]

This is all part of an effort at "making yourself look more friendly and open minded to the Western public. For example: Muslims who call themselves by a Western nickname gain more acceptances by their non Muslim colleagues. This can be an advantage because it reduces their suspicion of you as they consider you more open minded and less 'extreme' (religious.)."[74]

To get money, the jihadi-in-waiting should steal from non-Muslims: "Do not feel guilty if you take back a small amount of what they have stolen from us. Easy money Ideas: If you are an expert in credit card fraud, paypal/ebay scams, Phishing, hacking, or you know the secrets of a big company, then take advantage of your skills. If you can claim extra benefits from a government, then do so. If you can avoid paying taxes, then do so."[75]

How to Survive in the West details how jihadis should use the internet carefully, how they should communicate with each other, how they should keep in shape, and even how they should undertake weapons training using "Toy guns (Nerf guns), or Pellet guns or Paintball guns for target practice."[76] It also includes bomb-making instructions and tips on how to make sure one is not under surveillance. It goes into the *Charlie Hebdo* jihad massacre, explaining how the Kouachi brothers got their weapons and carried out their attack—making it clear that the Islamic State intends to train new cadres of jihadis to carry out an increasing number of jihad massacres in the United States and Europe.

They are coming.

Chapter Ten

HOW TO DEFEAT ISIS— AND WHY WE MUST

T he Islamic State is nothing less than the foremost evil force of our time.

It is, as Australian Prime Minister Tony Abbott has said, an "apocalyptic death cult."[1] In an age when the entire U.S. and European foreign policy establishment is geared toward negotiation, compromise, and accommodation, it is fanatically intransigent. The idea of reaching a negotiated settlement with ISIS is inconceivable.

The Islamic State wants the death of the United States and the free West. Many of its members want to die in the process of killing us. Like other jihadis, Islamic State members loudly proclaim their love for death. *Black Flags from Palestine* contains what it says is a quote from a Russian general, speaking of the jihadis in Chechnya: "How can you defeat an enemy who looks into the barrel of your Gun and sees Paradise?"[2]

This faith rules out the possibility that Islamic State jihadis will be deterred by the threat of death. They want to be killed, so that they can receive Allah's rewards for martyrs: the virgins, pearl-like boys, cool breezes, and non-intoxicating wine of Islamic Paradise. The old Cold War–era concept of Mutually Assured Destruction will not work in this context.

The Islamic State has published numerous calls for jihad terror attacks in the United States and the West, along with manuals to explain to young Muslims how they can carry out such attacks without being caught and imprisoned. They mean to drain our economy dry with counter-terror measures against an increasingly numerous and aggressive foe. They mean to kill us by means of the death of a thousand cuts.

As long as the Islamic State exists, the West will not have peace. As long as the Islamic State exists, the United States will not have peace.

Either the Islamic State will die, or we will.

But how to kill it?

Barack Obama's Foredoomed Plan

The Obama administration has been striking the Islamic State from the air and claiming great success. Of course, airstrikes alone have never won a war, and Obama is relying on Kurdish and other forces, supported by the U.S. from the air, to roll back the territory that the Islamic State controls. At the end of May 2015 it emerged that almost "75 percent of U.S. bombing runs targeting the Islamic State in Iraq and Syria returned to base without firing any weapons in the first four months of 2015, holding their fire mainly because of a lack of ground intelligence and raising questions about President Obama's key tactic in pushing back an enemy that continues to expand its territory in the war zone."[3]

In September 2014, the *New York Times* had reported that Obama "said he envisioned the Free Syrian Army's providing the ground presence needed to confront ISIS in Syria."[4] Obama told Chuck Todd of NBC, "We have a Free Syrian Army and a moderate opposition that we have steadily been working with that we have vetted. They have been on the defensive, not just from ISIL, but also from the Assad regime. And what—you know, if you recall, at the West Point speech that I gave, I said, we need to put more resources into the moderate opposition."[5]

There were at least two problems with Obama's plan:

1. The Free Syrian Army are allies of the Islamic State, not of the U.S. The "moderate opposition" to which Obama wanted to devote more resources was not actually opposing the Islamic State at all. Two months before Obama stated that he was depending upon the Free Syrian Army to fight against the Islamic State, several Free Syrian Army brigades had already pledged allegiance to the Islamic State.[6] And it was the Dawood Brigade, another group that had been aligned with the Free Syrian Army, that originally captured American journalist James Foley; when the Dawood Brigade pledged allegiance to the Islamic State, Foley fell into the hands of ISIS, and they beheaded him.[7]

The day after Obama said that he was depending on the Free Syrian Army to defeat the Islamic State, Bassel Idriss, the commander of an anti-Assad force aligned with the Free Syrian Army, declared, "We are collaborating with the Islamic State and the Nusra Front [al-Qaeda's representatives in Syria] by attacking the Syrian Army's gatherings in…Qalamoun…. Our battle is with the Assad regime, and it is on Syrian lands only."[8] In other words, they were not fighting against the Islamic State, either in Syria or Iraq.

Harakat Hazm, yet another group that was aligned with the Free Syrian Army and had received training and weapons from the United States, far from welcoming and helping to coordinate the U.S. airstrikes in Syria, denounced them as "an attack on the revolution."[9]

One Free Syrian Army fighter who joined the Islamic State and then labored to get others to follow suit observed in November 2014, "Isis now is like a magnet that attracts large numbers of Muslims."[10]

2. There are no "moderates"—and fighting the Islamic State is aiding Iran. There is no significant force in either Iraq or Syria that wants to establish a Western-style secular republic. The nation that stands to gain the most from the removal of the Islamic State from Iraq and Syria is Iran, where throngs chant "Death to America" at Tehran rallies as the tanks and rockets roll by. The U.S.-backed government in Baghdad is a weak client government of Iran, as is Bashar Assad's regime in Syria. Shi'ite militias have gone into action against the Islamic State in Iraq. The Islamic State must be removed, but if it is, the Iranians could end up controlling an arc of territory stretching from Baghdad to Beirut. There is simply no easy solution to this problem.

The Pentagon Becomes a Ministry of Propaganda

Apparently aware that Obama's plan, such as it was, to "degrade and ultimately destroy" the Islamic State had no chance of accomplishing that goal, and that any successes it did have would play into the hands of one of America's most vicious enemies, the Pentagon began to reassure the American people that all was well: the airstrikes were a huge success, and combined with ground forces from the area, they were recapturing large segments of Islamic State territory.

The mainstream media, always eager to make Barack Obama look good, began announcing the Islamic State's imminent demise late in 2014. The articles came in a steady stream: A CNN headline asked in November 2014, "Has ISIS Peaked? Terror Group Suffers Setbacks in Iraq."[11] The *Atlantic* announced in January 2015, "ISIS Is Losing Its Greatest Weapon: Momentum: Evidence Suggests That the Islamic State's Power Has Been Declining for Months."[12] Not to be outdone, CNN followed a few weeks later with "For ISIS, Tough Times as It Seeks to Regroup."[13] The *New York Times* announced on February 4, 2015, "ISIS Is Losing in Iraq."[14]

All this speculation about the Islamic State on its heels appeared to be confirmed on April 13, 2015, when the Pentagon announced: "ISIL is no longer the dominant force in roughly 25 to 30% of the populated areas of Iraqi territory where it once had complete freedom of movement."[15] On April 15, Vox buttressed this claim with its own report: "ISIS Is Losing."[16]

Just two days after this announcement, however, the U.S. military spokesmen had egg on their faces as the Islamic State placed the key city of Ramadi, just seventy miles from Baghdad, under siege, demonstrating all the characteristics of a confident, advancing force rather than a shattered, defeated, retreating one.[17]

Then on April 22 came definitive confirmation that the Pentagon had misled the public. The map the Pentagon had used to illustrate its claim that the Islamic State had lost 25 to 30 percent of its territory was inaccurate and misleading, leaving out or obscuring evidence that the U.S. airstrikes had not been successful: it showed territory the Islamic State had lost between August 2014—when the airstrikes started—and April 2015, but it didn't show what territory the Islamic State had gained during that same period.

Pentagon spokesman Colonel Steven Warren insisted that the omission was beside the point. "ISIL's own doctrine," he said, "says it must gain and hold territory. This map shows they are not achieving their stated goals." But he acknowledged that the map wasn't "meant to be a detailed tactical map—it is simply a graphic used to explain the overall situation." By that measure, it was highly misleading—it left out all of western Syria, where the Islamic State had made significant gains.[18]

During the 2003 American invasion of Iraq, Americans laughed as "Baghdad Bob"—Iraqi Information Minister Mohammed Saeed al-Sahhaf—repeatedly declared that the Iraqi Army was making huge gains and humiliating the Americans everywhere, and would soon throw them out of the country altogether, whereupon Allah would "roast their stomachs in hell"—when in reality, the U.S. was defeating Saddam Hussein's army with little difficulty.[19]

Twelve years later, Baghdad Bob could just as well have been the U.S. Secretary of Defense, triumphantly announcing that Allah would soon roast the stomachs of the Islamic State jihadis in hell.

But appearance would never conquer reality. As the Pentagon spun its misinformation, the Islamic State went from success to success.

Just a month and a day after the release of the deceptive map, Islamic State forces, using armored construction equipment and ten suicide bombers, breached the walls of Ramadi.[20] Within three days the city was firmly within ISIS control—and ISIS was within seventy miles of Baghdad.

So now the capital of Anbar Province, the heart of the "Sunni Awakening," where local Iraqi tribes first turned against al-Qaeda in Iraq to support U.S. forces in 2006—in other words, the home base of some of America's few potential strong allies against ISIS on the ground—has been absorbed into the caliphate. And the U.S. was reduced to blaming our weak allies in the Shia-dominated Iraqi Army: "What apparently happened is the Iraqi forces just showed no will to fight. They were not outnumbered," Secretary of Defense Ashton Carter said. "In fact, they vastly outnumbered the opposing force. That says to me, and I think to most of us, that we have an issue with the will of the Iraqis to fight [Isis] and defend themselves."[22]

The chairman of the defense and security committee in the Iraqi parliament wasn't having any of it: "Hakim al-Zamili … calls Carter's comments 'unrealistic and baseless.' He said the US should bear much of the blame for the fall of Ramadi, for its failure to provide 'good equipment, weapons

OSTRICH ALERT

ABC News chief White House correspondent Jonathan Karl: "Would you say that overall the strategy's been a success?"

White House press secretary Josh Earnest: "…Overall, yes."

—the White House continuing to claim success for its anti-ISIS strategy in the wake of the fall of Ramadi[21]

and aerial support' to the soldiers. Now he says the US military is seeking to 'throw the blame on somebody else.'"

While the Americans and Iraqis pointed fingers at each other, the Islamic State was consolidating its control of more newly captured territory—this time, in Syria—including most notably the city of Palmyra "and a nearby military airbase." Palmyra—just a hundred and fifty miles from the Syrian capital—was home to fifty thousand Syrians and also a UNESCO heritage site containing priceless Roman ruins.[23] Islamic State jihadis found immediate use for Palmyra's Roman amphitheatre, staging public executions there before a crowd of locals and ISIS fighters.[24]

Then, the next week, ISIS launched "a surprise assault" that "opened a new front in the multi-pronged war being waged by the extremist group across Iraq and Syria, and . . . underscored the Islamic State's ability to catch its enemies off guard." This new offensive in the Aleppo Province of Syria brought ISIS within striking distance of Azaz on the border with Turkey—and put the Islamic State on the verge of cutting off rival militant groups' supply lines and seizing control of border areas that would make smuggling weapons and foreign jihadis through Turkey all the easier.[25]

ISIS was winning the war.

The Only Way the Islamic State Can Be Defeated

There is only one way to defeat this kind of rogue state, short of a nuclear holocaust: by utterly defeating it and destroying the wellsprings of its ideological indoctrination. In the case of the Islamic State, nothing is much less likely than that these things will happen.

No ground force capable of recapturing the Islamic State's territories and preventing their reconquest is likely to be fighting ISIS, at least for the foreseeable future. America won't be doing it—not if Barack Obama has his way. The president campaigned on a promise to withdraw from Iraq and made good on his promise; the last thing he wants to do is betray the fact that the withdrawal was precipitous and ill-considered by committing U.S. ground forces to Iraq again.

Without a return of the Americans, it is hard to imagine what force on the ground *can* defeat the Islamic State. The Kurds withstood the ISIS siege of the Syrian border town of Kobani, but they have not been able to make significant advances into Islamic State territory. Bashar Assad has not been able to prevent the Islamic State from occupying ever larger portions of Syria—and threatening Damascus itself. The Shi'ite regime in Baghdad has (as per the Pentagon's misleading map) made some gains against Islamic State holdings in Iraq, but the Islamic State is not seriously threatened by it, and continues to advance elsewhere. The Turks appear unwilling to act, perhaps so that they can use the Islamic State's successes to their own advantage. King Abdullah of Jordan promised a massive retaliation against the Islamic State after its murder of Jordanian pilot Muath al-Kaseasbeh in February 2015, but took little real action.

That leaves Iran. Yet while they are aiding the Baghdad regime in actions against the Islamic State, the Iranians don't appear disposed to get into a full-scale war with the Islamic State. This reluctance may stem from their awareness of the fact that if they advance deeply into Sunni territory, they will face resistance even from people who despise the Islamic State.

The Ideological War

Even if the U.S. did invade and destroy the Islamic State, American troops can't remain in Iraq forever. As soon as they left, the vacuum could well be filled by an entity very like the Islamic State. The problem that the Islamic State poses will persist as long as the United States and the West are unwilling to confront the ideology that gave ISIS its impetus in the first place.

After American troops toppled Saddam Hussein, we installed a constitution that enshrined Sharia as the highest law of the land. This was in stark contrast to what should have been done: the explicit and enforced limiting of political Islam.

There are precedents: in October 1945, U.S. Secretary of State James Byrnes wrote to General Douglas MacArthur, directing him to restrict the influence of the Shintoism, the ideology that had fueled Japanese militarism, in postwar Japan:

> Shintoism, insofar as it is a religion of individual Japanese, is not to be interfered with. Shintoism, however, insofar as it is directed by the Japanese government, and as a measure enforced from above by the government, is to be done away with. People would not be taxed to support National Shinto and there will be no place for Shintoism in the schools. Shintoism as a state religion— National Shinto, that is—will go... Our policy on this goes beyond Shinto... The dissemination of Japanese militaristic and ultra-nationalistic ideology in any form will be completely suppressed. And the Japanese Government will be required to cease financial and other support of Shinto establishments.[26]

Allowing Islamic Sharia law into the constitutions of the U.S.-created Islamic (!) Republic of Afghanistan and Republic of Iraq in 2004 and 2005 was as foolhardy as it would have been to write emperor-worship and Shinto militarism into Japan's 1946 constitution.

Also providing an example for the modern day is the nineteenth-century British General Sir Charles Napier, who when he was Governor of Sindh in the British Raj was confronted by Hindu leaders angered by his prohibition of the practice of sati, the casting of widows upon their husbands' funeral pyres. Napier replied, "Be it so. This burning of widows is your custom; prepare the funeral pile. But my nation has also a custom. When men burn women alive we hang them, and confiscate all their property. My carpenters shall therefore erect gibbets on which to hang all concerned when the widow is consumed. Let us all act according to national customs."[27]

Of course it would be considered the height of ethnocentric impropriety to follow such examples today—either to confront ISIS on its own turf or to challenge mosques and Islamic schools in the U.S. and elsewhere to institute programs teaching against the Islamic State's core beliefs and actively discouraging young Muslims from joining it. Yet if this were done, many Muslims who don't want to live under Sharia any more than anyone else does would cast their lot with the free world; our ideas are better, our way of life is better, our civilization is better. But no one dares say that, or act upon it.

The only significant attempt that the United States government has made to confront the Islamic State's ideology is the State Department's Think Again Turn Away program, a rather embarrassing taxpayer-funded effort intended to make jihadists stop and think about what they're doing and lay down their arms, but which in practice amounts to little more than Twitter trolling of Islamic State supporters. Alberto Fernandez, coordinator of the State Department's Center for Strategic Counterterrorism Communications (CSCC), which oversees the program, explained in April 2014, "We are actually giving al Qaeda the benefit of the doubt because we are answering their arguments. The way I see it is we are participating in the marketplace of ideas."[28]

Since, however, the Obama administration is committed as a matter of policy not to discuss Islam and jihad in connection with terrorism, or to acknowledge that there is an ideology of violence and supremacism within Islam, it cannot confront jihadists even on Twitter—when it tries, it only betrays its failure to understand their perspective. When one jihadist on Twitter praised the Taliban's 2001 destruction of the ancient Buddhas of Bamiyan, the Think Again Turn Away program responded: "Destroying ancient culture out of hatred and backwardness are a feature of al Qaeda's ideology"—thereby demonstrating that the State Department has no understanding whatsoever of the jihadist imperative to destroy the relics of ancient non-Muslim civilizations so as to demonstrate the judgment of Allah and the victory of Islam.[29]

The quintessential example of the ineptitude, willful ignorance, and absolute ineffectiveness of the Think Again Turn Away program came in March 2015, when it tweeted as an example of the positive aspects of freedom of speech in the West a photograph of Muslim hard-liners in Britain manning an information table labeled "Shariah Law/Man Made Law: Which Is Better for Mankind?"[30] It is unclear how the State Department thought that a photo of Muslims spreading Sharia in the West would move them to stop trying to establish it in Iraq and Syria or anywhere else.

Even if the Islamic State were defeated and eradicated, there are Muslims around the world, including in the United States, who share its worldview, motives, and goals. If the caliphate disappears, they will not. And if no one effectively challenges their beliefs, they will continue waging jihad for decades to come.

I Have Seen the Future, Brother, It Is Murder

Since they are not fighting the Islamic State adequately on either the military or the ideological front, the United States and its allies can look forward to more of what they saw during the Islamic State's first year of existence: more bellicose threats, more Islamic jihad plots and attacks in the U.S. and Europe by individuals and groups, more Muslims from the West throwing everything away to join the Islamic State.

At very least, Muslims who leave the United States or other non-Muslim countries to wage jihad in the Islamic State should not be allowed back into their home countries; by joining or trying to join the Islamic State, they have declared their allegiance to an entity that is quite explicitly at war with their home country. Thus they should be treated as traitors. Yet even this obvious precaution against harboring jihadis and leaving ourselves need-lessly vulnerable to jihad attacks at home is not being taken: Homeland Security Secretary Jeh Johnson admitted in April 2015 that forty Muslims from the U.S. had already returned to America from the Islamic State. They were, he assured us, being closely watched: "We have in fact kept close tabs on those who we believe have left and those who've come back. A number have been arrested or investigated and we have systems in place to track these individuals." However: "But you can't know everything."[31]

Indeed. And at this point, one wonders if the Obama administration knows anything.

In any case, the fact that potential jihadis are being watched is no guar-antee that they will not carry out deadly attacks. After Man Haron Monis took customers at a chocolate café in Sydney's Martin Place hostage at gunpoint, forced them to display an ISIS flag, and ended up dead along with two of his hostages, Australian Prime Minister Tony Abbott admitted that Monis had been "well known to State and Commonwealth authorities" for, among other things, sending harassing letters to the relatives of soldiers who had been killed in Afghanistan and posting "graphic extremist [read: jihadi] material online."[32]

Only if there is a massive change in the political culture in Washington will effective action be taken against the Islamic State—or against the jihadis loyal to it in Western countries. How many more people will have to die before that change comes is anyone's guess. In the Islamic State, the free West has a foe that challenges it to its very core. This is not just a war against a rival that is grabbing territory to which it is not entitled. This is not even just a war between two competing ideologies and worldviews—it is very much that, although only one side is fighting on that basis, but it is more as well.

The challenge of the Islamic State is the challenge of destruction to cre-ation, of conflict to peace, of tyranny to freedom. It is, without hyperbole, the challenge of death to life. One teenage Muslim girl from France who joined the jihad in Syria in 2012 wrote to her mother, "Mum, you're too materialistic. All that matters is finding your daughter. You should know that I am no longer your daughter. I belong to Allah. I will never return to the land of the unbelievers. If your government of unbelievers should come to find me with an army, we will execute every last one of them, the Truth will win out, we are afraid of nothing. We love death more than you love life."[33]

We love death more than you love life. This is civilization's ultimate challenge. Will the lovers of death and destruction overwhelm and defeat those who love life and have created great civilizations that celebrate human creativity and achievement? Will all that is left of three thousand years of human civilization be reduced to rubble and a mindless religio-ideological lockstep?

The Islamic State is not just a challenge to Judeo-Christian Western civilization. It is a challenge to civilization itself—to the very idea of civilization.

And that is why, for all the advantages it enjoys today, it is doomed to fail. Life will always conquer death in the end. The human spirit will always prevail against the forces that would subjugate and enslave it.

Getting to that victory will not be easy. Besotted with propaganda and distraction, the West still doesn't know what it's up against. By the time it does, it may be impossible to avoid millions of deaths and unimaginable destruction, including that of the cultural and artistic patrimony of the Western world.

Yet if free souls prevail, and they will, the fight will not have been in vain.

And the lovers of life will rebuild again.

ACKNOWLEDGMENTS

Barack Obama once famously said: "If you've got a business—you didn't build that. Somebody else made that happen." He might say to me, "If you've got a book—you didn't write that. Somebody else made that happen."

I did write it, of course, but it took a village. Given the savagery and bloodlust of those about whom I have written here, I cannot name all of those who have provided me with information, guided my understanding, and informed my perspective in ways that show on every page of this book, but that doesn't dim my appreciation of them, and I hope this note will suffice to express that gratitude to them.

Meanwhile, once again my editor at Regnery, Elizabeth Kantor, has taken the inchoate mass I turned in to her like Michelangelo taking a block of marble, and has made from it, alas, not a David or a Pietà but a Robert Spencer book—and while this book is no David, that doesn't mean that she is no Renaissance-worthy artist. If there ever is a Renaissance of truth and honesty in America's public discourse, and Regnery authors have anything to do with it, her sculpting skills will have played a large role.

Thanks also to Harry Crocker, Patricia Jackson, and the entire marvelous and nonpareil Regnery team. If they were a sports team, they would be the New York Yankees, with Michelangelo batting cleanup, and opposing manager Obama sitting glumly in the dugout while his team takes a shellacking. Seriously, there is no better publishing house in the business, and I am proud that this is my eighth Regnery book.

My gratitude to some people is ongoing, for there are so many to whom the *sine qua non* label can be awarded. Chief among these is, of course, the great Jeffrey Rubin, without whom I might never have published a thing, and who at so many points gave me ideas, encouragement, and opportunities for which I can never overstate my gratitude. And my friend and colleague Pamela Geller has shown me by example how to maintain a healthful perspective and joy in life amid constant vilification and ongoing threats of blood and death. If there is any justice and historical memory, free people of successive generations will celebrate and laud her as one of the unsung heroes of this generation, a foremost champion of freedom in this rapidly darkening age.

It is for those free people of the future, if there are any, that I wrote this book.

NOTES

An ISIS Timeline

1. "The Islamic State," Mapping Militant Organizations, Stanford University, March 10, 2005.
2. Daniel L. Byman, "The Resurgence of al Qaeda in Iraq," Brookings, December 12, 2013.
3. Lee Ferran and Rym Momtaz, "ISIS: Trail of Terror," ABC News, February 23, 2015.
4. "ISIS Applies Its Own Laws in Raqqa," Al-Monitor, June3, 2013.
5. Adam Schreck (Associated Press), "Al-Qaeda Claims Responsibility for 'Bold Raid Blessed by God' After Hundreds Escape Abu Ghraib," *National Post*, July 23, 2013.
6. Ghazwan Hassan (Agence-France Presse), "Six Killed As Militants Overrun Iraq's Samarra," *Daily Star* (Lebanon), June 5, 2014.
7. Gwynne Dyer, "Iraq Falling in the Face of Jihadis," *Prince George Citizen*, June 13, 2014.

8.   Agence-France Presse, "Syria Says Giving Military Support to Kurds in Kobani," *Daily Star* (Lebanon), October 22, 2014.

9.   JohnLee Varghese, "3 Teenage American 'ISIS Jihadi Brides' Arrested in Germany While Trying to Flee to Syria," *International Business Times*, October 22, 2014.

10.   Sam Jones, "More than Half World's Countries Now Producing Jihadis," *Financial Times*, May 27, 2015.

11.   Lora Mofta, "ISIS Nuclear Weapon? Islamic State Claims It Can Buy Nukes from Pakistan with a Year in Dabiq Propaganda Magazine," *International Business Times*, May 23, 2015.

Introduction

1.   Adam Withnall, "Iraq Crisis: Isis Declares Its Territories a New Islamic State with 'Restoration of Caliphate' in Middle East," *Independent*, June 29, 2014.

2.   Ian Johnston, "The Rise of Isis: Terror Group Now Controls an Area the Size of Britain, Expert Claims," *Independent*, September 3, 2014; Janine di Giovanni, Leah McGrath Goodman, and Damien Sharkov, "How Does ISIS Fund Its Reign of Terror?," *Newsweek*, November 6, 2014.

3.   Barack Obama, "Statement by the President on ISIL," WhiteHouse.gov, September 10, 2014.

4.   David Remnick, "Going the Distance," *New Yorker*, January 27, 2014.

5.   Dan Merica, "ISIS Is Neither Islamic nor a State, says Hillary Clinton," CNN, October 7, 2014.

6.   "Syria, More Than 20 Thousand Foreign Fighters Have Joined the Jihad," Asia News, February 11, 2015.

Chapter One: Born of Blood and Slaughter

1.   Gary Gambill, "Abu Musab al-Zarqawi: A Biographical Sketch," Terrorism Monitor, vol. 2, issue 24 (December 15, 2004).

2.   Ibid.; Craig Whitlock, "Al-Zarqawi's Biography," *Washington Post*, June 8, 2006.

3.   Gambill, "Abu Musab al-Zarqawi."

4.   Ibid.

5.   Whitlock, "Al-Zarqawi's Biography."

6.   Aaron Y. Zelin, "The War between ISIS and al-Qaeda for Supremacy of the Global Jihadist Movement," Washington Institute for Near East Policy, June 2014.

7.   Gambill, "Abu Musab al-Zarqawi."

8.   Ibid.

9.   Whitlock, "Al-Zarqawi's Biography."

10. "'Zarqawi' Beheaded US Man in Iraq," BBC News, May 13, 2004; James Joyner, "Video: American Hostage Eugene Armstrong Beheaded [including selections from AP and Reuters reports]," Outside the Beltway, September 20, 2004.

11. Steven Stalinsky, "Dealing in Death," *National Review*, May 24, 2004.

12. Jeffrey Pool, trans., "Zarqawi's Pledge of Allegiance to Al-Qaeda: From Mu'asker Al-Battar, Issue 21," Terrorism Monitor, vol. 2, issue 24 (December 15, 2004).

13. "Purported bin Laden Tape Endorses al-Zarqawi," CNN, December 27, 2004.

14. Asif Haroon Raja, "From ISI to ISIL to IS to IS," *States Times*, August 2, 2014.

15. Chris McGreal, "Barack Obama Declares Iraq War a Success," *Guardian*, December 14, 2011.

16. Raja, "From ISI to ISIL to IS to IS."

17. McGreal, "Barack Obama Declares."

18. Ruth Sherlock, "How a Talented Footballer Became World's Most Wanted man, Abu Bakr al-Baghdadi," *Telegraph*, November 11, 2014.

19. Aaron Y. Zelin, "Al-Qaeda Disaffiliates with the Islamic State of Iraq and al-Sham," Washington Institute, February 4, 2014.

20. Adam Goldman, "Ohio Man Who Trained with Jabhat al-Nusra Is Indicted on Terrorism Charges," *Washington Post*, April 16, 2015.

21. Ibid.

22. Erin McClam, "'More Extreme Than Al Qaeda'? How ISIS Compares to Other Terror Groups," NBC News, June 20, 2014.

23. Linda Qiu, "David Gregory: Al-Qaida Cast Off ISIS as 'Too Extreme,'" Politi-Fact, August 13, 2014.

24. Mark Tran, "Who Are Isis? A Terror Group Too Extreme Even for al-Qaida," *Guardian*, June 11, 2014.

25. Steve Bird, "So Wicked That Even Al Qaeda Disowned Them: Letter Found at Bin Laden's Hideout Warned of Islamic State's Extreme Brutality," *Daily Mail*, August 10, 2014.

26. Translated document #SOCOM 2012 0000004 from the cache of documents found at Osama bin Laden's Abbottabad compound, *Washington Post*, pp. 5–6, http://www.washingtonpost.com/r/2010-2019/WashingtonPost/2012/05/03/Foreign/Graphics/osama-bin-laden-documents-combined.pdf.

27. The twenty-one-page letter found at bin Laden's Abbottabad compound did contain a principled argument from Islamic texts against causing unnecessary casualties among innocent Muslims in, for example, mosque bombings and suicide attacks in marketplaces. (See translated document #SOCOM 2012

0000004, pp. 11–21.) But that argument was aimed only obliquely against ISIS—its main target seems to have been the Pakistani Taliban. And as we shall see later in this chapter, ISIS founder Zarqawi developed an effective answer, firmly grounded in Islamic law and authorities, to the misgivings of his sometime sponsors in al-Qaeda about the savage tactics he favored. In fact the author of the al-Qaeda letter seems to be on the defensive when it comes to the rulings of Islamic jurisprudence on the treatment of Christians—at one point having to argue that "some of the rulings of the scholars concerning Jihad" no longer apply because "they were released when Islam was strong, mighty, and defensible." Perhaps his feeling that he wasn't on strong ground explains why he didn't want to confront ISIS on first principles—dismissing "the statements of the scholars" as "irrelevant" to the kind of tactical discussion he wanted to have: "We are here talking about the interest and the priorities not about the roots of the issue." (Ibid., p. 7). Somehow harder-line jihadis never seem to have much trouble justifying their atrocities from Islamic texts and rulings. It's any Muslim who argues for moderation—even when, as in this case, the relative "moderate" is an al-Qaeda spokesman!—that has the more difficult task.

28. "Look Who's Talking: John Brennan," Fox News, March 23, 2015.

29. "Jihadists 'Bulldoze Berm' Dividing Iraq from Syria," Agence France-Presse, June 11, 2014.

30. Adam Withnall, "Iraq Crisis: Isis Declares Its Territories a New Islamic State with 'Restoration of Caliphate' in Middle East," *Independent*, June 20, 2014.

31. Sherlock, "How a Talented Footballer."

32. Janine di Giovanni, "Who Is ISIS Leader Abu Bakr al-Baghdadi?," *Newsweek*, December 8, 2014.

33. Martin Chulov, "Isis: The Inside Story," *Guardian*, December 11, 2014.

34. Ashraf Khalil, "Camp Bucca Turns 180 Degrees from Abu Ghraib," *Los Angeles Times*, January 19, 2005.

35. Chulov, "Isis."

36. Sherlock, "How a Talented Footballer."

37. "Zawahiri's Letter to Zarqawi (English Translation)," Combating Terrorism Center at West Point, https://www.ctc.usma.edu/posts/zawahiris-letter-to-zarqawi-english-translation-2.

38. "Letter Addressed to Atiyah," from the tranche of documents taken from Osama bin Laden's compound and released by the Office of the Director of National Intelligence on May 20, 2015, http://www.dni.gov/files/documents/ubl/english/Letter%20Addressed%20to%20Atiyah.pdf.

39. Ali Ibrahim Al-Moshki, "AQAP Announces Support for ISIL," *Yemen Times*, August 19, 2014.

40. Paul Cruickshank, "Al Qaeda in Yemen rebukes ISIS," CNN, November 21, 2014.

41. Ibid.

42. "Top Commander of al Qaeda in Yemen: Beheadings Are 'Barbaric,'" CBS, December 8, 2014; Alessandria Masi, "Difference between Al-Qaeda and ISIS: Senior AQAP Leader Holds 'Press Conference,' Said Beheadings Are 'Big Mistake,'" International Business Times, December 8, 2014.

43. Ibid.

44. Marco Polo, *The Travels of Marco Polo*, trans. Henry Yule, ed. and annotated Henri Cordier (John Murray, 1920), chapter 23.

45. Bernard Lewis, *The Assassins: A Radical Sect In Islam* (Basic Books, 1967), 12.

46. Polo, *Travels*, chapter 24.

47. Ben McClellan, "Controversial Aussie Muslim Backs Right to Fight for Islamic State," *Daily Telegraph*, December 5, 2014.

48. Loubna Mrie, Vera Mironova, and Sam Whitt, "'I Am Only Looking Up to Paradise,'" *Foreign Policy*, October 2, 2014.

49. Muhammed Ibn Ismail Al-Bukhari, *Sahih al-Bukhari: The Translation of the Meanings*, trans. Muhammad Muhsin Khan (Darussalam, 1997), vol. 9, book 93, no. 7142.

50. Muslim ibn al-Hajjaj, *Sahih Muslim*, trans. Abdul Hamid Siddiqi, rev. ed. (Kitab Bhavan, 2000), no. 4554.

51. Ibid.

52. Bernard Lewis, *The Assassins: A Radical Sect In Islam* (Basic Books, 1967), 126.

53. Maulana Maudoodi, "The Mischief of Calling Muslims as *Kafir*," *Tarjuman al-Quran*, May 1935.

54. David Commins, *The Wahhabi Mission and Saudi Arabia* (I.B. Taurus, 2009), 31.

55. Yousaf Butt, "How Saudi Wahhabism Is the Fountainhead of Islamist Terrorism," Huffington Post, January 20, 2015.

56. "The Salafi Cult. The Modern Day Khawarij," http://wmneww.wahhabi.info/.

57. John Kerry, "Remarks on the Formation of the Iraqi Government," U.S. State Department, September 8, 2014.

58. On the idea that poverty causes terrorism, see, for example, Jeryl Bier, "Kerry: 'Root Cause of Terrorism' Is Poverty," *Weekly Standard*, January 15, 2014.

59.   Ashley Killough, "Strong Reaction to Obama Statement: 'ISIL Is Not Islamic,'" CNN, September 11, 2014.
60.   "Abu Mus'ab Al-Zarqawi: Collateral Killing of Muslims Is Legitimate," Middle East Media Research Institute, June 7, 2005.
61.   Ibid.
62.   "Zawahiri's Letter to Zarqawi."

Chapter Two: ISIS Comes to America

1.   Kevin Fasick, Amber Jamieson, and Laura Italiano, "Ax Attacker Wanted 'White People to Pay' for Slavery," *New York Post*, October 25, 2014.
2.   Ibid.
3.   Catherine Herridge, "Intel Memo Shows NYC Ax Attacker's Online Obsession with Radical Islam," Fox News, November 11, 2014.
4.   Fasick, Jamieson, and Italiano, "Ax Attacker Wanted."
5.   M. L. Nestel, "Sources: NYPD Hatchet Attacker May Have Been ISIS Supporter," Vocativ, October 23, 2014.
6.   Ab Muhammad al-'Adn n ash-Sh m , "Indeed Your Lord Is Ever Watchful," September 21, 2014, available at, https://ia801400.us.archive.org/34/items/mir225/English_Translation.pdf.
7.   Fasick, Jamieson, and Italiano, "Ax Attacker Wanted."
8.   Ibid.
9.   Adnani, "Indeed Your Lord Is Ever Watchful."
10.   Robert Spencer, "ISIL: 'If the US Bomb Iraq, Every American Citizen Is a Legitimate Target for Us,'" Jihad Watch, June 27, 2014.
11.   Missy Ryan, "Islamic State Threat 'Beyond Anything We've Seen': Pentagon," Reuters, August 21, 2014.
12.   Michael Zennie, "Somali-American Who Died Fighting for ISIS Cleaned Planes for Delta Airlines at Minneapolis Airport before He Joined Terrorist Group," *Daily Mail*, September 3, 2014.
13.   Jamie Weinstein, "ISIS Threatens America: 'We Will Raise the Flag of Allah in the White House,'" Daily Caller, August 8, 2014.
14.   Fasick, Jamieson, and Italiano, "Ax Attacker Wanted."
15.   "Feds Warn of ISIS-Inspired Threat against Police, Reporters in US," NBC, October 13, 2014.
16.   Adnani, "Indeed Your Lord Is Ever Watchful."
17.   Ibid.
18.   Ibid.
19.   Ibid.

20.   Ibid.
21.   Ibid.
22.   Ibid.
23.   Ibid.
24.   Ibid.
25.   Ibid.
26.   Ibid.
27.   Ibid.
28.   Ibid.
29.   Robert Spencer, "Brooklyn Cop Killer's FB Page: 'Strike Terror into the Hearts of the Enemies of Allah,'" Jihad Watch, December 20, 2014.
30.   Adnani, "Indeed Your Lord Is Ever Watchful."
31.   Charles C. Johnson, "Breaking, Exclusive: NYPD Cop Killer Worked for Muslim Terror Front Group," GotNews, December 23, 2014.
32.   John Hall, "ISIS Supports Ferguson Protesters: Islamic Militants Promise to Send Over 'Soldiers That Don't Sleep, Whose Drink Is Blood, and Their Play Is Carnage," *Daily Mail*, November 26, 2014.
33.   Allan Woods, "Martin Rouleau 'Died like He Wanted To,'" *Toronto Star*, October 20, 2014.
34.   "Martin Couture-Rouleau, Hit-and-Run Driver, Arrested by RCMP in July," CBC News, October 21, 2014.
35.   Woods, "Martin Rouleau 'Died like He Wanted To.'"
36.   Ibid.
37.   Ibid.
38.   Robert Spencer, "Canadian Hit-and-Run Jihadi: 'Work for Khilafah,'" Jihad Watch, October 21, 2014.
39.   Robert Spencer, "Facebook Page of Canadian Muslim Who Ran Down Soldiers Full of Qur'an Quotes, Support for Jihad," Jihad Watch, October 20, 2014.
40.   Ian Austen, "Hit-and-Run That Killed Canadian Soldier Is Called Terrorist Attack," *New York Times*, October 21, 2014.
41.   "Ottawa Shooting Suspect Michael Zehaf-Bibeau Had 'Very Developed Criminality,'" CTV News, October 23, 2014; Colin Freeze and Les Perreaux, "Suspected Killer in Ottawa Shootings Had Religious Awakening," *Globe and Mail*, October 22, 2014.
42.   Mike Hager, "Ottawa Shooter 'Confrontational' at North Vancouver Construction Site," *Vancouver Sun*, November 22, 2014.
43.   Susan Bibeau, "Statement of Susan Bibeau," Scribd.com, October 27, 2014, https://www.scribd.com/embeds/244415837/content?start_page=1&view_mode=scroll&show_recommendations=true.

44. "Charlie Hebdo: Gun Attack on French Magazine Kills 12," BBC, January 7, 2015.

45. Bob Orr, "How the French Terrorists Were Connected to al Qaeda, ISIS," CBS News, January 9, 2015.

46. "AQAP Announces Support for ISIL," *Yemen Times*, August 19, 2014.

47. Orr, "How the French Terrorists."

48. Ibid.

49. Chris Hughes, "Charlie Hebdo Massacre Predicted in Tweets: Did ISIS Plot Paris Terror Attack?," *Mirror*, January 8, 2015.

50. Zeina Karam, "ISIS, Al Qaeda Supporters Praise Charlie Hebdo Attack," Associated Press, January 10, 2015.

51. Robert Mendick, Nicola Harley and Harriet Alexander, "Amid the Terror, a Hero Who Lost His Life by Fighting Back," *Telegraph*, January 10, 2015.

52. "Translation of Paris Terrorist Video Claiming He Acted on Behalf of Islamic State," WarontheRocks.com, January 11, 2015.

53. Ibid.

54. *Mash'Allah* is literally "Allah has willed it," and is an expression of gratitude and joy among Muslims.

55. "Translation of Paris Terrorist Video."

56. Ibid.

57. Ray Sanchez and Wesley Bruer, "Two Illinois Men Arrested on Terror Charges," CNN, March 26, 2015.

58. Ibid.

59. Ibid.

60. Ibid.

61. Ibid.

62. "Islamic State in Illinois Planned Another Ft. Hood," *Investor's Business Daily*, March 27, 2015.

63. Sanchez and Bruer, "Two Illinois Men Arrested on Terror Charges."

64. "Terror Charges Filed against Topeka Man Accused of Fort Riley Bomb Plot for Islamic State," *Kansas City Star*, April 10, 2015.

65. Paul Farrell, "U.S. Army Recruit Accused of Plotting Jihad: 5 Fast Facts You Need to Know," Heavy.com, April 1, 2014.

66. "Terror Charges Filed against Topeka Man."

67. Ibid.

68. Ibid.

69. Ray Sanchez and Shimon Prokupecz, "New York Women Accused of ISIS-Inspired Bomb Plot," CNN, April 2, 2015.

70. Ibid.

ah Finance Watch, April 4, 2015.

NYPD Funeral," CBS News, April 3,

ISIS-Inspired Women Arrested in
," ABC News, April 2, 2015.

nen Accused."

NYPD Funeral."

R. Dowdy, "Bomb Suspects Noelle
s Devout Muslims with No Hint of
15.

Terror Plot Believed 'Armageddon'
15.

ts Noelle Velentzas and Asia Sid-

Terror Plot Believed 'Armageddon.'"

y Mcshane, "Queens Woman Sus-
Preschool," *New York Daily News,*

Prosecutors. Women Charged in Alleged Terror Plot Believed 'Armageddon.'"

87.   Badia, Parascandola, and Mcshane, "Queens Woman Suspected of Plotting."

88.   "Abu Bakr, Husband of Queens Muslima Noelle Velentzas Charged in Islamic Terror Bomb Plot Marched in the NYC Muslim Day Parades with Black Flag of Jihad," *Urban Infidel*, April 4, 2015.

89.   Ignaz Goldziher, *Introduction to Islamic Theology and Law*, trans. Andras and Ruth Hamori (Princeton University Press, 1981), 180–81.

90.   Ibn Kathir, *Tafsir Ibn Kathir* (*Abridged*) (Darussalam, 2000), vol. 2, p. 142.

91.   Dan Sewell, "Grand Jury Indicts Ohio Man Held in Capitol Terror Plot," Associated Press, January 22, 2015.

92.   Lisa Cornwall and Mitch Stacy, "Christopher Lee Cornell, Ohio Terrorism Suspect, Says He Would Have Shot Obama," Associated Press, March 6, 2015.

93.   Ibid.

94.   Pierre Thomas, Jack Date, Mike Levine, and Jack Cloherty, "Ohio Man Arrested for Alleged ISIS-Inspired Plot on US Capitol, FBI Says," ABC News, January 14, 2015.

95. Lydia Warren and Snejana Farberov, "'He Is One of the Most Peace-Loving People I Know': Father of Ohio-Born Muslim Convert, 20, 'Who Planned to Detonate Pipe Bombs in the U.S. Capitol' Insists His Son Is a 'Momma's Boy,'" Daily Mail, January 15, 2015.

96. Cornwall and Stacy, "Christopher Lee Cornell, Ohio Terrorism Suspect."

97. Sewell, "Grand Jury Indicts Ohio Man."

98. "Tariq Ramadan: 'ISIL Is Not Islamic,'" Al Jazeera, October 11, 2014.

99. "'Black Flag of Jihad Will Fly over London': Alarm over UK-Born Iraq Fighters' Threat," RT, June 16, 2014.

100. Robert Spencer, "US Convert to Islam Threatens to Kill Obama, Says ISIS Will Encompass World," Jihad Watch, June 22, 2014.

101. Michael Learmonth, "Grisly Twitter Hashtag #calamitywillbefallUS Is Battle-ground between ISIS, US in War for Minds," International Business Times, July 1, 2014.

102. "ISIS Magazine Shows Its Flag Flying over Vatican," ANSA, October 13, 2014.

103. Garth Kant, "Bachmann under 24/7 Guard after ISIS Threat," WorldNetDaily, October 20, 2014.

104. Mike Giglio and Munzer al-Awad, "Smuggler Says He Sent ISIS Fighters to Europe," BuzzFeed, November 11, 2014.

105. James O'Rourke and Akiko Matsuda, "Aron Wieder: Threat Won't Deter Me from Serving," Lohud.com, December 19, 2014.

106. Giglio and al-Awad, "Smuggler Says He Sent ISIS Fighters to Europe."

107. Jason Molinet, "ISIS Hackers Call for Homegrown 'Jihad' against U.S. Military, Posts Names and Addresses of 100 Service Members," New York Daily News, March 21, 2015.

108. Corey Charlton, "ISIS Release Latest Propaganda Video Showing Jihadists Threatening Another 9/11 and to 'Burn America,'" Daily Mail, April 12, 2015.

Chapter Three: Irresistible ISIS

1. Abdelhak Mamoun, "ISIS Has 30,000 Foreign Fighters from More Than 100 Countries," Iraqi News, May 29, 2015; Jack Moore, "5,000 Foreign Fighters Flock to Libya as ISIS Call for Jihadists, Newsweek, March 3, 2015.

2. Mamoun, "ISIS has 30,000 Foreign Fighters."

3. Lisa DeBode, "From Belgium to Syria and Back: How an Altar Boy Became an ISIL Admirer," Al Jazeera, March 5, 2015; "Popular Tunisian Rapper Alleg-edly Joins Islamic State Group," France 24, March 23, 2015; Chris Perez, "3 UK Teen Girls Arrive at ISIS Training Camp," New York Post, March 9, 2015; "Nine British Medics Feared to Have Crossed into Syria," BBC, March 22,

2015; Pierre Thomas, Mike Levine, and Jack Cloherty, "Tairod Nathan Webster Pugh: Former US Air Force Mechanic Charged with Trying to Join ISIS in Syria," ABC News, March 17, 2015; Ray Sanchez and Wesley Bruer, "Two Illinois Men Arrested on Terror Charges," CNN, March 26, 2015.

4. Erin Banco, "Why Do People Join ISIS? The Psychology of a Terrorist," International Business Times, September 5, 2014.

5. "Le Jihad: Nearly Half of European Jihadis in ISIL Are French Nationals," Sputnik News, April 9, 2015.

6. Jamie Crawford and Laura Koran, "U.S. Officials: Foreigners Flock to Fight for ISIS," CNN, February 11, 2015.

7. Robert Verkaik, "'Three Runaway Teen 'Jihadi Brides' Feared to Be Heading into the Clutches of British Women Leading ISIS Religious Police Who Dole Out Savage Beatings," Daily Mail, February 25, 2015; Madeline Grant and Damien Sharkov, "'Twice as Many' British Muslims Fighting for ISIS Than in UK Armed Forces," Newsweek, August 20, 2014.

8. Robert Mendick, Robert Verkaik, and Tim Ross, "Muslim MP: 2,000 Britons Fighting for Islamic State," Telegraph, November 23, 2014.

9. Sara Malm and Ted Thornhill, "Police Raise Security Levels as Rapper Dubbed 'the Goebbels of ISIS' Issues Sniper Video Declaring 'We Want British Blood,'" Daily Mail, April 19, 2015.

10. Daniel Piotrowski, "EXCLUSIVE: 'We're Thirsty for Your Blood': Playboy Jihadi's Widow Poses with Her Gun-Toting 'Clique' of Female Fanatics in Front of Flash BMW and Boasts of 'Five-Star Jihad' Lifestyle in Syria," Daily Mail, March 17, 2015.

11. Michael Zennie, "The American Computer Wiz Running Brutally Effective ISIS Social Media Campaign: College-Educated Son of Top Boston Doctor Is on FBI Most Wanted List," Daily Mail, September 4, 2014.

12. Jethro Mullen, "What Is ISIS' Appeal for Young People?," CNN, February 25, 2015.

13. Sarah Martin, "Internet Propaganda War Key for Islamic State," Australian, March 26, 2015.

14. "Terrorists 'Praise Allah' for Twitter," Worthy News, June 12, 2014.

15. Banco, "Why Do People Join ISIS?"

16. Mullen, "What Is ISIS' Appeal for Young People?"

17. Kevin Sullivan, "Three American Teens, Recruited Online, Are Caught Trying to Join the Islamic State," Washington Post, December 8, 2014.

18. "'ISIS Good at Propaganda & Marketing and Youngsters Buy into It,'" RT, April 15, 2015.

19. Christoph Reuter, Raniah Salloum and Samiha Shafy, "Digital Jihad: Inside Islamic State's Savvy PR War," *Spiegel*, October 8, 2014.
20. Ibid.
21. Maya Gebeily, "Shit ISIS Says," *Matter*, February 25, 2015.
22. Ibid.
23. Lachlan Markay, "Islamic State Hacks CENTCOM Twitter Feed as Obama Talks Cybersecurity," Washington Free Beacon, January 12, 2015.
24. Oliver Darcy, "'Islamic State Hacking Division' Posts Kill List with Purported Addresses of U.S. Military Members," TheBlaze, March 21, 2015.
25. Michael S. Schmidt and Helene Cooper, "ISIS Urges Sympathizers to Kill U.S. Service Members It Identifies on Website," *New York Times*, March 21, 2015.
26. Bill Briggs, "Military Spouses Hacked, Threatened by Alleged ISIS Sympathizer," NBC News, February 10, 2015.
27. Banco, "Why Do People Join ISIS?"
28. Maha Yahya, "The Ultimate Fatal Attraction: 5 Reasons People Join ISIS," *National Interest*, November 7, 2014.
29. Arie W. Kruglanski, "Joining Islamic State Is about 'Sex and Aggression,' Not Religion," Reuters, October 16, 2014.
30. Banco, "Why Do People Join ISIS?"
31. Holly Yan, "How Is ISIS Luring Westerners?," CNN, March 23, 2015.
32. Ibid.
33. Ibid.
34. Kruglanski, "Joining Islamic State Is about 'Sex and Aggression.'"
35. Gebeily, "Shit ISIS Says."
36. Ibid.
37. Ibid.
38. Graeme Wood, "What ISIS Really Wants," *Atlantic*, March 2015.
39. Ibid.
40. "Founder of Hizb Al-Tahrir in Chicago: The Caliphate Is Coming, and Britain and America Can Go to Hell," Middle East Media Research Institute, June 21, 2013.
41. Sullivan, "Three American Teens."
42. Ibid.
43. Ibid.
44. Lee Keath and Hamza Hendawi, "How Islamic Is Islamic State Group? Not Very, Experts Say," Associated Press, March 2, 2015.
45. Sullivan, "Three American Teens."
46. Ibid.

47. Michael Zennie, "Somali-American Who Died Fighting for ISIS Cleaned Planes for Delta Airlines at Minneapolis Airport before He Joined Terrorist Group," *Daily Mail*, September 3, 2014.

48. Mukhtar Ibrahim, "Jihad in Syria Lures Somalis from Minnesota," MPR News, June 12, 2014.

49. Meg Wagner, "Minnesota Dad-of-Nine Abdirahmaan Muhumed Killed Fighting for ISIS in Syria: Report," *New York Daily News*, August 28, 2014.

50. Ibrahim, "Jihad in Syria Lures."

51. Maury Glover, "'Challenges, Lack of Opportunity' Drove Suspected ISIS Fighter," KMSP, August 28, 2014.

52. Kruglanski, "Joining Islamic State Is about 'Sex and Aggression'"; Luke Salked, "UK Is Afraid I Will Come Back with the Skills I've Gained: Chilling Tweet of British Jihadist Fighting in Syria," *Daily Mail*, July 2, 2014.

53. Kruglanski, "Joining Islamic State Is about 'Sex and Aggression'"; Rob Williams, "British 'Primark Jihadist' from Portsmouth Is Killed while Fighting with Isis in Syria," *Independent*, August 11, 2014.

54. Michael S. Schmidt, "Canadian Killed in Syria Lives On as Pitchman for Jihadis," *New York Times*, July 15, 2014.

55. Ibid.

56. Ibid.

57. Banco, "Why Do People Join ISIS?"

58. Schmidt, "Canadian Killed in Syria."

59. Sullivan, "Three American Teens."

60. Mullen, "What Is ISIS' Appeal for Young People?"

61. Schmidt, "Canadian Killed in Syria."

62. Chris Greenwood, "Revealed: Benefits Mother-of-Two from Kent Once in All-Girl Rock Band Who Is Now Jihadi in Syria—and Wants to 'Behead Christians with a Blunt Knife,'" *Daily Mail*, August 31, 2014.

63. "Craigieburn ISIS Recruit Jake Bilardi Co-Founder of Children's Charity Soccer for Hope," Hume Leader, March 12, 2015.

64. Heather Saul, "Australian 'Isis Suicide Bomber' Jake Bilardi Wrote 4,300 Word Manifesto Vowing to Launch 'String of Bombing Attacks across Melbourne,'" *Independent*, March 12, 2015.

65. Jake Bilardi, "From Melbourne to Ramadi: My Journey," originally published at Bilardi's blog *From the Eyes of a Muhajir*, deleted from there and republished at slackbastard, March 12, 2015, http://slackbastard.anarchobase.com/?p=37774.

66. "Terror Teen: 'We'll Make 9/11 Look like Child's Play,'" News.com.au, March 10, 2015.

67.   Hamish MacDonald, Dan Good, Rym Momtaz, and Meghan Keneally, "Gunman and Two Others Dead in Sydney Hostage Crisis," ABC, December 15, 2014.

68.   Matt Brown, "Islamic State: Australian Teenager Jake Bilardi Believed to Be Involved in Suicide Bombing in Iraq," ABC.net.au, March 11, 2015.

69.   Jenny Deam, "Colorado Woman's Quest for Jihad Baffles Neighbors," *Los Angeles Times*, July 25, 2014.

70.   Ibid.

71.   Ibid.

72.   P. Solomon Banda and Dan Elliott, "Shock, Sadness after Teen's Arrest in Terror Case," Associated Press, July 3, 2014.

73.   "Woman Calls Self 'Servant of Allah,' Faces Sentencing for ISIS Plan," CNN, January 23, 2015.

74.   Deam, "Colorado Woman's Quest for Jihad."

75.   Ibid.

76.   Ibid.; "Coloradan in Terror Investigation Agrees to Change Plea to Guilty," CBS4Denver, August 11, 2014.

77.   "Woman Calls Self 'Servant of Allah.'"

78.   Deam, "Colorado Woman's Quest for Jihad."

79.   "Judge Hands Down 4 Year Sentence to 'Jihad Shannon,'" CBSDenver, January 23, 2015. "Woman Calls Self 'Servant of Allah.'"

80.   Deam, "Colorado Woman's Quest for Jihad."

81.   Michael Kosnar and Daniel Arkin, "Tairod Nathan Webster Pugh, U.S. Air Force Veteran, Charged with Trying to Join ISIS," NBC News, March 17, 2015.

82.   Pierre Thomas, Mike Levine, and Jack Cloherty, "Tairod Nathan Webster Pugh: Former US Air Force Mechanic Charged with Trying to Join ISIS in Syria," ABC News, March 17, 2015.

83.   Ibid.

84.   Sanchez and Bruer, "Two Illinois Men Arrested."

85.   "Islamic State in Illinois Planned Another Ft. Hood," Investor's Business Daily, March 27, 2015.

86.   Ibid.

87.   "Bangalore Police Arrest Pro-Jihad Twitter Handle User Mehdi Biswas, Book Him under Unlawful Activities Act," Indian Express, December 13, 2014.

88.   Subrata Nagchowdhury, "He Knew the Quran by Heart, Often Gave Us Lessons: Parents," Indian Express, December 14, 2014.

89.   Barney Guiton and Damien Sharkov, "Islamic State Supporters Hand Out Leaflets in Central London Promising 'Dawn of a New Era,'" *Newsweek*, August 12, 2014.

90. Pamela Brown and Wesley Bruer, "FBI Official: ISIS Is Recruiting U.S. Teens," CNN, February 4, 2015.

91. Andrew Kirell, "State Dept Spokeswoman Marie Harf: We Can't Beat ISIS Just by Killing Them," Mediaite, February 17, 2015.

92. Samantha Rollins, "France Says the Name ISIS Offensive, Will Call It 'Daesh' Instead," *Week*, September 17, 2014.

93. Nima Elbagir, Paul Cruickshank, and Mohammed Tawfiq, "Boko Haram Purportedly Pledges Allegiance to ISIS," CNN, March 9, 2015.

94. Charlie Spiering, "Obama: Climate Change Fueled Rise of Boko Haram, War in Syria," Breitbart, May 20, 2015.

95. Patrick Goodenough, "Kerry: Extremism Not Linked to Islam; Factors Include Deprivation, Climate Change," CNS News, October 17, 2014; John Kerry, "Remarks at a Reception in Honor of Eid al-Adha," U.S. Department of State, October 16, 2014.

96. Patrick Goodenough, "Kerry: Potential Terror Recruits Need 'More Economic Opportunities,'" CNS News, September 30, 2013.

97. Pamela Geller, "Shocking Video: Muslim Students at Brooklyn College Shout Support for ISIS," PamelaGeller.com, April 22, 2015.

98. Ibid.

99. Ibid.

100. Ibid.

101. Ibid.

102. Ibid.

103. Ibid.

104. "Exploding Misconceptions," *Economist*, December 16, 2010.

105. Carlos Lozada, "Does Poverty Cause Terrorism," National Bureau of Economic Research, n.d.

106. Abu Bakr al-Husayni al-Qurashi al-Baghdadi, "A Message to the Mujahidin and the Muslim Ummah in the Month of Ramadan," Al-Hayat Media Center, n.d.

Chapter Four: How They Did It—and Who's Trying to Stop Them

1.   "How Can Isis Afford Its Own Currency?," *Guardian*, November 16, 2014.

2.   Agence France Presse, "Iraq Lost 2,300 Humvees in Mosul: PM," *Daily Star* (Lebanon), May 31, 2015.

3.   Associated Press, "US Defense Secretary Says Fall of Ramadi Shows Iraqi Forces Lack Will to Fight ISIS," *Guardian*, May 24, 2015.

4.   Dexter Filkins, "The Real Problem in Iraq," *New Yorker*, May 19, 2015.

5.   Janine di Giovanni, Leah McGrath Goodman, and Damien Sharkov, "How Does ISIS Fund Its Reign of Terror?," *Newsweek*, November 6, 2014.

6.   Ibid.

7.   Karen Leigh, "ISIS Makes Up to $3 Million a Day Selling Oil, Analysts Say," Syria Deeply, July 28, 2014.

8.   David E. Sanger and Julie Hirschfeld Davis, "Turkey Fails to Cut Islamic State Oil Revenue Despite US Pressure," *Sydney Morning Herald*, September 14, 2014.

9.   Ibid.

10. Ibid.

11. "Pentagon: Oil Is No Longer ISIS' Main Source of Income," Al Arabiya, February 5, 2015.

12. Di Giovanni, Goodman, and Sharkov, "How Does ISIS Fund Its Reign of Terror?"

13. Ibid.

14. Ibid.

15. Bruce Golding, "Jihadi Barbarians Demanded $100M Ransom for Foley's Life," *New York Post*, August 20, 2014.

16. Jethro Mullen and Junko Ogura, "ISIS Apparently Demands Release of Terrorist to Spare Japanese Hostage," CNN, January 26, 2015.

17. Jon Gambrell and Mari Yamaguchi, "Japan Weighs Ransom in Islamic State Threat to Kill Hostages," Associated Press, January 20, 2015.

18. Di Giovanni, Goodman, and Sharkov, "How Does ISIS Fund Its Reign of Terror?"

19. Evan Bleier, "Christian Held Hostage for Five Months by ISIS Tells How He Was Made to Call His Parents while Being Electrocuted so They Would Hear the Screams and Pay a Ransom," *Daily Mail*, March 21, 2015.

20. Di Giovanni, Goodman, and Sharkov, "How Does ISIS Fund Its Reign of Terror?"

21. Ahmed ibn Naqib al-Misri, *Reliance of the Traveller ('Umdat al-Salik): A Classic Manual of Islamic Sacred Law*, trans. Nuh Ha Mim Keller (Amana Publications, 1999), o9.14.

22. Abu'l Hasan al-Mawardi, *al-Ahkam as-Sultaniyyah (The Laws of Islamic Governance)* (Ta-Ha Publishers, 1996), 192.

23. "Obama: ISIS 'Unintended Consequence' of Invading Iraq, 'Which Is Why We Should Aim Before We Shoot,'" Real Clear Politics, March 17, 2015.

24. "Transcript: President Obama Iraq speech," BBC, December 15, 2011.

25. Riyadh Mohammed, "ISIS Burns 8000 Rare Books and Manuscripts in Mosul," Fiscal Times, February 23, 2015.

26. Julian Robinson, "ISIS Thugs Take a Hammer to Civilisation: Priceless 3,000-Year-Old Artworks Smashed to Pieces in Minutes as Militants Destroy Mosul Museum," *Daily Mail*, February 26, 2015.

27. "Ancient Artefacts Destroyed in Iraq," News.com.au, February 27, 2015.

28. Jean Marc Mojon, "Widespread Outrage after IS Bulldozes Ancient Iraq City," Agence France Presse, March 6, 2015; Ahmed Rasheed and Isabel Coles, "Islamic State Militants Raze Iraq's Ancient Hatra City: Government," Reuters, March 7, 2015; Gianluca Mezzofiore, "Iraq: Isis Blows Up 10th Century Assyrian Catholic Monastery near Mosul," International Business Times, March 10, 2015.

29. Perry Chiaramonte, "ISIS Reportedly Selling Christian Artifacts, Turning Churches into Torture Chambers," Fox News, December 23, 2014.

30. John Hall, "Tearing Down the Graves: Now ISIS Turn Their Savagery on the Dead by Pulling Down Monuments and Smashing Tombs in Syrian Cemetery," Daily Mail, March 30, 2015.

31. Sinan Salaheddin and Sameer N. Yacoub, "Iraqi Libraries Ransacked by Islamic State Group in Mosul," Associated Press, January 31, 2015.

32. "Ancient Artefacts Destroyed in Iraq," News.com.au, February 27, 2015.

33. Abu Isa Muhammad at-Tirmidhi, *Jami' at-Tirmidhi*, translator anonymous, book 10, hadith 85, no.1049, Sunnah.com; "Islamic State (ISIS) Destroys Christian Graves in Mosul," Middle East Media Research Institute, April 16, 2015.

34. "Islamic State Seizes Syria's Ancient Palmyra," BBC News, May 21, 2015.

35. Kareem Shaheen, "Syria: Isis Releases Footage of Palmyra Ruins Intact and 'Will Not Destroy Them,'" *Guardian*, May 27, 2015.

36. Flora Drury, "ISIS Fanatics Summon Crowd to Ancient Roman Amphitheatre of Palmyra to Execute 20 Men," *Daily Mail*, May 27, 2015.

37. "Kuwaiti Preacher, ISIS Call for Demolition of Egypt's Sphinx, Pyramids," RT, March 9, 2015.

38. Raymond Ibrahim, "Italy: Muslims Destroy and Urinate on Virgin Mary Statue," Raymond Ibrahim: Islam Translated, January 17, 2015.

39. Robert Spencer, "Italy: Screaming Phrases from the Qur'an, a 67-Year-Old Muslim Devastates a Church in Trento," Jihad Watch, January 6, 2015.

40. Robinson, "ISIS Thugs Take a Hammer to Civilisation."

41. "Kuwaiti preacher, ISIS Call for Demolition."

42. Robert D. Kaplan, *Balkan Ghosts: A Journey Through History* (Picador, 2014), xiv.

43. This idea is based on a saying attributed to Muhammad: "Do not leave an image without defacing it or a high grave without leveling it" (Sahih Muslim 969).
44. "10 Historical Sites Destroyed by ISIS and Why They Matter," CBC, March 13, 2015.
45. Ibid.
46. Ibid.
47. Ibid.
48. Ibid.
49. Ibid.
50. Ibid.
51. Ibid.
52. Joseph Mahmoud, "As Jihadists Destroy Mosul's Church of the Immaculate Virgin, Chaldeans Get Ready for Unity Synod in Baghdad," Asia News, February 6, 2015.
53. "ISIS Blows up Catholic church in Mosul," *Rudaw*, December 26, 2014.
54. "ISIS Destroys Assyrian Churches, Hostages Still Being Held," AINA, March 16, 2015; "ISIL Destroys Historical Church in Mosul," World Bulletin, March 10, 2015.
55. "ISIS Destroys Armenian Genocide Memorial Church in Der Zor," Armenian Weekly, September 21, 2014.
56. "ISIS Blow up Tikrit's Green Church," ANSA, September 25, 2014
57. John Hall, "Another Blow to Christianity and Civilisation: ISIS Destroy 4th Century Mar Benham Monastery in Iraq," *Daily Mail*, March 19, 2015.
58. ISIS Destroys Assyrian Churches, Hostages Still Being Held," AINA, March 16, 2015.
59. "10 Historical Sites Destroyed by ISIS."
60. Yasmine Hafiz, "ISIS Destroys Jonah's Tomb in Mosul, Iraq, as Militant Violence Continues," Huffington Post, July 25, 2014.
61. "Islamic State Destroys Ancient Mosul Mosque, the Third in a Week," Associated Press, July 27, 2014.
62. "Ancient Artefacts Destroyed in Iraq," News.com.au, February 27, 2015.
63. "10 Historical Sites Destroyed by ISIS"; "ISIS Destroys Shrines, Shiite Mosques in Iraq," Agence France Presse, July 5, 2014.
64. "ISIS Militants Destroy Shiite Mosque, Execute Muezzin," Agence France-Presse, August 15, 2014; "ISIS Destroys Shrines, Shiite Mosques in Iraq," Agence France Presse, July 5, 2014.
65. "ISIL Destroys Two Shia Religious Sites in Iraqi City of Mosul," Press TV, June 25, 2014.

66. Praveen Swami, "ISIS Insurgents Wage War on History," *Hindu*, June 29, 2014.

67. Abdelhak Mamoun, "Urgent: ISIS Destroys Historical Al-Arbain Mosque in Tikrit," Iraqi News, September 25, 2014.

68. Faraj Obaji, "YPG Official: Airstrikes Not Enough to Protect Kobani," Al-Monitor, October 14, 2014; "YPG Retakes the Entire City of Ayn al- Arab 'Kobani' after 112 Days of Clashes with IS Militants," Syrian Observatory for Human Rights, January 26, 2015.

69. Patrick Cockburn, "Isis in Kobani: US Resupplies Kurdish Fighters by Plane— then Turkey Allows Reinforcements through Its Border," *Independent*, October 20, 2014.

70. Elad Benari, "ISIS: Fighting 'Infidels' Takes Precedence over Fighting Israel," Arutz Sheva, July 8, 2014.

71. Rita Katz, "ISIS in Ramadi: The Terrifying Truth behind Islamic State's Latest Capture," International Business Times, May 19, 2015.

72. "Iraqi Forces Battle Islamic State Jihadists in Ramadi, Kirkuk," Agence France Presse, November 27, 2014.

73. "Baghdad Halts Ramadi Refugee Flow after Capture by IS," BBC News, May 23, 2015; Tim Lister, "ISIS's Victory in Ramadi: Five Lessons," CNN, May 22, 2015.

74. Jack Moore, "'4,000-Strong' Christian Militia Formed to Fight ISIS in Northern Iraq," *Newsweek*, February 4, 2015.

75. Susan Berry, "Exiled Archbishop of Mosul: 'I Have Lost My Diocese to Islam; You in the West Will also Become Victims of Muslims,'" Breitbart, August 18, 2014.

76. Moore, "'4,000-Strong' Christian Militia."

77. Samuel Smith, "Fla. Army Veteran Recruits US Soldiers to Fight ISIS by Joining 'Veterans Against ISIS' Militia," *Christian Post*, March 3, 2015.

78. Ibid.

Chapter Five: Inside the Islamic State

1. "12 Rules for Living Under ISIS: Follow or Be Killed," Clarion Project, January 28, 2015.

2. Ibid.

3. Ghazi Balkiz and Alexander Smith, "What Life Is like Inside ISIS' Capital City of Raqqa, Syria," NBC News, September 25, 2014.

4. "12 Rules for Living Under ISIS."

5. Ibid.

6. Ibid.

7.   Ibid.

8.   Ibid.

9.   Adam Taylor, "The Rules in ISIS' New State: Amputations for Stealing and Women to Stay Indoors," *Washington Post*, June 12, 2014.

10.   Ibid.

11.   Ibid.

12.   Ibid.

13.   Ibid.

14.   Ibid.

15.   "IS Militants Punish Citizens with 80 Lashes if Seen Wearing Football Team Jerseys," *Free Press Journal*, April 25, 2015.

16.   Damien Gayle, "All-Female Islamic State Police Squad Tortured New Mother with Spiked Clamp Device Called a 'Biter' after She Was Caught Breastfeeding in Public," *Daily Mail*, December 30, 2014.

17.   Priya Joshi, "Isis: Man Accused of 'Witchcraft' Decapitated in Town Square," International Business Times, April 8, 2015.

18.   Jay Akbar and Simon Tomlinson, "ISIS Burn Woman Alive for Refusing to Take Part in 'Extreme Sex Act' Reveals UN Official, as the Islamist Fighters' Sadism Becomes Even More Depraved," *Daily Mail*, May 26, 2015.

19.   Benjamin Hall, "'You Want to Kill': ISIS Deserter Recounts Training, Torture and Terror," Fox News, November 6, 2014.

20.   Matthew Fisher, "Convert to Islam or Face the Sword, Iraqi Christians Told by Sunni Extremists," Postmedia News, June 22, 2014.

21.   Steph Cockcroft, "How to Live as a Christian in Raqqa: ISIS Release Seven Rules for Followers of Rival Faith, Including Praying out of Earshot of Muslims and Never Mocking Islam," *Daily Mail*, December 23, 2014.

22.   Ibid.

23.   "Syria Crisis: ISIS Imposes Rules on Christians in Raqqa," BBC, February 27, 2014.

24.   Cockcroft, "How to Live as a Christian in Raqqa."

25.   Ibid.

26.   Ibid.

27.   Ibid.

28.   Ibid.

29.   Cockcroft, "How to Live as a Christian in Raqqa"; "Syria Crisis: ISIS Imposes Rules."

30.   "Syria Crisis: ISIS Imposes Rules."

31.   *'Umdat al-Salik*, o11.5(6).

32. "Islamic State Warns Those Who Refuse Islam Will Die like Ethiopians in Libya Video," *Morning Star News*, April 24, 2015.

33. Patrick Cockburn, "Life under Isis: The Everyday Reality of Living in the Islamic 'Caliphate' with Its 7th Century Laws, Very Modern Methods and Merciless Violence," *Independent*, March 15, 2015.

34. Balkiz and Smith, "What Life Is like inside ISIS' Capital."

35. Ben Hubbard, "Wanted in Saudi Arabia: Executioners," *New York Times*, May 18, 2015.

36. Molly Crabapple, "Scenes from Daily Life Inside ISIS-Controlled Mosul," *Vanity Fair*, February 5, 2015.

37. Balkiz and Smith, "What Life Is like inside ISIS' Capital."

38. Alexander Smith, "Shopkeepers Selling Cigarettes in Mosul under ISIS Face 80 Lashes," NBC News, November 10, 2014.

39. Gianluca Mezzofiore, "Syria: Isis Chief Executioner Found Beheaded with Cigarette in His Mouth," International Business Times, January 6, 2015.

40. Heather Saul, "Life under Isis in Raqqa: The City Where Smoking a Cigarette Could See You Publicly Flogged, Imprisoned and Even Decapitated," *Independent*, February 13, 2015.

41. Ibid.

42. Maya Gebeily, "Shit ISIS Says," *Matter*, February 25, 2015.

43. John Hall, "'I Saw ISIS Playing with a Severed Head as if It Was a Football. They Killed Children in front of Their Parents': Refugees in Yarmouk Reveal Atrocities They Have Seen since Islamic State Took over the Camp," *Daily Mail*, April 8, 2015.

44. Heather Saul, "Isis Fighters 'Crucify' 17-Year-Old Boy in Syria," *Independent*, October 17, 2014.

45. Adam Withnall, "Isis Throws 'Gay' Men Off Tower, Stones Woman Accused of Adultery and Crucifies 17 Young Men in 'Retaliatory' Wave of Executions," *Independent*, January 18, 2015.

46. Jay Akbar, "ISIS Publicly Executes Two 'Spies' and Crucifies Another as Armed Insurgents and Young Boys Watch," *Daily Mail*, February 14, 2015.

47. "ISIS Graphic Photos Shows 2 Most Horrific Executions," AlAlam, April 9, 2015.

48. John Hall, "Slaughtered for Their Entertainment: Crowds Gather to Watch the Barbaric Murder of Jordanian Pilot on Specially Erected Giant Screens on the Streets of Raqqa … and Cheer When the Airman Goes up in Flames," *Daily Mail*, February 4, 2015.

49. Christopher Reuter, "The Terror Strategist: Secret Files Reveal the Structure of Islamic State," *Spiegel*, April 18, 2015.

50. Balkiz and Smith, "What Life Is like inside ISIS' Capital."

51. "Revealed: The Islamic State 'Cabinet', from Finance Minister to Suicide Bomb Deployer," *Telegraph*, July 9, 2014.

52. Julian E. Barnes, "Several Islamic State Leaders Have Been Killed in Iraq, U.S. Says," *Wall Street Journal*, December 18, 2014.

53. Charles Lister, "Islamic State Senior Leadership: Who's Who," Brookings Institution, October 20, 2014.

54. Ibid.

55. Ibid.

56. Ibid.

57. "Revealed: The Islamic State 'Cabinet.'"

58. Lister, "Islamic State Senior Leadership."

59. Ibid.

60. Ibid.

61. Ibid.

62. "Revealed: The Islamic State 'Cabinet.'"

63. Ibid.

64. Ibid.

65. Lister, "Islamic State Senior Leadership."

66. Ibid.

67. Ibid.

68. Ibid.

69. Ibid.

70. Ibid.

71. "Revealed: The Islamic State 'Cabinet.'"

72. Lister, "Islamic State Senior Leadership."

73. Ibid.

74. Ibid.

75. Ibid.

76. "Revealed: The Islamic State 'Cabinet.'"

77. Lister, "Islamic State Senior Leadership."

78. Ibid.

79. Ibid.

80. Sophie Alexander, "Jihadi Doctor Stands with Severed Head in Her Hand as Kids Look on in Horror," *Daily Star*, September 8, 2014.

81. Marga Zambrana, Hazar Aydemir, and Emma Graham-Harrison, "Nine British Medics Enter Isis Stronghold to Work in Hospitals," *Guardian*, March 21, 2015.

82. John Hall and Robert Verkaik, "ISIS Execute Ten Doctors after They Refused to Treat Wounded Members of the Terror Group in Iraq," *Daily Mail*, April 10, 2015.

83. "Islamic State Health Service? ISIS Launch British-Inspired NHS," RT, April 24, 2015.

84. "Perth Doctor Joins ISIS Medical Team in 'Jihad for Islam' against the West," News.com.au, April 25, 2015.

85. Sam Prince, "Photo: First 'Official' Birth Certificate for ISIS," Heavy, April 26, 2015.

86. "'Cubs of the Caliphate'—ISIS Recruits 400 Children since January," *Jerusalem Post*, March 24, 2015.

87. Zeina Karam, "Some Signs of Tension Emerge among Islamic State Militants," Associated Press, February 19, 2015.

88. Jamie Dettmer, "ISIS Barbarians Face Their Own Internal Reign of Terror," Daily Beast, February 6, 2015.

89. Karam, "Some Signs of Tension Emerge."

90. Dettmer, "ISIS Barbarians Face Their."

91. Ibid.

92. "Islamic State 'Has Executed 116 Foreign Fighters Who Were Members of Group in Past Six Months after They Tried to Return Home,'" *Daily Mail*, December 29, 2014.

93. "ISIS Kills Own Fighters Who Tried to Flee," Al Arabiya, March 10, 2015.

94. "Islamic State 'Has Executed 116 Foreign Fighters.'"

95. Ruth Sherlock, "How a Talented Footballer Became World's Most Wanted Man, Abu Bakr al-Baghdadi," *Telegraph*, November 11, 2014.

96. Janine di Giovanni, "Who Is ISIS Leader Abu Bakr al-Baghdadi?," *Newsweek*, December 8, 2014.

97. Ibid.

98. Sherlock, "How a Talented Footballer."

99. Ibid.

100. Ibid.

101. Di Giovanni, "Who Is ISIS Leader Abu Bakr al-Baghdadi?"

102. Sherlock, "How a Talented Footballer."

103. Mariam Karouny, "Leader of Iraq Insurgents Is Jihad's Rising Leader," Reuters, June 11, 2014.

104. Ibid.

105. Vasudevan Sridharan, "Iraqi Isis Leader Abu Bakr al-Baghdadi 'Severely Injured and Flees to Syria,'" International Business Times, July 5, 2014.

106. Abdelhak Mamoun, "Urgent: ISIS Leader Abu Bakr al-Baghdadi Seriously Injured by Air Strike According to Al Arabiya," Iraqi News, November 8, 2014.

107. Kieran Corcoran, "ISIS Terror Chief 'Believed Dead': Iraqi Military Confirm Warlord WAS Injured in US-Led Airstrike as Speculation Grows Feared Jihadist Perished in Attack," *Daily Mail*, November 9, 2014.

108. Ian Black, "Islamic State Leader Baghdadi Reportedly Resurfaces after Claims US Strike Killed Him," *Guardian*, November 13, 2014.

109. Martin Chulov and Kareem Shaheen, "Isis Leader Abu Bakr al-Baghdadi 'Seriously Wounded in Air Strike,'" *Guardian*, April 21, 2015.

110. Pamela Engel and Michael B. Kelley, "Report: ISIS leader Abu Bakr al-Baghdadi Was 'Seriously Wounded' in a March Airstrike—Pentagon Denies," Reuters, April 21, 2015.

111. Jack Moore, "ISIS Replace Injured Leader Baghdadi with Former Physics Teacher," *Newsweek*, April 22, 2015.

112. Pamela Engel, "ISIS Leader Baghdadi Is Reportedly 'Unable to Move' after a Spinal Injury," Business Insider, April 27, 2015.

113. "ISIS Chief Abu Bakr al-Baghdadi Is Dead Says Radio Iran," IndiaToday, April 27, 2015.

114. Moore, "ISIS Replace Injured Leader."

115. Ibid.

116. Barbara Starr, Nick Paton Walsh, and Hamdi Alkhshali, "ISIS' No. 2 Leader al-Afri Killed in Airstrike, Iraq Says," CNN News, May 14, 2015.

117. Nancy A. Youssef, "Iraq's B.S. about Killing ISIS Bosses," Daily Beast, May 13, 2015.

118. Matt Watts, "Ringo Starr Takes on IS over Beatles Nickname: 'It's Bulls**t …We Stood for Peace and Love," *London Evening Standard*, September 4, 2014.

119. Ibid.

120. Souad Mekhennet and Adam Goldman, "'Jihadi John': Islamic State Killer Is Identified as Londoner Mohammed Emwazi," *Washington Post*, February 26, 2015; "'Jihadi John' Named as Mohammed Emwazi from London," BBC, February 26, 2015.

121. "'Jihadi John' Named as Mohammed Emwazi from London."

122. Ibid.

123. Corinne Lestch, "Tech-Savvy Terrorist from Boston Believed to Be Running ISIS' Social Media Arm," *New York Daily News*, September 4, 2014.

124. "FBI offers $50,000 Reward for Terrorism Suspect Ahmad Abousamra, Alleged Co-Conspirator with Tarek Mehanna," *Boston Globe*, October 3, 2012.

125. "Man Accused in Boston Terror Plot Is Son of Former Muslim American Society Leader: Father Moves Out of Town Weeks after Son Questioned by the FBI," Americans for Peace and Tolerance, October 23, 2009.

126. Ibid.

127. Michael Zennie, "The American Computer Wiz Running Brutally Effective ISIS Social Media Campaign: College-Educated Son of Top Boston Doctor Is on FBI Most Wanted List," *Daily Mail*, September 4, 2014; "FBI Offers $50,000 Reward."

128. "Man Accused in Boston Terror Plot."

129. Smiley Jr. and Sweet, "FBI Adds Stoughton High Grad."

130. Colneth Smiley Jr. and Laurel J. Sweet, "FBI Adds Stoughton High Grad to Most Wanted Terrorists List," *Boston Herald*, December 18, 2013.

131. Shelley Murphy and Milton J. Valencia, "Details Emerge on Plot Suspects," *Boston Globe*, October 23, 2009; "Dr. Abdul Abou-Samra Receives Prestigious National Institutes of Health Training Grant—Award Will Prepare Future Leaders of Endocrine Research," Wayne State University, June 28, 2010, http://research.wayne.edu/rwnews/article.php?id=656; "Man Accused in Boston Terror Plot Is Son."

132. Noreen S. Ahmed-Ullah, Sam Roe and Laurie Cohen, "A Rare Look at Secretive Brotherhood in America, *Chicago Tribune*, September 19, 2004.

133. Mohamed Akram, "An Explanatory Memorandum on the General Strategic Goal for the Group in North America," May 22, 1991, Government Exhibit 003-0085, U.S. vs. HLF, et al. P. 7 (21).

134. Noah Rothman, "GOP'er Louie Gohmert and FBI's Robert Mueller Explode Over Investigation into Boston Bombers," Mediaite, June 13, 2013.

135. Joe Dwinell, "Top ISIS Deputy, of Stoughton, Reportedly Killed in Iraq," *Boston Herald*, June 2, 2015.

136. Robert Verkaik, "'Three Runaway Teen 'Jihadi Brides' Feared to Be Heading into the Clutches of British Women Leading ISIS Religious Police Who Dole out Savage Beatings," *Daily Mail*, February 25, 2015; Harriet Sherwood et al., "Schoolgirl Jihadis: The Female Islamists Leaving Home to Join Isis Fighters," *Guardian*, September 29, 2014.

137. Sherwood et al., "Schoolgirl Jihadis."

138. Ibid.

139. Ibid.

140. Ibid.

141. Jake Wallis Simons and Chris Greenwood, "Exclusive: Father Who Blamed Police for Not Stopping His Daughter Joining ISIS Attended 2012 Rally Led

by Hate Preacher Anjem Choudary and Attended by Lee Rigby Killer," *Daily Mail*, March 26, 2015.

142. Verkaik, "'Three Runaway Teen 'Jihadi Brides.'"
143. Ibid.
144. Ibid.
145. Sherwood et al., "Schoolgirl Jihadis."
146. Ashley Fantz and Atika Shubert, "From Scottish Teen to ISIS Bride and Recruiter: The Aqsa Mahmood Story," CNN, February 24, 2015.
147. Sherwood et al., "Schoolgirl Jihadis."
148. Fantz and Schubert, "From Scottish Teen to ISIS Bride"; Sherwood et al., "Schoolgirl Jihadis."
149. Russell Myers, "British Female Jihadis Running ISIS 'Brothels' Allowing Killers to Rape Kidnapped Yazidi Women," *Mirror*, September 10, 2014.
150. Gianluca Mezzofiore, "Iraq: Yazidi Girls 'Raped in Public' and Sold to Isis Fighters before Release," International Business Times, April 9, 2015.
151. Richard Engel and James Novogrod, "ISIS Terror: Yazidi Woman Recalls Horrors of Slave Auction," NBC News, February 13, 2015.
152. Zachary Davies Boren, "Yazidi Sex Slave Escapes Isis to Tell Her Story: 'They Took Us away like Cattle,'" *Independent*, December 22, 2014.
153. Emily Feldman, "Slave to Terror," Mashable, September 16, 2014.
154. Ibid.
155. Richard Engel and James Novogrod, "ISIS Terror: Yazidi Woman Recalls Horrors of Slave Auction," NBC News, February 13, 2015.
156. Ibid.
157. Charlotte Alter, "Girls Who Escaped ISIS Describe Systematic Rape," *Time*, April 16, 2015.
158. "ISIS 'Executes 100 Deserters' in Syria's Raqqa," Al Arabiya, December 20, 2014.
159. Ibid.
160. "Ex-U.S. Detainees now ISIS Leaders," CBS News, n.d.
161. Ibid.
162. Ibid.
163. Ibid.
164. Ibid.
165. Ibid.
166. Ibid.
167. Ibid.
168. Ibid.
169. Hall, "'You Want to Kill.'"

170. Andrew Johnson, "Man Who Escaped ISIS: They Want to Plan an Attack 'More Brutal' than 9/11," National Review, January 25, 2015; Michael Dorstewitz, "Prisoner who Escaped ISIS Captivity Tells NBC: They Want Something Bigger than 9/11," BizPac Review, January 25, 2015.

171. Michael Dorstewitz, "Prisoner Who Escaped ISIS Captivity Tells NBC: They Want Something Bigger than 9/11," BizPac Review, January 25, 2015.

172. "Ex-U.S. Detainees now ISIS Leaders," CBS News, n.d.

173. Ibid.

174. Barnes, "Several Islamic State Leaders Have Been Killed."

175. Lister, "Islamic State Senior Leadership."

176. Ibid.

177. "Revealed: The Islamic State 'Cabinet.'"

178. Lister, "Islamic State Senior Leadership."

179. Hamdi Alkhshali, Jason Hanna and Michael Martinez, "Hussein Deputy, Insurgent Leader al-Douri Killed, Iraqi TV Reports," CNN, April 17, 2015.

180. Jack Moore, "ISIS Replace Injured Leader Baghdadi with Former Physics Teacher," Newsweek, April 22, 2015.

181. "How Can Isis Afford Its Own Currency?," Guardian, November 16, 2014.

182. "Iraqi Dealers Confirm ISIS Hoarding Gold, Precious Metals to Issue Currency—Report," RT, November 21, 2014.

183. "Cracking the Code behind ISIS' New Currency," Vocativ, November 22, 2014.

184. "How Can Isis Afford Its Own Currency?"

185. "ISIS Allegedly Issues 'Caliphate' Passport," Al Arabiya, July 5, 2014.

186. Yasser Allawi, "ISIS Issues 11 Rules for Journalists in Deir Ezzor," Syria Deeply, October 7, 2014.

Chapter 6: The Caliphate: What It Means and Why It Matters

1. Ahmed ibn Naqib al-Misri, Reliance of the Traveller ('Umdat al-Salik): A Classic Manual of Islamic Sacred Law, trans. Nuh Ha Mim Keller (Amana Publications, 1999), xx.

2. Ibid., Section o9.8.

3. Raymond Ibrahim, "Egypt's Sisi: Islamic 'Thinking' Is 'Antagonizing the Entire World,'" Raymond Ibrahim: Islam Translated, January 1, 2015.

4. Michele Antaki, "El-Sisi Modifies Stance on Islamic Reform at Davos," American Thinker, January 25, 2015.

5. Mahmoud Mourad and Yara Bayoumy, "Special Report: Egypt Deploys Scholars to Teach Moderate Islam, but Skepticism Abounds," Reuters, May 31, 2015.

6.   "Prominent Scholars Declare ISIS Caliphate 'Null and Void,'" Middle East Monitor, July 5, 2014.

7.   Islamic State, "This Is the Promise of Allah," June 29, 2014, http://myreader. toile-libre.org/uploads/My_53b039f00cb03.pdf.

8.   Ibid.

9.   This is apparently a reference to the devastation the Arab armies wrought upon the Byzantine and Sassanid Persian Empires in the seventh century. The Byzantine Empire, however, continued on for another 800 years, although it never recaptured its prior glory.

10. Islamic State, "This Is the Promise of Allah."

11. Ibid.

12. Ibid.

13. Ibid.

14. "Isis Video 'Shows al-Baghdadi Alive' after Death Rumours," BBC, July 5, 2014.

15. Abu Bakr al-Husayni al-Qurashi al-Baghdadi, "A Message to the Mujahidin and the Muslim Ummah in the Month of Ramadan," Al-Hayat Media Center, n.d.

16. Ibid.

17. Ibid.

18. Ibid.

19. Al-Baghdadi, "A Message to the Mujahidin."

20. Ibid.

21. Ibid.

22. "Hammond: James Foley Murder an 'Utter Betrayal' of Britain," Channel 4 News, August 14, 2014.

23. Al-Baghdadi, "A Message to the Mujahidin."

24. Ibid.

25. Ibid.

26. Ibid.

27. Ibid.

28. Ibid.

29. Ibid.

30. Ibid.

31. Qur'an 7:128.

32. Al-Baghdadi, "A Message to the Mujahidin."

33. Ibid.

34. Ibid.

35. Oliver Duggan, "Abu Bakr al-Baghdadi Ridiculed for Flashy Wristwatch," *Telegraph*, July 6, 2014.

36. Aaron Short, "Terrorist Leader Sports $7K Watch during Religious Address," *New York Post*, July 6, 2014.

37. Mario Ledwith, "Terror Warlord al-Baghdadi Denounces the West—but Is Spotted Wearing '£3,500 James Bond Wristwatch,'" *Daily Mail*, July 6, 2014.

38. "'Follow My Every Word and You Too Will Have a Rolex'; Islamic State Leader Wears Luxury Watch to First-Ever Public Address," Twitchy, July 6, 2014.

39. Daniel Politi, "ISIS Leader Mocked for Wearing Expensive Wristwatch in First Public Appearance," Slate, July 6, 2014.

40. Ibn Ishaq, *The Life of Muhammad: A Translation of Ibn Ishaq's Sirat Rasul Allah*, trans. A. Guillaume (Oxford University Press, 1955), 327; Daniel Greenfield, "ISIS Caliph of All Muslims Wears Stolen $6000 Watch," FrontPage Magazine, July 6, 2014.

41. Ishaq, *The Life of Muhammad*, p. 503; Greenfield, "ISIS Caliph of All Muslims."

42. Ishaq, *The Life of Muhammad*, p. 324; Greenfield, "ISIS Caliph of All Muslims."

43. Ahmed Rashid, *Taliban* (Yale University Press, 2001), 42.

44. Craig Pyes, Josh Meyer and William C. Rempel, "Officials Reveal Bin Laden Plan," *Los Angeles Times*, May 18, 2002.

45. "Algerian Terror Group Seeks Zarqawi's Help," UPI, May 2, 2006.

46. Brynjar Lia, *The Society of the Muslim Brothers in Egypt* (Ithaca Press, 1998), 28.

47. "Hasan Al-Banna and His Political Thought of Islamic Brotherhood," IkhwanWeb, The Muslim Brotherhood's Official English website, May 13, 2008, http://www.ikhwanweb.com/article.php?id=17065.

48. Lia, *The Society of the Muslim Brothers*, 80.

49. Shaker El-sayed, "Hassan al-Banna: The Leader and the Movement," Muslim American Society, http://www.maschicago.org/library/misc_articles/hassan_banna.htm.

50. Hasan Al-Banna, "Toward the Light," *Five Tracts of Hasan Al-Banna*, trans. Charles Wendell (University of California Press, 1978), 126.

51. Caroline Fourest, *Brother Tariq: The Doublespeak of Tariq Ramadan*, trans. Ioana Wieder and John Atherton (Encounter Books, 2008), 20

52. Charles Wendell, "Introduction," *Five Tracts of Hasan Al-Banna*, trans. Charles Wendell, (University of California Press, 1978), 3.

53. Ali Ibrahim Al-Moshki, "AQAP Announces Support for ISIL," *Yemen Times*, August 19, 2014.

54. Rita Katz, "Interactive Map: The Islamic State's Global Network of Pledged and Supporting Groups," SITE Intel Group, February 17, 2015.

55. Katz, "Interactive Map"; Barnaby Lo, "Muslim Rebels in Philippines Vow Allegiance to IS," CCTV.com, September 17, 2014; Alessandria Masi, "Where to Find ISIS Supporters: A Map of Militant Groups Aligned with the Islamic State Group," International Business Times, October 9, 2014.

56. 'Jola Sotubo, "Boko Haram: Terrorist Group Changes Name to 'Islamic State in West Africa,'" Pulse, April 23, 2015.

57. Lo, "Muslim Rebels in Philippines"; Masi, "Where to Find ISIS Supporters."

Chapter 7: The Caliphate's Bloody History

1. Bukhari, vol. 5, book 64, no. 4428.

2. Bukhari, vol. 4, book 56, no. 2977.

3. Bukhari, vol. 5, book 64, no. 4431. The material in parentheses here was added by the Saudi translator of the hadith of Bukhari; the word Al-Mushrikun is generally translated as "unbelievers" or "polytheists"; literally, it refers to those who commit shirk, that is, the association of partners with Allah in worship.

4. Muslim, book 31, no. 5877.

5. Muslim, book 31, no. 5916.

6. Ibn Ishaq, p. 183. Bukhari, vol. 4, book 55, no. 2741.

7. Bukhari, vol. 4, book 55, no. 2741.

8. Tirmidhi, vol. 1, book 46, no. 3673, Sunnah.com, http://sunnah.com/urn/635490.

9. Fred Donner, *Muhammad and the Believers at the Origins of Islam* (The Belknap Press of Harvard University Press, 2010), 100–1.

10. Bukhari, vol. 9, book 88, no. 6922; cf. vol. 4, book 56, no. 3017.

11. H. U. Rahman, *Chronology of Islamic History, 570–1000 CE* (Ta-Ha Publishers, 1999), 55–57.

12. See, for example, Abdullahi Ahmed An-Na'im, *Islam and the Secular State: Negotiating the Future of Shari`a* (Harvard University Press, 2009), 60.

13. "Islam: A Complete Code of Life," Islamweb.net, http://www.islamweb.net/emainpage/articles/111867/islam-a-complete-code-of-life.

14. Abubakr Asadulla, *Islam vs. West: Fact or Fiction?: A Brief Historical, Political, Theological, Philosophical, and Psychological Perspective* (iUniverse, 2009), 42.

15. Bukhari, vol. 5, book 62, no. 3668.

16. Rahman, *Chronology of Islamic History, 570–1000 CE*, 59–60, 63–64.

17. John Gilchrist, *Jam' Al-Qur'an, The Codification of the Qur'an Text: A Comprehensive Study of the Original Collection of the Qur'an Text and the Early Surviving Qur'an Manuscripts* (MERCSA, 1989), http://www.answering-islam.org/Gilchrist/Jam/index.html.

18. Bukhari, vol. 6, book 66, no. 4987.

19. *The History of al-Tabari*, vol. 11, *The Challenge to the Empires*, trans. Khalid Yahya Blankinship (State University of New York Press, 1993), 147.

20. Rahman, *Chronology of Islamic History, 570–1000 CE*, 65–68.

21. *The History of al-Tabari*, vol. 12, *The Battle of al-Qadisiyyah and the Conquest of Syria and Palestine*, trans. Yohanan Friedmann (State University of New York Press, 1992), 167.

22. Bukhari, vol. 4, book 58, no. 3162.

23. John Esposito, *Islam: The Straight Path* (Oxford University Press, 1998), 34.

24. "Muslim Conquests in Egypt and Iran," MacroHistory and World Timeline, n.d., http://www.fsmitha.com/h3/islam08b.htm.

25. "Professor Harald Suermann: The Idea That the Copts Received the Muslims as Liberators is No Longer Tenable," *On Coptic Nationalism*, February 2, 2014, https://copticliterature.wordpress.com/2014/02/02/professor-harald-suermann-the-idea-that-the-copts-received-the-muslims-as-liberators-is-no-longer-tenable/.

26. Robert G. Hoyland, *Seeing Islam as Others Saw It: A Survey and Evaluation of Christian, Jewish and Zoroastrian Writings On Early Islam* (Darwin Press, 1997), 121.

27. Bat Ye'or, *The Decline of Eastern Christianity Under Islam: From Jihad to Dhimmitude* (Fairleigh Dickinson University Press, 1996), 274.

28. Ibid., 271–72.

29. Ibid., 275.

30. Daniel J. Sahas, "The Face to Face Encounter Between Patriarch Sophronius of Jerusalem and the Caliph Umar ibn al-Khattab: Friends or Foes?," in *The Encounter of Eastern Christianity With Early Islam*, Emmanouela Grypeou, Mark Swanson, and David Richard Thomas, eds. (Brill, 2006), 38.

31. Hoyland, *Seeing Islam As Others Saw It*, 69.

32. Steven Runciman, *A History of the Crusades*, vol. 1 (Cambridge University Press, 1951), 4.

33. Hoyland, *Seeing Islam As Others Saw It*, 72–73.

34. Runciman, *A History of the Crusades*, vol. 1, 3.

35. "Khalifa Umar bin al-Khattab–Death of Umar," Alim.org, http://www.alim.org/library/biography/khalifa/content/KUM/19/2.

36. *Agh.*, VII, 13 (quoted in Goldziher, 118).

37. Bukhari, vol. 5, book 62, no. 3699.

38. Bukhari, vol. 6, book 65, no. 4784.

39. Rahman, *Chronology of Islamic History, 570–1000 CE*, 77–79.

40. Ibid., p. 83.

41. *The History of al-Tabari*, vol. 16, *The Community Divided*, trans. Adrian Brockett, (State University of New York Press, 1997), 52–166, passim; Akbar Shah Najeebabadi, *The History of Islam*, vol. 1 (Darussalam, 2000), 455.

42. *The History of al-Tabari*, vol. 17, *The First Civil War*, trans. G. R. Hawting (State University of New York Press, 1996), 1–110, passim; Najeebabadi, *The History of Islam*, vol. 1, 462–77.

43. Rahman, *Chronology of Islamic History, 570–1000 CE*, 59.

44. *The History of al-Tabari*, vol. 17, *The First Civil War*, trans. G. R. Hawting (State University of New York Press, 1996), 110–42, *passim*.

45. Rahman, *Chronology of Islamic History, 570–1000 CE*, 88–89.

46. Ibid., 90–91.

47. "Sunni Cleric Says Iraq Caliphate Violates Sharia," Agence France-Presse, July 5, 2014.

48. Ibid.

49. Rahman, *Chronology of Islamic History, 570–1000 CE*, 99–101.

50. Akbar Shah Najeebabadi, *The History of Islam*, vol. 2 (Darussalam, 2001), 79–80.

51. Ibid., 109–11, 140–46.

52. Rahman, *Chronology of Islamic History, 570–1000 CE*, 131.

53. Theophanes the Confessor, *The Chronicle of Theophanes*, trans. Harry Turtledove, (University of Pennsylvania Press, 1982), p. 93.

54. Ahmad Hasan Dani, *History of Civilizations of Central Asia: The Crossroads of Civilizations: A.D. 250 to 750* (Motilal Banarsidass Publishers, 1999), 459.

55. G. R. Hawting, *The First Dynasty of Islam: The Umayyad Caliphate AD 661–750* (Routledge, 2002), p. 92.

56. Rahman, *Chronology of Islamic History, 570–1000 CE*, 137–38.

57. Ibid., 243.

58. Ibid., 255.

59. Ibid., 260.

60. Ibid., 272.

61. John Esposito, ed., *The Oxford History of Islam* (Oxford University Press, 1999), 692.

62. *The Oxford History of Islam*, 692.

63. Rahman, *Chronology of Islamic History, 570–1000 CE*, 153.

64. Philip K. Hitti, *The Arabs: A Short History* (Regnery, revised edition, 1970), 137.
65. María Rosa Menocal, *The Ornament of the World: How Muslims, Jews, and Christians Created a Culture of Tolerance in Medieval Spain* (Little, Brown, 2002), 281.
66. Harold Bloom, "Foreword," in Menocal, *The Ornament of the World*, 15.
67. Richard Fletcher, *Moorish Spain* (University of California Press, 1992), 172–73.
68. Norman A. Stillman, *The Jews of Arab Lands: A History and Source Book* (The Jewish Publication Society of America, 1979), 56.
69. Fletcher, *Moorish Spain*, 108.
70. Ibid., 96–97.
71. Andrew Bostom, *The Legacy of Islamic Antisemitism* (Prometheus, 2007).
72. Norman A. Stillman, *The Jews of Arab Lands: A History and Source Book* (The Jewish Publication Society of America, 1979), 56.
73. "Leading Sunni Sheikh Yousef Al-Qaradhawi and Other Sheikhs Herald the Coming Conquest of Rome," MEMRI, December 6, 2002.
74. Ye'or, *The Decline of Eastern Christianity*, 113, 115.
75. Thomas Sowell, *Conquests and Cultures: An International History* (Basic Books, 1998), 192.
76. Godfrey Goodwin, *The Janissaries* (Saqi Books, 1997), 36–37.
77. Lord Kinross, *The Ottoman Centuries* (Morrow Quill, 1977), 477.
78. Ibid., 501.
79. Ye'or, *The Decline of Eastern Christianity*, 399–400.
80. Ibid., 406.
81. Ibid., 417.
82. Rudolph Peters, *Islam and Colonialism* (Mouton Publishers, 1979), 90.
83. Kinross, *The Ottoman Centuries*, 410.
84. H. C. Armstrong, *The Gray Wolf* (Penguin Books, 1937), 206.
85. Philip Mansel, *Constantinople: City of the World's Desire, 1453–1924* (St. Martin's Griffin, 1995), 414.
86. Armstrong, *The Gray Wolf*, 205.

Chapter 8: Is the Islamic State Islamic? (Is the Pope Catholic?)

1. Brittany M. Hughes, "State Dept. on Beheading of U.S. Journalist: 'This Is Not about the United States,'" CNS News, August 21, 2014.
2. "Crowd Gathers to Show Support of ISIS Takeover of Mosul," Middle East Media Research Institute, June 12, 2014.

3. "Transcript: President Obama's Remarks on the Execution of Journalist James Foley by Islamic State," *Washington Post*, August 20, 2014.

4. "French Govt to Use Arabic 'Daesh' for Islamic State Group," France 24, September 18, 2014.

5. Adam Taylor, "'Daesh': John Kerry Starts Calling the Islamic State a Name They Hate," *Washington Post*, December 5, 2014.

6. "Is It IS, ISIS, ISIL or Maybe Daesh?," Associated Press, September 12, 2014.

7. "'This Week' Transcript: DHS Secretary Jeh Johnson," ABC News, February 22, 2015.

8. Khaleda Rahman, "Corporal Punishment ISIS-Style: Boy Flogged 60 Times in Town Square for Calling Terror Group the Wrong Name," *Daily Mail*, February 12, 2015.

9. Shounaz Meky, "Egypt's Dar al-Ifta: ISIS Extremists Not 'Islamic State,'" Al Arabiya, August 24, 2014.

10. Daniel Boffey, "'Islamic State' Is a Slur on Our Faith, Say Leading Muslims," *Observer*, September 13, 2014.

11. Ab Muhammad al-'Adn n ash-Sh m , "Indeed Your Lord Is Ever Watchful," September 21, 2014, https://ia801400.us.archive.org/34/items/mir225/English_Translation.pdf.

12. "Syria, More than 20 Thousand Foreign Fighters Have Joined the Jihad," Asia News, February 11, 2015; Jack Moore, "5,000 Foreign Fighters Flock to Libya as ISIS Call for Jihadists, *Newsweek*, March 3, 2015.

13. Loren Thompson, "Five Reasons the ISIS Fight Isn't about Islam," *Forbes*, February 26, 2015.

14. Alroy Menezes, "ISIS Kills 50 Syrian Soldiers, Beheads Many in Raqqa," International Business Times, July 26, 2014.

15. Chelsea J. Carter, "Video Shows ISIS Beheading U.S. Journalist James Foley," CNN, August 20, 2014.

16. "Lebanon/IS: Soldier Beheading a War Crime if Confirmed," Human Rights Watch, September 1, 2014.

17. Andrew Marszal and Raf Sanchez, "Steven Sotloff Beheaded by Islamic State—Latest," *Telegraph*, September 3, 2014.

18. "David Haines—Obituary," *Telegraph*, September 14, 2014.

19. Fazul Rahim and Alexander Smith, "ISIS-Allied Militants Behead 15 during Afghanistan Offensive: Official," NBC News, September 26, 2014.

20. "Jund al-Khilafah in Algeria Beheads French Hostage in Video," SITE Intelligence Group, September 24, 2014.

21. Greg Botelho, Michael Pearson, and Phillip Taylor, "ISIS Executes British Aid Worker David Haines; Cameron Vows Justice," CNN, September 13, 2014.

22. Steven Nelson, "Peter Kassig's Conversion Unlikely to Halt ISIS Headsman, Experts Say," *US News & World Report*, October 6, 2014.

23. "IS Beheads Peter Kassig, Challenges U.S. to Send Ground Troops," SITE Intelligence Group, November 16, 2014.

24. Karin Laub, "Japanese Hostage Kenji Goto Seen Beheaded in ISIS Video, Bringing Abrupt End to Negotiations to Free Him," *National Post*, January 31, 2015.

25. Justen Charters, "ISIS Declares War on 'The Cross': 21 Christians Beheaded in Barbaric New Video from the Islamic State," IJ Review, February 25, 2015.

26. Rukmini Callimachi, "The Horror before the Beheadings," *New York Times*, October 25, 2014.

27. Stuart Ramsay, "IS Hostages Subjected to Execution Rehearsals," Sky News, March 10, 2015.

28. Ahmed ibn Naqib al-Misri, *Reliance of the Traveller ('Umdat al-Salik): A Classic Manual of Islamic Sacred Law*, trans. Nuh Ha Mim Keller (Amana Publications, 1999), o9.13.

29. "Egyptian Shaykh: Jihad Is Solution to Muslims' Financial Problems," *Translating Jihad*, May 31, 2011.

30. Natasha Culzac, "James Foley Beheading Was an 'Utter Betrayal of Britain', Says Philip Hammond," *Independent*, August 24, 2014.

31. "Video: Shaykh al-Huwayni: 'When I Want a Sex Slave, I just Go to the Market and Choose the Woman I Like and Purchase Her,'" *Translating Jihad*, June 11, 2011.

32. Raymond Ibrahim, "Video: Kuwaiti Activist: 'I Hope That Kuwait Will Enact a Law for…Sex Slaves,'" *Translating Jihad*, June 22, 2011.

33. Raymond Ibrahim, "Muslim Woman Seeks to Revive Institution of Sex-Slavery," FrontPage Magazine, June 6, 2011.

34. Graham Smith and Damien Gayle, "Grooming Gang Found Guilty: Nine Men Shared Girls Aged 13 to 15 for Sex and Raped One up to Twenty Times a Day," *Daily Mail*, May 8, 2012; Dominic Casciani, "More than 2,000 Children 'Victims of Sex Grooming,'" BBC, June 29, 2011; James Tozer, "Police 'Hid' Abuse of 60 Girls by Asian Takeaway Workers Linked to Murder of 14-Year-Old," *Daily Mail*, April 8, 2011.

35. "Rotherham Child Abuse Scandal: 1,400 Children Exploited, Report Finds," BBC News, August 26, 2014.

36. Brandon Gee, "Sex Trafficking Trial Unusual in Scope: As Many as 23 Will Face Jury Simultaneously," *Tennessean*, February 28, 2012.

37. Zachary Davies Boren, "Yazidi Sex Slave Escapes Isis to Tell Her Story: 'They Took Us away Like Cattle,'" *Independent*, December 22, 2014.

38. Rose Troup Buchanan, "Isis Fighters Barter over Yazidi Girls on 'Slave Market Day'—the Shocking Video," *Independent*, November 3, 2014.

39. "Islamic State (ISIS) Releases Pamphlet on Female Slaves," Middle East Media Research Institute, December 4, 2014.

40. Ibid.

41. Kirk Semple, "Yazidi Girls Seized by ISIS Speak Out after Escape," *New York Times*, November 14, 2014.

42. "Islamic State (ISIS) Publishes Penal Code, Says It Will Be Vigilantly Enforced," Middle East Media Research Institute, December 17, 2014.

43. Bukhari, vol. 8, book 86, no. 6829.

44. Bukhari, vol. 8, book 86, no. 6777.

45. "Islamic State (ISIS) Publishes Penal Code."

46. Sami Aboudi and Suleiman Al-Khalidi, "Clerics Denounce Burning Alive of Pilot as un-Islamic," Reuters, February 4, 2015.

47. Bukhari, vol. 9, book 88, no. 6922.

48. Bukhari, vol. 1, book 10, no. 657.

49. Ibn Ishaq, p. 515.

50. "The Burning of the Murtadd Pilot," *Dabiq* 7 (March 2015): 6–8, http://media.clarionproject.org/files/islamic-state/islamic-state-dabiq-magazine-issue-7-from-hypocrisy-to-apostasy.pdf.

51. Ibid., 5.

52. Bukhari, vol. 1, book 4, no. 233.

53. Haroon Moghul, "The Atlantic's Big Islam Lie: What Muslims Really Believe about ISIS," *Salon*, February 19, 2015.

54. Patrick Goodenough, "ISIS Publication Aims to Lure Recruits; Justifies Atrocities by Citing Mohammed," CNS News, September 2, 2014.

55. Patrick Goodenough, "Kerry: Extremism Not Linked to Islam; Factors Include Deprivation, Climate Change," CNS News, October 17, 2014.

56. Caner K. Dagli, "The Phony Islam of ISIS," *Atlantic*, February 27, 2015.

57. Tom Heneghan, "Muslim Scholars Present Religious Rebuttal to Islamic State," Reuters, September 26, 2014.

58. Ibid.

59. Daniel Pipes and Asaf Romirowsky, "Hamas in the Florida Classroom," FrontPage Magazine, January 27, 2004; "Dr. Jamal Badawi," Discover the Networks, http://www.discoverthenetworks.org/individualProfile.asp?indid=1009; "Bosnia: Muslim Spiritual Leader Urges More Sharia Law," AdnKronos International, August 17, 2009; Robert Spencer, "Why Can't Muslims Debate? (Again)," Jihad Watch, January 9, 2012; Ramadan Al Sherbini, "Top Cleric Denies 'Freedom to Choose Religion' Comment," GulfNews, July

25, 2007; Hamza Yusuf, "The Real Teddy Bear Tragedy," Faith Street, December 6, 2007; Ed Husain, "Taking Passports Would Only Raise the Jihadist Threat," *London Evening Standard*, September 2, 2014; Robert Spencer, "The Hypocrisy of the Fatwa against Terrorism," PJ Media, December 24, 2013; Muzammil Siddiqi, Discover the Networks, http://www.discoverthenetworks.org/individualProfile.asp?indid=1061.

60.   Sharona Schwartz, "'My Jihad': CAIR Ad Campaign Tries to Rebrand 'Jihad' as a Positive Word," TheBlaze, January 7, 2013.

61.   See, for example, Harris Zafar, "Pastor Nadarkhani, Islam and Punishment for Apostasy, Huffington Post, March 12, 2012; Qasim Rashid, "Shariah Law: The Five Things Every Non-Muslim (and Muslim) Should Know," Huffington Post, November 4, 2011.

62.   Garrett Mitchell, "Muslim Group in Tempe Pushes back against ISIS Extremism," The Republic, May 30, 2015.

63.   See, for example, "The Truth about Shari'a: What Sharia Is and Is Not," CAIR Iowa, n.d., http://www.cair-iowa.org/news-action-alerts/the-truth-about-shari-a.

Chapter 9: On the Islamic State's To-Do List (Rome, Non-Muslims, and the Final Showdown)

1.   Abu Bakr al-Baghdadi, "A Message to the Mujahedin and the Muslim Ummah in the Month of Ramadan," July 1, 2014.

2.   "Founder of Hizb Al-Tahrir in Chicago: The Caliphate Is Coming, and Britain and America Can Go to Hell," Middle East Media Research Institute, June 21, 2013.

3.   Ibid.

4.   Islamic State, *Black Flags from Rome (Europe)*, 2015, 3.

5.   Ibid., 3, 28.

6.   Ibid., 28.

7.   Ibid., 3.

8.   Ibid., 8.

9.   Ibid., 10.

10. Ibid., 14.

11. Ibid.

12. Ibid., 15.

13. Ibid.

14. Ibid., 20.

15. Ibid., 21.

16.   Ibid.
17.   Ibid., 23.
18.   Ibid., 25.
19.   Ibid.
20.   Ibid., 28.
21.   Ibid., 26.
22.   Ibid., 35.
23.   Ibid., 39.
24.   Katie Zavadski, "These 10 People Were Also Named Al Qaeda's Most Wanted," *New York* magazine, January 14, 2015.
25.   Islamic State, *Black Flags from Rome (Europe)*, 40.
26.   Ibid., 45.
27.   Ibid., 46.
28.   Ibid., 64.
29.   Ibid., 68.
30.   "Handwritten ISIS Notes 'in Front of Rome, Milan Monuments,'" ANSA, April 28, 2015.
31.   Islamic State, *Black Flags from Rome (Europe)*, 4.
32.   Muslim, book 41, no. 6924.
33.   Islamic State, *Black Flags from Rome (Europe)*, 81.
34.   Ibid.
35.   "King Abdullah of Jordan Says Pilot's Reported ISIL Murder Does Not Resemble Islam," *Telegraph*, February 3, 2015.
36.   Islamic State, *Black Flags from Palestine (Magic, Deception & War)*, 2015, 7.
37.   Ibid., 2.
38.   Ibid.
39.   Ibid., 13, 22.
40.   Ibid., 25.
41.   Ibid.
42.   Ibid., 26.
43.   Ibid.
44.   Ibid., 28.
45.   Ibid., 30.
46.   Ibid., 33.
47.   Ibid., 45.
48.   Ibid., 42.
49.   Ibid., 53.
50.   Ibid., 62.
51.   Ibid., 117.

52. Ibid, 62.
53. Ibid., 89.
54. Ibid., 94.
55. Ibid., 95.
56. Ibid., 99.
57. Ibid.
58. Ibid., 103.
59. Ibid., 104.
60. Ibid., 109.
61. Ibid., 114.
62. Ibid.
63. Ibid.
64. Abu-Dawud Sulaiman bin Al-Aash'ath Al-Azdi as-Sijistani, *Sunan abu-Dawud*, Ahmad Hasan, translator, Kitab Bhavan, 1990, no. 4324.
65. Muslim, no. 6985; Islamic State, *Black Flags from Palestine (Magic, Deception & War)*, 132.
66. Jane Onyango-Omara, "Activists: Islamic State Seizes More than Half of Syria," *USA Today*, May 21, 2015.
67. "What Is Islamic State?," BBC News, September 26, 2014.
68. Islamic State, *How to Survive in the West*, 2015, 2.
69. Ibid., 5.
70. Surah al-Tawbah is the Qur'an's ninth chapter, which contains its clearest exhortations to kill and subjugate unbelievers, including Jews and Christians.
71. Islamic State, *How to Survive in the West*, 5.
72. Ibid., 7.
73. Ibid., 8.
74. Ibid., 9.
75. Ibid., 14.
76. Ibid., 20.

Chapter 10: How to Defeat ISIS—and Why We Must

1. Daniel Hurst, "Tony Abbott Intensifies Rhetoric about Isis, Calling It an 'Apocalyptic Death Cult,'" *Guardian*, September 30, 2014.
2. Islamic State, *Black Flags from Palestine (Magic, Deception & War)*, 2015, 130.
3. Jacqueline Klimas, "U.S. Bombers Hold Fire on Islamic State Targets amid Ground Intel Blackout," *Washington Times*, May 31, 2015.
4. Julie Hirschfeld Davis, "Obama to Present Case for Broader U.S. Mission against Militants," *New York Times*, September 7, 2014.

5.   Jordan Schachtel, "Daily Jihad: Obama's 'Vetted' Free Syrian Army Joining Forces with Islamic State Terror Group," Breitbart, September 9, 2014.

6.   "FSA Brigades Pledge Allegiance to ISIS in Al Bukamal, East Syria," Zaman Alwasl, July 7, 2014.

7.   Erin Banco, "James Foley Allegedly Used as Token of Allegiance by Group That Joined ISIS," International Business Times, August 20, 2014.

8.   Elise Knutsen, "Frustration Drives Arsal's FSA into ISIS Ranks," *Daily Star*, September 8, 2014; Schachtel, "Daily Jihad: Obama's 'Vetted' Free Syrian Army."

9.   Patrick J. McDonnell, "Lack of Reliable Partners in Syria Poses Daunting Challenge to U.S.," *Los Angeles Times*, September 23, 2014.

10. Mona Mahmood, "US Air Strikes in Syria Driving Anti-Assad Groups to Support Isis," *Guardian*, November 23, 2014.

11. Tim Lister, "Has ISIS peaked? Terror Group Suffers Setbacks in Iraq," CNN, November 14, 2014.

12. Daveed Gartenstein-Ross, "ISIS Is Losing Its Greatest Weapon: Momentum: Evidence Suggests That the Islamic State's Power Has Been Declining for Months," *Atlantic*, January 6, 2015.

13. Tim Lister, "For ISIS, Tough Times as It Seeks to Regroup," CNN, January 28, 2015.

14. Kenneth M. Pollack, "ISIS Is Losing in Iraq. But What Happens Next?," *New York Times*, February 4, 2015.

15. Jim Michaels, "Pentagon: ISIL Pushed out of 25% of Its Territory," *USA Today*, April 14, 2015.

16. Zack Beauchamp and Johnny Harris, "ISIS Is Losing. Watch How and Why It's Happening," Vox, April 15, 2015.

17. Hamdi Alkhshali, Arwa Damon and Jethro Mullen, "Ramadi Could Fall as ISIS Militants Lay Siege, Iraqi Official Warns," CNN, April 15, 2015.

18. Tim Mak, "Exclusive: Pentagon Map Hides ISIS Gains," Daily Beast, April 22, 2015.

19. "M.S.S. Updates," http://www.welovetheiraqiinformationminister.com/.

20. Hamdi Alkhshali, "ISIS on Offensive in Iraq's Ramadi, Taking over Mosque and Government Buildings," CNN News, May 15, 2015.

21. "White House: Obama's Strategy against the Islamic State Has 'Overall' Been a Success," Washington Free Beacon, May 19, 2015.

22. Associated Press, "US Defense Secretary Says Fall of Ramadi Shows Iraqi Forces Lack Will to Fight ISIS," *Guardian*, May 24, 2015.

23. Anne Barnard and Hwaida Saad, "ISIS Fighters Seize Control of Syrian City of Palmyra, and Ancient Ruins, *New York Times*, May 20, 2015; Greg Botelho,

"ISIS Is 'Everywhere' in Syria's Ancient City of Palmyra," CNN News, May 22, 2015

24. Oliver Lane, "ISIS Puts Captured Roman Amphitheatre Back into Use as Venue for Execution for Entertainment," Breitbart, May 30, 2015.

25. Liz Sly, "While Nobody Was Looking, the Islamic State Launched a New, Deadly Offensive," *Washington Post*, June 1, 2015.

26. John David Lewis, "'No Substitute for Victory': The Defeat of Islamic Totalitarianism," *The Objective Standard*, vol. 1, no. 4, Winter 2006–2007.

27. William Napier, *History Of General Sir Charles Napier's Administration Of Scinde* (Chapman and Hall, 1851), 35.

28. Tim Hume, "Why the U.S. Government Is 'Trolling' Jihadists on Social Media," CNN, April 18, 2014.

29. Ibid.

30. Martin Beckford and Abul Taher, "Internet Gaffe by US Government as UK Extremist's Sharia Law Photo Used in Free Speech Ad," *Daily Mail*, March 15, 2015.

31. Lesley Stahl, "Homeland Security: Homeland Security Secretary Jeh Johnson Talks about the Evolving Role of His Department's Massive Security Efforts," CBS News, April 5, 2015.

32. Lorna Knowles, "Sydney Siege: Man behind Martin Place Standoff Was Iranian Man Haron Monis, Who Had Violent Criminal History," Australian Broadcasting Corporation, December 15, 2014.

33. Marialaura Conte, "With Isis, because I Love Death More than You Love Life," Oasis, March 4, 2015.

INDEX